YOUTH AND GENERATION

SAGE was founded in 1965 by Sara Miller McCune to support the dissemination of usable knowledge by publishing innovative and high-quality research and teaching content. Today, we publish more than 750 journals, including those of more than 300 learned societies, more than 800 new books per year, and a growing range of library products including archives, data, case studies, reports, conference highlights, and video. SAGE remains majority-owned by our founder, and on her passing will become owned by a charitable trust that secures our continued independence.

Los Angeles | London | Washington DC | New Delhi | Singapore

YOUTH AND GENERATION

RETHINKING CHANGE AND INEQUALITY IN THE LIVES OF YOUNG PEOPLE

DAN WOODMAN AND JOHANNA WYN

Los Angeles | London | New Delhi
Singapore | Washington DC

Los Angeles | London | New Delhi
Singapore | Washington DC

SAGE Publications Ltd
1 Oliver's Yard
55 City Road
London EC1Y 1SP

SAGE Publications Inc.
2455 Teller Road
Thousand Oaks, California 91320

SAGE Publications India Pvt Ltd
B 1/I 1 Mohan Cooperative Industrial Area
Mathura Road
New Delhi 110 044

SAGE Publications Asia-Pacific Pte Ltd
3 Church Street
#10-04 Samsung Hub
Singapore 049483

Editor: Chris Rojek
Assistant editor: Gemma Shields
Production editor: Tom Bedford
Copyeditor: Audrey Scriven
Proofreader: Rosemary Campbell
Indexer: Jessica Crofts
Marketing manager: Michael Ainsley
Cover design: Jennifer Crisp
Typeset by: C&M Digitals (P) Ltd, Chennai, India
Printed in Great Britain by Henry Ling Limited at
The Dorset Press, Dorchester, DT1 1HD

Library of Congress Control Number: 2014940527

British Library Cataloguing in Publication data

A catalogue record for this book is available from
the British Library

ISBN 978–1–4462–5904–7
ISBN 978–1–4462–5905–4 (pbk)

For Louis and Corinne, and for Evan, Michael, Julia, Natalie, Malte and James

TABLE OF CONTENTS

ABOUT THE AUTHORS

Dr Dan Woodman is the TR Ashworth Senior Lecturer in Sociology in the School of Social and Political Sciences at the University of Melbourne. He is an Associate Editor of the *Journal of Youth Studies* and Vice President for Australia, New Zealand and Oceania of Research Committee 34: Sociology of Youth within the International Sociological Association. His work focuses on the sociology of generations, individualisation and inequality among young people, and the impact of insecure work and variable employment patterns on young people's relationships.

Professor Johanna Wyn is Director of the Youth Research Centre in the Melbourne Graduate School of Education at The University of Melbourne, Australia and a Fellow of the Academy of Social Sciences Australia. Her work focuses on young people's learning and wellbeing, on their transitions and on what kinds of knowledge and skills professionals who work with young people in these settings need in the twenty-first century.

ACKNOWLEDGEMENTS

This book is a culmination of thinking about the concept of generations and its value to youth studies that began almost a decade ago (Wyn and Woodman, 2006). These ideas about the concept of generations have been further developed to support new arguments in this book. We have also expanded on ideas that were first presented in joint and individual publications. In particular some elements of Chapter 3 first appeared in Woodman (2009, 2010) and Chapter 4 in Woodman (2011a). Chapter 7 also draws on arguments from work presented elsewhere (Woodman, 2011b, 2012, 2013). Likewise Chapter 5 draws on insights from Cuervo and Wyn (2012, 2014) and Woodman and Wyn (2013).

Our thinking draws on the Life Patterns research programme, a longitudinal panel study of two cohorts of Australian youth, based in the Youth Research Centre at the University of Melbourne. The first stage of the programme commenced in 1991, with a cohort of young people who had just completed their secondary education. A second cohort of school leavers was recruited in 2005/6. The lead investigator during the early years of the research programme was Peter Dwyer, and in 2002 Johanna became the lead investigator. Combined, the two of us have approximately three decades' experience of research with the Life Patterns programme (Johanna since the project began and Dan since 2005). In 2014 the research team includes Hernan Cuervo, Graeme Smith, Julia Coffey, Jessica Crofts and Lesley Andres. Along with two anonymous readers, these colleagues have generously given of their time to comment on draft chapters of this book. Jessica also expertly compiled the index, and Anne Farrelly, also at the Youth Research Centre, assisted with tracking down missing references.

Since 1998 the Life Patterns research programme has been funded by a number of grants from the Australian Research Council. Previous to 1998 the study received funding from the Australian National Training Authority. We are grateful to the participants who have continued to give their time over many years. Thanks are also due to the professional support provided by Sage, particularly our editors Gemma Shields and Tom Bedford.

1

CONTINUITY AND CHANGE

Young people experience a world that is significantly different from the world their parents knew as young people. These young lives are being changed alongside large-scale transformations in education, work and relationship formation in many parts of the globe. Although these changes are clearly documented in North America, Western Europe and Australia (Vosko, 2003; Bynner, 2005; Leccardi and Ruspini, 2006; Andres and Wyn, 2010), they are not limited to the Global North. The expansion of higher education, rapid integration into a global economy and contested and changing possibilities for relationship and household formation are also creating profound changes in many former communist-bloc countries (Roberts, 2007; Roberts and Pollock, 2009) and across Asia, Africa and South America (Nilan and Feixa, 2006; Tranberg-Hansen et al., 2008).

These changes have been driven by the implementation, sometimes under duress, of 'market' reforms, opening domestic markets to international trade, liberalising labour laws and pushing to increase individual investment in post-secondary education (Marquardt, 1996; Ball et al., 2000; Thrupp, 2001; Nilan and Feixa, 2006). While the impacts of these changes are far from limited to the young, it is the experience of youth that has been most reshaped by this wave of reform. They as a group are most affected by education and labour market changes and are also among the group most likely to be experimenting with new ways of living in response to new conditions, such as those facilitated by new digital technologies, and to be pushing for social change.

While young people in some parts of the world are seen as politically apathetic, under some conditions (including high youth unemployment and undemocratic government) they are driving significant political change. Young people have been at the centre of the social movements attempting to reshape North Africa and Western Asia (or the 'Middle East'). Structural changes in the experience of youth have been one of the major catalysts of these uprisings. Driven in part by experiments with democracy, demands for human rights and supported by the rise of a 'digital generation', the revolutionary movements in 2011 in Tunisia and Egypt for example have also been fostered by highly educated but unemployed young people who have embraced the call to further their education but have not been rewarded with the job opportunities promised (Castells, 2012: 66; Herrera, 2012).

Youth unemployment and the poor employment conditions facing young people are not only a problem in the Global South. Even if it is yet to lead to uprisings elsewhere, this does not mean that young people in the Global North are not suffering or protesting. In a reversal of the direction in which influence among youth cultures is often assumed to flow, the Occupy Movements that sprang up in many parts of the Global North in recent years, with its catch cry of 'we are the 99 per cent', were a response to precarious conditions of employment once squarely associated with the Global South, but now also spreading across the North (Beck, 2000; Standing, 2011). The Occupiers in New York City and elsewhere also drew their inspiration in part from the example of the revolutionaries of North Africa and West Asia (Castells, 2012).

At a time of unprecedented investment by governments and young people in further education, unemployment and temporary and precarious employment are also on the rise for young people across the world, making it appear unlikely that the 'neoliberal bargain' that promises individuals a return for their investment in human capital can be maintained (Brown et al., 2011; ILO, 2013). This could shape a generation. Considerable evidence has been amassed to show that unemployment and even precarious employment in the late teens and twenties have a scarring effect on young people, correlating with relatively poorer employment prospects and conditions into middle age and beyond. This has been found in countries of the Global North, like France (Chauvel, 2006), and also countries like Brazil in the Global South (Cruces et al., 2012).

Despite the apparent significance of these changes, recent youth research shows the enduring nature of patterns of structural inequality over time. In response to this, there has been a chorus of voices within youth studies highlighting the risk of exaggerating change. Researchers caution against relying on a simplified account of the past to create the appearance of a contrast with the present (Goodwin and O'Connor, 2005), or failing to recognise that the same groups of people are the 'winners and losers' (Roberts, 2003). Gender, class, ethnicity, disability and other social divisions continue to profoundly shape outcomes. If new possibilities for young lives have been created, it appears to be only a smaller group of privileged young people who really get to make choices about their future (MacDonald and Marsh, 2005; Roberts, 2007). In other words, it can often seem that the more things change, the more they stay the same (MacDonald, 2011). Understanding the dynamic between continuity and change is one of the central challenges for youth sociology today.

This book addresses the complex issue of the interrelated transformations of societies and individual biographies and how these impact on the social dynamics of inequality in young people's lives. We agree with youth researchers who suggest that interrogating the relationship between continuity and change is the substance of the promise and challenge of youth studies. Robert MacDonald (2011: 440, emphasis in original) for example believes that it is the '*asking* of these sorts of questions – questions about social change, social continuity, about inequality and the position of young people's transitions in these processes – that ... gives youth studies its particular appeal and purpose'. This view is also the foundation for arguably the most influential youth studies text of the past two decades, Andy Furlong and Fred Cartmel's (2007 [1997]) *Young People and Social Change*. These authors concisely state how concerns about the balance between continuity and change set the central questions for contemporary research:

> Young people today are growing up in different circumstances to those experienced by previous generations; changes which are significant enough to merit a reconceptualization of youth transitions and processes of social reproduction. In other words, in the modern world young people face new risks and opportunities ... But the greater range of opportunities available helps to obscure the extent to which existing patterns of inequality are simply being reproduced in different ways. (Furlong and Cartmel, 2007: 8–9)

In many ways our book takes up the spirit and challenge expressed in these words. The changes occurring around the world in the experience of youth point towards the need for a reconceptualisation in youth studies. Our concern however is that the view embedded in the second half of this quotation has been far more influential than the first in youth studies, and represents a common, but we will argue limited, way of thinking about inequality as evidence against social change. While it is rare to find a youth researcher who would contest absolutely that significant change in the experience of youth has occurred, it is common for youth researchers to assert that fundamental social stratification is simply reproduced *despite* change (Roberts, 1995; Lehmann, 2004; Evans, 2007). To some extent this is also expressed by Furlong and Cartmel (2007: 8), who emphasise 'that there are powerful sources of continuity; young people's experience continues to be shaped by class and gender'.

In this book we aim to rethink how the relationship between change and inequality is understood in youth studies, based on the starting point that this 'reproduction' of inequality is not simple, and that the creation of inequality is not opposed to but integral to change. We argue that if youth researchers are to understand the emergence of new patterns of inequality, it will be necessary to develop conceptual approaches that can analyse entrenched (and new) forms of inequality as part of the process of change. Too often these elements are seen in opposition, creating a conflation of 'continuity' and inequality. This is sometimes represented by the claim that because older forms of stratification have changed the outcome is a reduction in inequality. More commonly, continuity and inequality are conflated through arguments that evidence of inequality is evidence against change.

While youth researchers should contest accounts of youth that downplay inequality, the more significant challenge facing youth studies is that too often simply showing that class or gender still matters is seen as an important contribution in itself, and, as such, limits the analysis in some youth research from more fully understanding the contemporary dynamics and changing nature of inequality (Woodman, 2009: 253). As such, we also argue that new risks and inequalities do not simply mask old forms of inequality, but are central to the way inequalities, including those of class and gender, are being made afresh in contemporary conditions. To put this rather simplistically, creating a balance sheet that places change in young lives in one column and inequality in the other will not realise the promise of youth studies. This promise is not achieved through simply tracing social change, or highlighting patterns of continuity, but through showing how the two are intertwined.

Individualisation

One of the contributing factors to the conflating of inequality with continuity is a widely held belief that influential contemporary sociological theory both overemphasises change and downplays inequality. A shared point of departure for much contemporary sociological theory is that a series of shifts that began in the latter parts of the twentieth century are reshaping both the self and society (Giddens, 1991; Beck, 1992; Bauman, 2001; Sassen, 2008; Archer, 2012). Although the details vary, these theorists argue that a qualitatively new form of social organisation is emerging that impacts on how people imagine and build their biographies. In youth studies in particular, the concept of individualisation as proposed by Ulrich Beck and colleagues (Beck, 1992, 2007; Beck and Beck-Gernsheim, 2002), has been extensively discussed and critiqued. The 'individualistion thesis' is consistently interpreted as making two key claims. The first is that social structures, such as gendered role expectations about work and motherhood and the class structuring of education and employment opportunities, are weakening. The second is that in the space left in the wake of these weakening structures the work of shaping the future increasingly becomes the active responsibility of each person who can and must now make choices about their future.

Sociological youth research is an obvious area of study to put claims about the biography to the test and there is a substantial body of research that gives unequivocal evidence of patterns of inequality and their continuity over time. Based on consistent findings of the persistence of inequality, many youth researchers have heavily criticicised theories of individualisation for either de-emphasising, or worse, actively denying the (unchanging) nature of inequality (see Andres et al., 1999; Evans, 2002, 2007; Lehmann, 2004; Brannen and Nilsen, 2005, 2007; McLeod and Yates, 2006; Roberts, 2010, among others). We acknowledge the important contribution that these researchers have made to cataloging patterns of inequality, and some aspects of their theorising of it. However, the conclusion that theories of individualisation do not enable an account of inequality is too simplistic. The theory of individualisation is complex, presenting apparent contradictions that require interpretation. We argue, however, that the way individualisation has been predominantly understood in youth studies has missed one of this theory's central claims. This oversight is not primarily because of the theory's own ambiguities, although they do exist, but because the individualisation thesis has become a trope employed as a foil to emphasise empiricist analyses of inequality.

We offer an analysis of the individualisation thesis that opens up a more nuanced understanding of how key elements of the theory work (Woodman, 2010). The concept of individualisation offers a sense of the active work that people must do to shape their lives. Yet far from proposing a weakening of social structure that frees individuals to shape their own lives, individualisation indexes an unequal but spreading challenge of keeping the biography from breaking into pieces in the face of new structural constraints, which are contradictory or ambivalent in their demands (Beck and Beck-Gernsheim, 2002: 22).

While we use the individualisation thesis, this book is not a straightforward application of the concept of individualisation to thinking about youth. Despite arguing that people must now actively shape the biography in new ways, most of the individualisation theorists say relatively little about the detail of how people actually respond to the changes that individualisation brings. We use the idea of individualisation as a description of the conditions of contemporary youth, taking it as a starting point but using a variety of other theories, including Bourdieu's theory of habitus and concepts from post-colonial theories often considered to be incompatible with individualisation. Our analysis does not interpret individualisation to be a privilege of the most resourced to make choices about the biography, but sees it as a structural challenge faced most acutely by the least resourced. This becomes a point of departure for theorising the way that inequality is made in contemporary conditions among young people, including by class, gender and race.

We draw on a range of theories because the challenge of analysing young lives in context is complex. We explore the processes through which social relations create unequal outcomes to understand how these processes interrelate. Attending to the interrelation of different institutions and actors that shape contemporary conditions can highlight changes in the meaning and function of aspects of social life that would otherwise appear unchanging over time. For example, Saskia Sassen (2008) in defending her claims about the profound impacts of globalisation highlights how social arrangements and shared beliefs, such as the idea of sovereignty, can endure over time while coming to play a much more significant and sometimes radically different part in a social formation over time. As we have already mentioned, the changing nature of youth labour markets and conditions of employment is a significant dynamic impacting on young people across the world. Understanding this dynamic requires an understanding of new global processes.

Sassen (2008) argues that economic globalisation, including the rise of non-state economic actors such as multinational firms, could not have happened without the highly developed financial and legal mechanisms within nation states. These mechanisms, which once strengthened the nation state, have become disembedded from the context in which they originated, to be repositioned to serve cross-national actors' purposes (such as forcing opening national economies to global trade) (Sassen 2008: 13–14). For our purposes we use and develop the concept of generations to provide a conceptual anchor for investigating the complex intertwining of change and continuity in the production of inequality in the lives of contemporary young people.

Generation

In the context of the rise of theories proposing a new modernity and their impact in youth studies, Ken Roberts (2003: 27–8) has argued '[w]e need progress, not more restarts … Constantly seeking new approaches, perspectives and paradigms is a recipe for stagnation … We have foundations, an impressive track record of youth research, on which to build. Why kick past achievements away?' There is an intuitive truth in this claim. In part this book returns to and affirms the importance of the longstanding focus on transitions, cultures, class, gender and race in youth sociology. However, our way forward is neither to start from scratch nor to refuse to jettison what we have.

While unequal outcomes for different groups of young people remain predicable to a significant degree, they do not emerge from an abstract or inevitable social logic. Instead they are the outcomes of institutional arrangements adjusting to social change, and through people actively maintaining distinctions and advantages over others in new conditions. For example, at the same time as education has become more important, the outcome of this investment in education has become more tenuous, with secure professional employment elusive for many and casual employment at the lower ends of the service industry growing rapidly (Furlong and Kelly, 2005; Andres and Wyn, 2010). It is only through rethinking our frameworks for contemporary conditions that youth research can remain relevant and reaffirm its core concepts such as class, gender, race and identity (Woodman and Threadgold, 2011).

In this spirit, one of our conceptual strategies is to follow a long tradition in sociology of reinventing older conceptual frameworks to better fit new times and new places (Abbott, 2001). As well as drawing on a relatively recent conceptual contribution, the theory of individualisation, we return to some of the oldest sociological thinking about young lives in the form of Karl Mannheim's (1952 [1923]) essay on generations. The sociology of generations is part of a broader tradition that asks not only how youth transitions and cultures have or have not changed, but also how the very meaning of youth as a relational concept is shaped by contemporary conditions (Allen, 1968; Lesko, 1996; Mizen, 2002; Blatterer, 2007). Along with other authors who use frameworks that emphasise a relational understanding of youth (but who may not embrace the term 'generations'), we argue that the changing patterns of work, study and living arrangements mentioned in the opening of this chapter point to a new socio-historical economic and policy formation that does not simply change the timing of transitions or young people's leisure practices, but more foundationally transforms the types of adulthood available and the possibilities open to young people (Wyn and Woodman, 2006).

While this broader tradition of attending to the relational shaping of youth continues to be influential in youth studies, the sociology of generations can provide tools for focusing thinking about continuity and change. Mannheim (1952) highlights that at particular points in time a generation of young people will face conditions different enough from those facing their parents (in their youth) that the rules for how to achieve a basic sense of ontological security, let alone sense of success, will have to be rewritten. It is the young generation that rewrites these rules. Mannheim's theory, however, does not present a generation as an homogeneous group of young people. He argues that a generation is made up of sometimes radically different and potentially politically opposed 'generational units' (Mannheim, 1952: 8). According to Mannheim, class was one of the significant elements that contributed to the heterogeneity of a social generation. These units are groupings that, while sharing the same generation, react in different ways to the conditions of their times due to their different social positions.

We argue that this central element of Mannheim's framework was overlooked by youth researchers in large part because of a similar conflation of continuity and inequality to that which influences youth research today. Mannheim's theory of generations was, to the detriment of youth studies, largely abandoned as the notion of generations was linked to an implicit and homogenising type of generationalism in the work of mid-twentieth-century functionalist sociology that was heavily critiqued by subcultural scholars in the 1970s.

While we hold that Mannheim's (1952) theory of generations continues to be valuable for thinking about youth, for our purposes his framework needs updating. One limitation is his focus on politics. His theorising tends to rest on the potential for a shared consciousness to emerge among some sections of a generation as a catalyst for political movements, neglecting other more mundane and affective forms of generational subjectivity. To attend equally to everyday and embodied forms of subjectivity created in the context of generational conditions, and to ask how they are entangled in the creation of contemporary inequalities, we draw on the concept of habitus taken from Pierre Bourdieu (1990). Bourdieu is often associated not just with the theorising of inequality but also with proposing a relatively mechanical theory of social reproduction. By highlighting points in his work where Bourdieu theorises social change, and by showing that neither Beck's theory of individualisation or the concept of generation downplays inequality, we argue that we can legitimately create what for some may seem like an improbable theoretical combination. Drawing on this combination, we propose using a concept of internally differentiated social generations as a useful frame for investigating class, gender, race and, although they are not our focus here, potentially other social divisions such as those related to disability, sexuality and health in a changing social world.

New Life Patterns

In the mid-twentieth century Robert Nisbet (1962) argued that sociology cannot, on the whole, mimic the procedures and methods of the natural sciences, but instead does and should mix 'art and science'. Some sociology is closer to art and some to the empirical procedures of the natural sciences. Nisbet makes a related distinction between 'grasp' and 'reach' sociology. Grasp sociology is close-grained empirical analysis of the details, while reach sociology treats data as a starting point for making larger claims and speculates on future trends. This book presents sociology as a mix of grasp and reach. In building our case for rethinking change and inequality in the lives of young people we draw on theories and data from around the world, almost unavoidably given the current political economy of academic knowledge, with a focus on the Global North. It is not, however, a detailed empirical monograph or an overview of current research from across the world. Many of our examples come from our own work on the Australian-based longitudinal mixed-methods 'Life Patterns' research programme, with the fuller empirical detail available in other publications that we will reference along the way.

Life Patterns has followed the transitions of two cohorts of young Australians across two decades. The first stage of the programme commenced in 1991, following a cohort of young people who had just completed their secondary education. A second cohort were recruited in the mid-2000s, and finished secondary school in 2006. Despite fifteen years difference in their age in many essential ways their lives have been the same, shaped by the ongoing expansion of education and a decline in the youth labour market with a recession in Australia in the early 1990s from which it never fully recovered. The significant difference between the two is that the first cohort experienced the digital revolution, the shift in mobile phone and internet technology to generally affordable and ubiquitous modes of communication, in their teens while the second cohort have lived their entire lives with this technology part of their everyday experience. Apart from this the experiences and attitudes of the two cohorts appear to have much more in common with each other than with the preceding (Baby Boomer) generation (Wyn et al., 2008). While the experiences of the participants in this research programme will differ from that of other young people in other places, the analysis of their experiences helps us both to investigate the impact of social changes that are widely experienced and provide a case study for illuminating what we see as the limitations of current conceptualisations of inequality in youth research.

As we will show in the coming chapters, the Life Patterns participants have been reshaping patterns of parenthood, marriage, cohabitation and work. They have, to greater and lesser degrees depending on the resources they have available to them, needed to rethink adulthood in terms not dependent on stability, security and continuity, and have also needed to see themselves as responsible for their outcomes even in the face of significant structural barriers. This does not make them all the same. As will become clearer in coming chapters, highly stratified life chances and the ways that young people have worked within the conditions they face have created relatively complex, diverse, and also unequal life pathways and outcomes. Using the birth of the cohort who graduated from secondary school in 1991 as our reference, we refer to this long generation in Australia as the post-1970s generation (Dwyer and Wyn, 2001). Such a categorisation is unlikely to fit perfectly in other parts of the world, and could no doubt be challenged, depending on the criteria used, even for Australian young people.

The possibility that the categorisation of generations may differ does not diminish the value of using the social generations lens that we advocate in this book. The concept of social generations is too fuzzy, and the world itself too complex, for 'objective' criteria on when one generation ends and another begins to be agreed upon. The identification of a generation, or the boundaries of a generational unit, will necessarily have a heuristic quality. By reviving the concept of social generation for use in sociological youth studies, we are not arguing that at some point in recent history the experience of youth, globally, was so radically transformed that everything significant was either reversed or made insignificant in one moment. Young people's lives and attitudes are not alien to those of the generation before. Indeed, the Life Patterns research shows that the post-1970s generation had hopes that were similar to those we associate with the 'Baby Boomer' and other generations – fulfilling work, security of work and relationships and a happy family life (Andres and Wyn, 2010). In the coming chapters we highlight many generational commonalities as well as tensions and note that factors that shaped the experience of youth in previous eras and other places have not 'disappeared' but may be playing a new role in new times and places. Generation is hence a valuable concept for orienting investigations in a changing world where old divisions have to be actively reinforced and even made anew to continue.

Structure of the Book

The lives of young people today are not the same as they were for members of the post-war baby boom in their youth. Using the concepts of 'social generation' and 'individualisation', developed with the help of many other theoretical resources, we aim to provide a framework for the widely-shared goal of understanding patterns of inequality in changing times. We begin to build our argument in Chapter 2 by sketching out the current conditions of young lives in different parts of the world, including the shift of cultural, economic and political influence away from Europe and North America, before turning to the specific conditions in Australia. We focus on the expansion of educational participation, the creation of new forms of consumption, youth cultures, and the changing nature of work on a global scale. The chapter shows that far from making the social divisions of class, gender, location and race long identified by sociologists irrelevant, these changes appear to point to new ways in which longstanding inequalities are being produced and entrenched. This raises the question of which conceptual tools provide the most effective grasp of the processes creating inequality in the context of changing times, which we take up in the chapters that follow.

In Chapter 3, using changes in the experience of youth traced out in Chapter 2 as a backdrop, we discuss debates about change and inequality in youth studies. Our particular focus is on the individualisation thesis (Beck, 1992). In one way our aim is deflationary, to show that the concept of individualisation is not as radical or innovative as many assume and that it has many points of resonance and overlap with unlikely sources, such as theories of intersectionality or hybridity. Our aim, however, is also to show that, given the concept of individualisation is not the radical denial of social structure that some assume, it nonetheless raises key points about the conditions of contemporary life for young people that are often overlooked.

Above all, we argue that some of the responses to the individualisation thesis in youth studies conflate inequality with continuity, limiting at least some contemporary youth research from fulfilling its promise.

Throughout the chapter we revisit debates about individualisation and the 'reflexive' shaping of life chances to create an alternative understanding of the concept that is both well supported by the writings of the authors who developed the thesis and by empirical patterns identifiable in the lives of young people in the Life Patterns research programme. We understand the individualisation thesis as issuing a challenge to researchers to reconceptualise class, gender and race for contemporary conditions, in which an ever greater number of incompatible or unreachable demands are foisted upon young people. As such, we also argue for thinking of reflexivity as an effort to hold together competing and sometimes seemingly incompatible demands. In everyday life, and across the biography, we hold that it is not the most privileged but the least who are likely to face the greatest demands to be reflexive.

Chapter 4 builds the conceptual basis for our approach to youth studies. We show how the relatively neglected work of Karl Mannheim (1952) on the sociology of generations provides a foundation for thinking more productively about the relationship between change and inequality in young lives. While in need of some updating, the concept of a social generation points towards a framework that enables an understanding of social change and of inequality. Mannheim distinguishes three primary components of a generation: the cultural and structural conditions in which a generation is shaped; the ways that young people develop particular dispositions in the context of these conditions; and differences between groups of young people sharing a generation (which he calls different 'generational units'). As a generational unit is on one dimension defined by their difference to the generation before and on another by its differences with other units within the same generation, it can provide the basis for a framework that explicitly enables an analysis of the active recreation of stratification in the context of social change.

In Chapters 5 and 6 we apply this generational framework to engage with the two most influential streams of contemporary youth research. While the sociology of youth is constituted by a loose constellation of approaches and interests, including studies of crime and deviance, leisure, family life and sexuality (Griffin, 1993), summaries of youth sociology widely recognise that for the last quarter of a century or so the field has had two dominant streams, a transitions approach and a cultures approach (Cohen, 2003). In these chapters we aim to show that a social generation frame provides another way to bridge the concerns of the two approaches and to better bring together their separate insights.

In Chapter 5 we turn to the value and limitations of recent transitions research, which traces young people's movements in and out of education, employment, relationships and housing arrangements. We argue that, while it has been and remains a valuable dimension of youth studies, the transitions paradigm and common understandings of the metaphor of transition reflect an underpinning in theories of youth development. This heritage makes it difficult for researchers to see beyond the boundaries of the transition from youth to adulthood, and hence to also see beyond debates about whether transitions are delayed or messy to ask about the relational construction of youth and adulthood. The meaning of adulthood, that which is being transitioned 'to', can change over time (Blatterer, 2007; Silva, 2012). Without a proper concept of generation, youth researchers can misdiagnose generational conditions and the subjectivities with which they are intertwined as simply a change in the timing of transition, or as the invention of an entirely new life stage (Arnett, 2004).

In Chapter 6 we apply our generational framework to an analysis of the relationship between change and inequality in youth cultural forms. We situate our analysis within ongoing debates about whether these forms are 'post-subcultural'. Since the subcultural approach tied to the Centre for Contemporary Cultural Studies (CCCS) first emerged in the 1970s, a stream of research has developed and strengthened over time that challenges the CCCS's key claim that the most significant youth cultural forms can be understood as subcultures of larger class cultures. Recent 'post-subculture' concepts such as neo-tribalism have been proposed as better able to capture contemporary modes of cultural practice and group belonging. In this chapter we suggest that the tendency to conflate evidence of inequality with evidence against change (which has tended to frame debates about individualisation) is arguably even starker on both sides of the post-subcultural debate in this stream of youth research. This has led post-subcultural theorists to simplify the position of the subcultural approach and fail to see continuities. It has also emboldened critics of post-subcultural approaches to over-emphasise the extent to which post-subcultural theorists have dismissed structural inequality and hence themselves pass over too quickly the substance of the challenge of tracing inequalities in new times.

As with the concept of individualisation, we interpret the post-subcultural turn less as a denial of structured inequality than as pointing to the challenge of tracing the impact of unequal resources in the context of the seemingly more fragmentary but still profoundly powerful sets of social structures in contemporary modernity. We finish the chapter by arguing that a biographical approach provides a way to understand youth cultural practices in the context of 'youth transitions' and generational change. This entails investigating young people's multiple engagements – in education, employment, cultural forms and relationships – and how they interact. Particularly in the context of individualising social structures, investments and demands in one sphere may or may not articulate easily with those in other spheres. Certain work practices for example may make participating in some leisure forms impossible.

In Chapters 7 and 8 we apply a biographical approach to examples taken from the Life Patterns research programme and return to larger questions about the challenges for youth research in the coming decades. Chapter 7 investigates the way the temporal structures of society are shaped for the current generation of young people in Australia, including by the rise of new information–communication technologies. Time is implicitly central to youth studies. Transitions research investigates the movement from one status to another and cultural research has focused on practices that unfold over time and the changing temporal orientation of youth cultural groupings. Yet concepts of time are rarely explicitly developed in youth studies. In this chapter we argue that focusing on the temporal structure of everyday life can clarify the nature of social change and its relationship to forms of inequality.

The chapter focuses on the impact of insecure and variable work on relationships with others, suggesting that the experience of youth is made in everyday life through synchronising social practices with significant others, and variable work patterns can make this harder. The timetables and rhythms of young people's lives have become more unstable and fragmented and hence less likely to neatly align with those of their friends and family unless active effort is expended synchronising lives and scheduling time together. This structural desynchronisation points to new forms of time-based inequality that impact on the way that young people and their networks of significant others can use the passing of time to build resources, enjoy the present, and shape the future. The chapter is hence a concrete example of the way that inequalities that in the abstract have a long history, such as control over time, are coming to function in new ways.

In Chapter 8 we turn to place. The changing experience of youth is not homogeneous across space. Space, place and mobility need to be part of any conceptualisation of youth. Youth research has tended to neglect place, but driven by human geography youth researchers are beginning to pay more attention to place and mobility and the way that these shape opportunities and identities (Nayak, 2003; Hopkins, 2010; MacDonald et al., 2010; Farrugia, 2014). In Australia, and possibly other countries, a significant marker of this generation's experience may be the need to coordinate varying 'non-standard' work hours, and also for many the timetables set by educational institutions, with the wish and need to regularly spend time with significant others. In other societies generational patterns are more significantly established through revolutionary social action, such as North Africa, partly in response to a lack of employment opportunities commensurate with growing levels of education, or through social transformations involving the extension of educational opportunities and flows from rural to urban settings, such as China.

The book finishes with a short conclusion. The conditions that shape youth experience vary across place and social position. Not only will these conditions vary across space, but the concepts that will help youth researchers to understand this experience may also be somewhat different in different places. Yet despite these differences the lives of young people around the globe are increasingly interconnected, which makes it almost impossible to avoid an awareness of other ways of life. While a global generation as an homogeneous entity is an impossibility, youth studies will need conceptual devices to analyse the way that the current young generations around the world are connected by digital technology, new demands for education, the impact of neoliberal economic pressures and associated forms of inequality, which in different ways shape all young lives.

2

GLOBAL CHANGE AND INEQUALITY

Youth studies can be central to developing an understanding of the dynamics of global economic, social, cultural and political changes that will play out over the next quarter of a century and their impact on young people. The economic opportunities and unprecedented levels of inequality within and across countries that are emerging as key aspects of these transformations will impact directly on youth: on what youth means and how it is experienced. For example, some have argued that we are witnessing the emergence of an 'Asian Century', influencing the whole world but driven in part by unprecedented change in the Asia–Pacific region, where 60 per cent of the world's young people live (UNESCAP, 2013a: 1). The expansion of the economies of some of the largest countries in Asia (for example, China, India and Indonesia) is creating new and powerful middle classes and elites, whose consumption needs are driving new economic activity in many countries. This expansion will create new opportunities (for example, markets that will open up new areas of production and consumption) and also new risks (poverty, ill health and social exclusion).

Young people are already centrally implicated in the expansion of educational participation around Asia and other parts of the Global South, and in the creation of new forms of consumption, youth cultures and the changing nature of work. Global economic, social and political relationships will increasingly shape the nature of youth as a social category – and the kinds of adulthoods that are possible. Therefore, we would argue that the future of youth studies lies in understanding forces that go beyond the borders of the nation state to impact on young people's lives, even if these processes must always be understood in local contexts.

Social science alone has the unique capacity to enable us to understand how our world is shaped by human endeavour, to understand the dynamic of inequality and how we can change it. This was the motivation for the social scientists who contributed to the birth of social science during the Industrial Revolution beginning around 1750. For example, the work of Marx, Durkheim and Weber, seen as among the significant figures in the founding of sociology, was motivated by a desire to understand the revolutionary forces that were changing the nature of economic life throughout the nineteenth and into the early twentieth century and their implications for social life (Giddens, 1971). Their contributions to understanding how economic structures create relationships of inequality (Marx), of the role of religion and of culture in building subjectivities that favour particular forms of economic activity (Weber), and of the dynamics of social integration and of social fragmentation (Durkheim), were instrumental in not only creating new understandings of social life, but also supporting people and organisations to work towards greater equality and social integration.

Periods of significant change have also galvanised social science in other ways. For example, first wave feminism arose in the late nineteenth and early twentieth centuries (including for example the work of Virginia Wolff, Mary Wollstonecraft and Marie Stopes) responding to the impact of industrialisation on women. The second wave feminist theories in the 1960s and 1970s (including for example the work of Simone de Beauvoir, Betty Friedan, Juliet Mitchell, Luce Irigaray, Nancy Chodorow and Mary Daly) were a direct response to the inequalities between men and women in the post-Second World War era, and to the failure of traditional academic work to address gender inequality. Today feminist thinkers are currently reimagining a third wave of feminist thought for contemporary conditions (Fraser, 2005).

Arguably, we are again living in times of significant social change that call on the social sciences to produce the concepts and frameworks that will enable an understanding of transformation. In this book we affirm the promise of youth studies to interpret the dynamics of social change in relation to young people, and to contribute to the building of socially just and enabling societies in the coming decades. In the following sections we briefly discuss the transformations unfolding around the global, with a focus on those that have the most significant impact on young people. We argue that three developments have made a significant impact on the nature of youth across many contexts: firstly, the universal push to increase levels of educational participation; secondly, increasing rates of urbanisation; and thirdly, the globalisation of youth labour markets. After tracing contemporary patterns of change and inequality globally, we turn to Australia and its similarities and differences from these broader patterns. In this context we discuss the failure of a market-based approach (also known as neoliberalism) to live up to the promise of economic security based on educational credentials and expanding, high-skills labour markets. We argue that market-based policies are creating new levels of national and international inequality with significant implications for the risks that young people bear, creating new forms of precarity and impacting on young people's health and wellbeing. This chapter concludes with a discussion of the challenges for youth studies in fulfilling its promise, and the conceptual tools that are needed, to make sense of the situation of young people today.

Education, Urbanisation and Employment

The challenge of youth studies in the context of the global changes that are alluded to above is considerable. The three dynamics (increasing rates of participation in education, new forms of work associated with global labour markets and increased urbanisation) are often described as new forms of mobility or 'mobilities' in the youth studies literature (see Chapter 8). These forms of mobility are related to and supported by advances in digital communication that enable increasingly sophisticated forms of connectivity, and they impact directly on young people's wellbeing (social, physical and economic) and their citizenship and political engagement. While these developments bring opportunities for young people, the evidence is that they also bring significant risks. Across all these domains, as we will discuss in more detail below, the trend is towards increasing inequalities within and between nations.

Rates of participation in tertiary education are increasing in almost all countries as governments use education as a tool for supporting economic growth. This expansion is based on the premise that education creates a demand for skilled labour and will ensure national competitiveness in increasingly global labour markets (Brown et al., 2011; OECD, 2011). The goal of achieving universal participation in secondary education is supported by the finding that workers with upper secondary education earn higher salaries than those with lower levels of education, and that unemployment decreases as educational attainment increases (OECD, 2010). Hence government policies assume a close relationship between increased educational participation by young people and economic prosperity. Statistical analysis by UNESCO shows that there has been a five-fold increase in tertiary students world-wide since 1970, with the most intense acceleration in participation since 2000 (UIS, 2009). This is one part of a broader trend for young people to stay longer in education and enter the labour market later than previous generations (Mason and Lee, 2012: 1).

Increasing rates of educational participation have contributed to the migration of young people from rural to urban and regional centres where secondary and tertiary educational institutions are in the vast majority located. Tertiary education is one of the factors pushing migration by young people to metropolitan centres, nationally and internationally. In 2007 over 2.8 million students were enrolled in educational institutions outside their country of origin, with an annual increase of around 5.5 per cent (UIS, 2009: 36). China sends most students to international destinations, and the US hosts most international students, followed by the UK, France, Australia, Germany, Japan, Canada and South Africa. These countries host 71 per cent of the world's international students (UIS, 2009: 36–7). However, China, the Republic of Korea and New Zealand have become increasingly popular destinations for tertiary students (UIS, 2009: 43).

These trends mean that young people in all countries are increasingly subject to the transition regimes of educational participation, to the extent that these regimes transcend national borders; they are global. Transition regimes, a term employed by du Bois-Reymond and Stauber (2005: 63), refer to the institutional processes, practices and discourses of the education systems, labour markets and welfare systems that shape the meaning and experience of youth through institutional transition points and statuses, such as the completion of secondary education or entry into full-time employment. Examples of this process are provided by Kelly (2006) who shows how transition regimes in Australia circumscribe the horizons of identity for young people, and by Mizen (2004) who provides an analysis of how welfare systems in the UK define the meaning of youth.

The scale and pace of urbanisation over the last decades are also influenced by labour markets. As we discuss in other chapters in this book (see for example Chapters 5 and 8) the concentration of youth in urban areas is a distinguishing feature of this generation of young people. It impacts on their relationships with place and has implications for the temporal complexities that they have to manage. The prevalence of urbanisation amongst young people has contributed to a sense of urban ubiquity in youth studies that obscures the relevance of place and the interrelationships between rural and urban places.

The process of urbanisation has been especially striking in some Asian countries. More than half of the world's mega-cities (i.e. 13 out of 22) are found in Asia and the Pacific and seven of the world's ten most populated cities (i.e. Tokyo, Delhi, Shanghai, Mumbai, Beijing, Dhaka and Kolkata) are in the Asian region. These mega-cities are drivers of regional and global economic activity. They are attractive to industries seeking the efficiency of economies of scale and they are centres of cultural activity, creativity and diversity (Kraas, 2007). For these reasons, cities are also very attractive to young people (Tranberg-Hansen et al., 2008).

Young people are also implicated in changing patterns of employment. The idea of 'entering the labour market' is usually understood as the step that young people take after they have become qualified and are seeking employment in a field or occupation that recognises their educational qualification. However, although the transition from education into work is often portrayed in this linear way to reflect the shift from one status (student) to another (worker) the reality, ever since tertiary education became normative (for example, in the 1990s in Australia), is that young people mix (or juggle) study and work over a period of ten years or more (Andres and Wyn, 2010).

The prevalence of mixing work and study over extended periods of time is supported by analyses of youth labour markets that reveal the extent to which precarious work is spreading across the globe. There is no clear definition of precarious work. For example, Omerbasic's (2012) discussion of such work amongst young people points out that in Denmark part-time, fixed-term and temporary agency work is often not considered to be precarious work. This term is reserved for work that is 'involuntary', or that has insufficient working hours to secure work-based benefits and employment security. But other analyses of precarious work, such as the analysis of precarious work amongst young people in the OECD by Scarpetta and Sonnett (2012), argue that the widespread scale of temporary work for young people creates precarity. On average, nearly 40 per cent of young people in the OECD aged 15–24 are employed in temporary work, and this rises as high as 50 per cent in Slovenia, Poland, Spain, Sweden, Portugal, France, Germany and Switzerland (Scarpetta and Sonnett, 2012: 7). Research on the nexus between education and employment for young people in France identifies the 'scarring effect' of unemployment and precarious work. Chauvel (2010) states that France (and by implication other countries with similar youth employment patterns) is facing long-term scarring effects, both on individual lives and for welfare regimes (which depend on high levels of labour market engagement by the young). Chauvel argues that a *génération précaire* is emerging in France, made up by well-educated young people who are the children of upwardly mobile Baby Boomers who will never have the employment opportunities of their parents. This generation, he says, will bear the (scarring) effects throughout their lives of reduced opportunities in their youth.

This section has drawn attention to global processes impacting on young people in the current generation. We hold that educational institutions and labour markets today increasingly constitute a global transition regime. These processes include the expansion of transition regimes in which almost universal completion of secondary education is a reality in developed countries and a goal in developing countries, and in which tertiary education is increasingly normative. As young people in various countries and locations spend longer in education they experience common generational effects, including increased or new forms of dependence on their families, or the state, for a longer time than the previous generation, and increased levels of financial stress as they struggle to finance their education and to meet debts incurred during their education years (ILO, 2013). One of the other effects of these global transition regimes is increased youth mobility, as young people shift from rural to urban areas to access secondary and tertiary education, and as an elite go offshore to access educational institutions in other countries. Finally, the transition regime of education contributes to precarious work, as young people seek flexible employment to survive financially through the student years and yet often remain stuck in less secure employment after they graduate despite their credentials. In the face of these changes, inequalities between young people continue and in many cases are exacerbated.

Inequality

As in the past, understanding inequality is the central challenge for a relevant youth studies. The dynamics of global change identified above bring new patterns of inequality between individuals, groups, regions and nations. Far from making social division in the form of social class, race, gender and location irrelevant, social change is forging new forms of inequality and at the same time also reinscribing older inequalities in new ways. Each of the key dimensions of social change impacting on young people that we have identified above is associated with widening inequalities. The questions youth studies faces are twofold: what does inequality look like and what conceptual tools provide the most useful grasp of the processes creating, and potentially alleviating, inequality? We take up these questions throughout the book. Here we identify some of the important indicators of inequality in relation to young people and consider the implication of new inequalities for our understanding of youth and generation.

Inequality and the market

In an article on poverty in the Pacific, Abbott (2007) argues that the region is experiencing increased levels of poverty and hardship. The difficulties being experienced in some Pacific countries (the Cook Islands, Fiji, Kiribati, Samoa, Tuvalua and Tonga for example) are attributed to the global financial crisis and other 'global externalities', to concern about the impact of climate change on these countries, and to high levels of migration from rural to urban areas within these countries (2007: 61). People in these countries are experiencing daily difficulties in meeting their needs. The fact that young people are particularly impacted by these conditions, resulting in poor health, poor school attendance and low rates of school completion, means that the cycle of poverty and marginalisation is difficult to break. Abbott identifies an increase in rates of HIV as being one of the outcomes of these new patterns of widespread poverty. Abbott's description of the integration of Pacific Island economies and societies into global markets provides an illustration of how these processes create new, wider and widening gaps between those who have resources and those who do not:

> Increases in user charges for government services, particularly for health and education place particular burdens on low-income households. Even where education is nominally free, there are frequently additional costs now imposed by schools for books, materials, and building and maintenance funds, often as a result of funding cut-backs or simply lack of resources from national budgets. Introducing improved transport and communication services raises demand and the need to pay for them. Promoting the private sector increases the availability of goods and services and also the need for money with which to purchase them. (2007: 67)

Indeed, the logic of markets (as the central driving mechanism of neoliberal government policies) appears to demand the existence or even creation of inequalities within and across countries. For example, Connell (2013) argues that new mechanisms and technologies have been developed specifically to enhance inequality in education, thereby creating the sense of a need to make choices in new educational markets or risk missing out. Connell argues that in order to encourage parents to buy privatised educational services, the risk of being a 'loser' has to be created and publicised. In other words, a central dynamic in creating educational markets is the creation of a relative scarcity of positive outcomes, so that education has a competitive value on global markets. Connell argues that the high-stakes testing being taken up in more and more countries is a mechanism for the identification and from there the publication of lists of winners and losers. Although high-stakes testing (e.g. national standardised tests) remains a popular strategy for governments there is widespread evidence of the negative impact of such testing on students' wellbeing, including its potential to impact on their self-esteem and lower teachers' expectations of students (Perrone, 1991; Stiggins, 1999; Gregory and Clark, 2003; Schroeder, 2006). There is also evidence of negative effects on service delivery and professional–parent relationships and the stress, anxiety, pressure and fear experienced by students (Polesel et al., 2012: 4). Lingard (2011) also highlights the global influence of quasi markets as a strategy adopted by neoliberal governments through the privatisation of public policy and public policy delivery. Echoing Connell's analysis, Lingard argues that through organisations such as the OECD there has been a global shift towards quasi markets (in education) and the discourse of citizens as consumers exercising choice (2011: 367).

On a global scale the gap between rich and poor is as large as ever. A report by UNICEF finds that the world's top 20 per cent of the population enjoys 70 per cent of total income and the world's richest quintile gets 80 per cent of the global income (UNICEF, 2011: vii). It also notes that children and young people are overrepresented in the lowest groupings, with approximately 50 per cent of the world's children and young people living below the $2 a day poverty line. This continues while the income for the world's richest people has increased, with the largest gains made by the top 1 per cent of the world's wealthy. The OECD has identified an increasing reliance on wage-earning and the decreasing role of welfare, benefits and tax redistribution as central factors in the spectacular widening of inequality in many OECD countries, including the USA and Australia (2011: 18). Since the early 2000s, the direct relationship between globalisation and inequality had been identified in a raft of reports (see for example, ILO, 2004, 2008, 2010; Sutcliffe, 2004; United Nations, 2005; IMF, 2007; OECD, 2008; Ravallion, 2008).

In developing countries increasing and chronic levels of poverty impact on young people directly through health and wellbeing. For example, UNICEF (2011) offers conclusive evidence in its analysis of household survey data from across the developing world. In particular, this report compares children and young people from developing country households in the poorest income quintile with those in the richest income quintile of the same country. It finds that those in the poorest income quintile are nearly three times as likely to be underweight; less likely to attend school; and, for girls, three times as likely to get married before the age of 18 as their peers in the richest income quintile (UNICEF, 2011: 37).

Other dimensions of inequality include the effects of increasing rates of urbanisation, especially in developing economies, and gender-based discrimination. For example, the Economic and Social Commission for Asia and the Pacific (ESCAP), a commission of the United Nations, found that in the Asia–Pacific region poverty is growing faster in urban than rural areas as the proportion of people living in urban slums increases exponentially (UNESCAP, 2013b: 3). This report also documents the expansion of urban slums and growing inequality within cities. There is also evidence that these developments favour men over women. For example, overall young women have more difficulty than young men in finding work. In some countries women are especially disadvantaged in the labour market (for example in the Middle East and North Africa) and the ILO (2010: 5) found that in most countries (with the exception of the European Union and developed economies) the gap between young women's and young men's participation in paid work widened between 2007 and 2009.

The discussion above has drawn on recent reports to illustrate just some of the dimensions of inequality that have emerged over the last decades and that are anticipated to increase in the future. We turn now from the bigger global picture to the Australian context, looking at population trends among younger people that show examples of these broader processes in Australia. In the following chapters we will draw on examples from our own research, undertaken within this Australian context, in developing our proposals for the sociology of youth.

Australia in a Changing World

Census data from the Australian Bureau of Statistics (ABS, 2013) point to significant changes in patterns of work, education and relationships and a growing cultural diversity. Some of the more substantial shifts are summarised in Table 2.1.

Table 2.1 Comparison of trends for young people 18–34 years in Australia 1976 and 2011

Trend	1976 (%)	2011 (%)
Education		
Non-school qualification	30	52
Bachelor degree or higher	5	26
Attending an educational institution	Men 17	Men 25
	Women 10	Women 28
Work		
Labour-force participation	Men 88	Men 79
	Women 54	Women 69
Part-time employment	11	34
Identity and relationships		
Married	64	29
Median age of first marriage	Men 24	Men 30
	Women 21	Women 28
Born overseas	23	27
Place of birth	*UK/Ireland 36*	*UK/Ireland 10*
(percentage of those born	*Rest of Europe 40*	*Rest of Europe 7*
overseas)	*Asia 11*	*Asia 53*
Religion	No religion 12	No religion 29
	Christian 74	Christian 50
	Other 14	Other 21

Source: Australian Bureau of Statistics (2013) *Australian Social Trends: Young Adults Then and Now*, Cat. No. 4102.0, April 2013 (data from Australian Census 1976, 2011)

The life context of young Australians has been changing steadily since well before 1976, but changes have been rapid and pronounced in the past thirty-five years. At the beginning of the twentieth century attending university was exceptionally rare, and while there was some growth after the Second World War, between 1975 and today there has been a boom in enrolments. Between 1975 and 2008 the Australian university sector expanded from 19 universities and 175,000 students to 39 universities (and over 150 non-university tertiary providers) educating 772,000 students (Department of Education, Employment and Workplace Relations, 2009). This doubling in the number of universities and more than quadrupling in the number of students in little more than three decades has shifted going to university from an elite to a mass experience. As Table 2.1 shows in 1976 only 1 in 20 (5 per cent) of Australians aged 18–34 had a Bachelor degree or higher, while by 2011 this was 26 per cent.

Focusing on 25–34 year olds, when most will have had time to complete a degree, it is clear there has been significant change in even the past ten years. Between 2002 and 2012 the proportion of this group with at least a Bachelor qualification increased from 25 per cent to 37 per cent (ABS, 2012a). While young men are much more likely to undertake post-compulsory school-ing, including attending university, than their fathers, the greatest growth has occurred for young women who have overtaken men in enrolment numbers in higher education (ABS, 2013).

In contrast to the relatively sequential patterns of education and then employment for many of their parents, the overwhelming majority of post-secondary school students in contemporary Australia are also workers, with estimates of between two-thirds to almost three-quarters of university stu-dents working during the semester (ABS, 2008; Devlin et al., 2008). This mixing of work and study explains why the number of people aged 18–34 in paid employed has not shown an equivalent decrease as the length of time in education has expanded. Table 2.1 shows that the number of men aged 18–34 in paid employment has dropped somewhat (from 88 to 79 per cent) since 1976. Yet at the same time the number of women in paid work in this age bracket has increased by the greater margin of 15 per cent (from 54 to 69 per cent). Driven by women's increased participation in the workforce, overall participation in employment across the ages of 18–34 has actually increased from 71 to 74 per cent between 1976 and 2011, even as educational partici-pation has expanded (ABS, 2013).

Patterns of working hours have also changed since 1976, such that the once standard 40-hour week is now only the experience of a minority. On the one hand, as Table 2.1 shows, there has been a tripling of part-time employment among the 18–34 age bracket (from 11 to 34 per cent), and this is most likely linked in part to the large proportion of young people combining paid work with study or unpaid care work. On the other hand, those still in full-time employment are much more likely to be working more than 40 hours a week, increasing from 25 to 38 per cent (ABS, 2013).

Whether full-time or part-time, young people in employment are more likely than their parents at the same age to be working with reduced job security. In 1982 fewer than 1 in 10 employees were on what is called in Australia a 'casual contract', but this has now more than doubled to a fifth of the Australian workforce (Shomos et al., 2013: 78), including almost half (48 per cent) of employed 15–24 year olds (ABS, 2008). A casual contract comes with a small pay loading but with the removal of security of tenure and leave entitlements, and little legislative protection over number of hours to be worked and the period of notice required before patterns of work are changed (Campbell, 2004).

Relationships

As more young men and women are pursuing further education and facing a changing labour market, new patterns of intimate relationships and family formation are also emerging. Table 2.1 shows that the likelihood of an Australian aged 18–34 being married more than halved between 1976 and 2011, with the age of first marriage now 30 for men and 28 for women (compared to 24 and 21 in 1976). Compared to their parents, the current generation are also less likely to have children and much more likely to have their first child after the age of 30 (ABS, 2005).

Alongside a later age of marriage, the percentage of 18–34 year olds still living with at least one parent has increased, but less significantly, from 21 to 29 per cent. The more significant change in living arrangements has been the increase in, and growing social acceptance of, de-facto living arrangements. The percentage of the Australian population unmarried but cohabiting tripled between 1982 and 2006 (to 14 per cent). This is not evidence of the end of the institution of marriage however, and the nature and extent of the change are better highlighted by the percentage who now cohabit before marriage. In the 1960s only approximately 5 per cent of people cohabited before marriage, while by 2006 the number was 15 times higher at 75 per cent (Buchler et al., 2009).

Diversity

While general patterns are evident in the data presented in Table 2.1, there is also now a greater diversity of experience. As most young people are studying longer, taking longer to establish themselves in the labour market and to marry and start families than their parents, it has also become more common for young Australians to have children while in their mid-teens and leave school at this point (Australian Institute of Health and Welfare, 2011).

Alternative living arrangements and relationship types, including same-sex relationships, are also more accepted than ever before. This is arguably linked to a relative weakening of the hold of Christian religious belief in Australia. As Table 2.1 shows, more 18–34 year old Australians now profess no religious faith than in 1976 (29 per cent from 12 per cent), and there is a greater diversity of faiths, with a 24 per cent drop in the number of young people identifying as Christian (74 to 50 per cent) and a rise in those professing other beliefs (14 to 21 per cent). Relatedly, the ethnic background of young people in Australia has also changed significantly since 1976. The number of young Australians born overseas coming from various parts of Asia has increased almost fivefold (11 to 53 per cent).

Continued inequality

Despite these changes, however, the divisions that have long been a primary focus of sociological analysis – such as class, gender, race and place – continue to shape how youth is experienced for different groups. While the expansion of higher education has opened up new opportunities across the social spectrum, socio-economic status also continues to impact on educational attainment. Using the Socio-Economic Indexes for Areas (a widely used place-based measure of socio-economic disadvantage in Australia), the Australian Bureau of Statistics (2009b) has shown that young people aged 20–24 years from the most disadvantaged 20 per cent were approximately one third as likely to have completed or be undertaking a Bachelor-level degree compared to young people from the most advantaged 20 per cent of areas (19 to 54 per cent). Young people from the city are similarly almost twice as likely to attend university as young people in rural areas (James, 2001), and despite a small narrowing of the gap, indigenous status remains one of the strongest correlates of reduced opportunity. In 2011 indigenous Australian were 32 per cent less likely to complete secondary school than non-indigenous young people, and were almost four times less likely to achieve a Bachelor-level degree (ABS, 2012b).

Furthermore, inequalities do not equalise out even if young people from disadvantaged groups do manage to enter higher education. Young people from lower socio-economic backgrounds are less likely to attend the most prestigious universities or enrol in the more prestigious courses (James et al., 2004). After graduation, gender patterns become particularly stark. While young women now represent the majority of graduates, and are arguably the group that has most benefitted from the rapid expansion of further education, a significant pay gap continues to favour men. This gender gap appears immediately upon graduation, with female full-time graduate employees earning 4 per cent less than their male counterparts. The gap is even higher with a postgraduate qualification, with men's median earnings 18 per cent higher than women's in the first year after completing a Master's degree by coursework (ABS, 2012c).

In the context of these changes, young people's wellbeing may be suffering. Some patterns of physical health are very positive. In particular, young Australians are less likely to die than at any previous point in history. Patterns of mental illness and psychological distress are, however, less positive. Rates for many mental illnesses are highest among young people and this trend may be getting worse, and again many of the standard sociological variables correlate with patterns of health inequality (Eckersley, 2011). While rates are similarly high across socio-economic groups, among those aged 16–24 young women are 7 per cent more likely to suffer a mental disorder than young men and indigenous young people are more than twice as likely to do so as their non-indigenous peers (Australian Institute of Health and Welfare, 2011). Other longstanding social divisions that have only more recently become the focus for sustained sociological attention also correlate with mental health. Despite many changes for the better in attitudes towards sexuality in Australia, it is same-sex attracted young people who appear to face the greatest pressures on their wellbeing. This group are approximately three times as likely as their peers to report anxiety or depression (ABS, 2008).

The Failure of the Neoliberal Promise

In Australia, as elsewhere, new transition regimes position education as a tool for economic development and labour market competitiveness. These regimes institutionalise the presumed but increasingly less secure links between education and labour markets for individuals and for economies. As we will discuss in Chapter 5, the notion of youth transitions is often synonymous with the transition from education into the labour market, a point that Kelly (2006) emphasises through his analysis of the necessity of the entrepreneurial self to making a successful transition in times of uncertainty. The impact of these transition regimes, and their failures, is evidenced in the statistical patterns above.

The global financial crisis from 2008 onwards has highlighted the weakness of the link between educational qualifications and labour markets. Although in general educational qualifications are associated with better employment conditions in the long term, the value of educational credentials as a strategy for gaining secure and meaningful employment is being undermined. For example, a recent report on youth unemployment in Denmark makes the point that although 'education and employment are inseparable in the Danish context', after the global financial crisis education no longer protects young people from part-time and insecure work (Omerbasic, 2012). A report from the International Labour Organisation (ILO) argues that increasing rates of unemployment for young people in many countries, including Australia, are creating a 'generation at risk' (ILO, 2013). This report shows that although the global financial crisis of 2008 exacerbated unemployment levels, rising rates of unemployment for the young had become a 'persistent and growing trend' and irregular employment and informal labour have been increasing since before the crisis (ILO, 2013: 1). The ILO identifies a 'mismatch' between the skills that are required in new labour markets and those that young people have (leading to the identification of a new category of young people: the 'over-educated'), as well as a lack of quality employment opportunities (ILO, 2013: 1). Research on labour markets in the Asia Pacific region concludes that for young graduates 'the potential benefits from earlier investments are not fully realized' due to a lack of job opportunities in labour markets in the region (Mason and Lee, 2012: 80).

Indeed, we would argue that the neoliberal promise of a close nexus between education and employment for young people was never realised. As Quinlan (2012) points out, precarious work has been a constant feature of labour markets in many countries since the late 1970s, even for those with higher levels of education. This challenges one of the key assumptions underpinning neoliberal economic regimes – that investment in education (by individuals and governments) is necessarily an investment in secure, high-quality work. This theme is taken up by Brown and colleagues (2011) who say that the investment in education by individuals has not been matched by the other part of the 'neoliberal bargain', namely the promise of jobs and rewards. In the global competition for jobs the apparent value of investing in knowledge building has largely failed to materialise. Instead, young people are faced with a high-skill, low wage labour market. Brown and colleagues' analysis of the nexus between education and employment in the USA finds that the free market approach that underpins neoliberal government policies is driving down the value of education as employers draw on global labour markets to find the cheapest sources of labour

(Brown et al., 2011). This enables employers to employ graduates in parts of the world where costs of living (and hence the price of labour) are low, driving down the global price of labour. For example, the Australian-based site freelancer.com.au claims to be the world's largest outsourcing marketplace, offering to provide labour for 'any project' from one of Freelancer's 9.6 million global bank of 'freelancers' at 'a fraction of the cost' (of regular labour markets presumably).

Brown and colleagues also describe the development of a 'new Taylorism' in which labour is reduced to discrete skills that are bought on the open market. This process undermines the professionalism of occupations (for example, in law, education, medicine or engineering), fundamentally changing the meaning of professional work. As they point, out the meaning of jobs is changing, and profession and job titles such as manager, consultant, academic or engineer no longer tell us as much as they used to about income, job security, career opportunities, or where these jobs are. These developments combine to create what these authors refer to as an 'opportunity trap' in which people are forced to spend time, effort and money on activities that may have little purpose in achieving their goals.

The impact of the failure of the neoliberal promise on young people has yet to be fully understood. However, some clues are provided by Berlant (2011) who explored the idea of 'cruel optimism' as a description of how people navigate situations of incoherence and precariousness. She describes the development of strategies for survival and modes of adjustment for getting by when fantasies of the good life become unsustainable. She also discusses the affective structure of optimism that sustains fantasies of the good life in the face of growing evidence of their improbability, arguing that optimism becomes cruel when 'the very pleasures of being inside a relation have become sustaining regardless of the content of the relation' (Berlant, 2011: 24). We interpret this to mean that being engaged in education (for example) gives young people a sense of achievement and progress, despite the evidence that educational qualifications are a blunt tool for achieving job security. She argues that embedded conditions of precariousness have given rise to a 'crisis of ordinariness' (i.e. a focus on 'small things', like adjusting the definitions of which categories of disadvantaged qualify for social security support, rather than addressing the causes of poverty) and analyses a range of situations in which individuals have developed strategies of survival and adjustment to the incoherence and precariousness of life (Berlant, 2011: 10). Many of the descriptions of young people's lives presented in this book resonate with her analysis.

The role of young people in the Arab Spring uprisings from 2009 onwards underlines the potentially significant political implications when the gap between the expectations for employment of an educated generation and the reality becomes unbearable. As Khalaf and Khalaf (2011) highlight, the Arab Spring has a social history grounded in the raised aspirations and globally connected networks of young people. In many of the Middle Eastern countries (including Egypt, Tunisia and Libya) where young people mobilised against traditional leaders, more than half the population were under the age of 35 (Khalaf and Khalaf, 2011). In these countries, even precarious work was dwarfed by the extent of youth unemployment. The ILO reports that the Middle East had the highest rates of youth unemployment of all regions in the world, where youth represented 44 per cent of the unemployed (ILO, 2013: 19).

Theory in Youth Studies

The social changes that are central to this book constitute a challenge to youth researchers because they involve new dynamics that interact with and reshape older dynamics and processes. This means that youth researchers need to be especially attentive to, and reflexive about, their use of theories and concepts. For example, as this chapter argues, inequality is a central dynamic impacting on young people's lives. We acknowledged at the outset of this chapter that the emergence of inequalities during the Industrial Revolution and beyond was one of the factors that drove theorists to consider the relationship between individuals and societies – including the ways in which economic processes contribute to (unequal) social structures and in which cultures, including religions, both reflect and contribute to contemporary economic processes. Systematic social inequality was a central motivation for the development of theories of class, culture and the impacts of the division of labour, and for the development of first and second wave feminist theory. We would argue that in late modernity, while class, gender, religion and culture continue to shape people's lives in profound ways, their analysis requires paying attention to the specific ways in which this occurs in current contexts.

As we will explore in Chapter 3, the issue of how to characterise contemporary dynamics of class and gender (in particular) has become a central debate in youth studies. To say that there has been change is not to say that social divisions no longer matter. On the contrary, as this book argues throughout, in many respects social change has brought an intensification of inequality. Existing social forms can take on new significance and even meaning in different social formations over time (Sassen, 2008), and it is important to understand what this looks like in different contexts and how young people themselves make sense of their circumstances in everyday life.

We agree with Ball (2006) who argues for the necessity and violence of social theory, pointing out that theories are heuristic devices, necessary for making sense of social life. This becomes a problem when we lose sight of the work that theories do in making aspects of social life visible and obscuring others. This is because the positions we take and the theories we use play a significant role in making the objects of our research (to paraphrase Ball, 2006: 3–4). As Ball also explains, over-identification with one theory risks making the world more orderly than it is. For these reasons, the theoretical concepts that frame our analysis of young people's lives in a time of change are broad-based ones that enable us to draw on the work of a range of theorists, and, we recognise, in drawing on these theorists, that theories are never complete (Ball, 2006: 5).

In working with theory in this book we are also aware of the critique of Northern Theory and the promotion of Southern Theory by Connell. Connell asks how 'the social location of a group of thinkers is significant for the ideas they produce' (2007: 268) and concludes that in order to recognise the validity of nonmetropolitan experience it is necessary to challenge the terms in which theory is constituted (2007: 381). A central element of this is to move beyond the Eurocentrism of sociological theorising and embrace sociological research that is by academics and about societies that are outside the metropole.

This chapter sets the larger context of inequalities in a global context and explores what these mean for youth. Strictly speaking, in Connell's terms of reference for Southern Theory, the perspectives covered in the following chapters would fall short because they are informed by theories that derive from the Global North. However, from the international and global perspective that informs this book, and recognising the idea of the Asian Century, Australian youth studies is positioned on the border between North and South. Australian youth research continues to engage largely with theoretical traditions and empirical research that derive from the Global North, but Australia is also part of the Asian region, and shares much with other countries along the Pacific Rim. It may take another generation of youth sociologists to deeply engage with Southern conceptual traditions and empirical studies and to understand what this means. While to some extent our position allows a double perspective on the global situation, we cannot claim to represent a Southern perspective, and are not sure that one either exists or is desirable. This book remains primarily oriented towards theories and debates coming from the Global North, using these to think about empirical patterns in Australia (and elsewhere). We will return to the challenge of understanding these global division and interconnections in Chapter 8 as well as the concluding chapter, noting that the focus of youth studies will need to shift towards Asia, where the majority of young people in the world are currently located and will be in the future, creating a challenge for the field to draw on intellectual resources and concepts developed outside of Europe and North America.

Conclusion

To accept Connell's critique of the limiting effects of Northern Theory may not mean that we need to abandon the concepts that have been used previously to instead create or draw on different theories. Instead we may be able to enrich and rework those we have. The inequalities between young people within countries are often stark, but the divisions between the North and South tend to be even more immense. To equate these would be ethically and politically suspect as well as empirically unjustifiable. Yet at the same time, the pressures and opportunities of economic and cultural globalisation are reshaping young people's lives in both the Global South and North, creating new interconnections and relationships that transcend the binary of North/South. There are also new relationships forged by the digital revolution, which while not equalising lives create a new awareness about how others are living and new imaginaries amongst young people.

There is also growing evidence that the 'neoliberal promise' (supported by global transition regimes) is failing young people. This book is intended to provide a starting point for a new way of conceptualising continuity and change for these conditions, asking not whether gender, race and class shape young lives but how in the context of global connections this takes place. We begin to build this framework in the next chapter.

3

INDIVIDUALISATION

In the previous chapter we set the scene by tracing the impact of global neoliberal transition regimes, focusing in detail on how education, employment and relationship patterns in Australia have changed between the 1970s and today. Many youth researchers hold that current sociological theories aiming to diagnose the nature of the large-scale changes we discussed in that chapter either underemphasise or worse actively deny the ongoing relevance of inequality. One of these theories in particular, the 'individualisation' thesis (Beck, 1992), arguing that institutional transformations are creating a demand for greater biographical decision making, has been pivotal in youth researchers coming to this conclusion.

Recent debates about change and inequality in youth studies have to a significant degree proceeded through an empirically grounded critique of the individualisation thesis on social change. To summarise and simplify a huge diversity of work, a general consensus about the individualisation thesis exists in two parts. The first is that the thesis might correctly identify some significant changes that have occurred in much of the Global North, and to some extent maybe even beyond, particularly a greater 'messiness' or non-linearity in the institutionalised pattern of young lives. The second is that it has none-the-less tended to exaggerate the extent of change and failed to recognise far more significant continuities in the ways that class, gender and race continue to shape outcomes.

In this chapter we trace the way these views have informed the debate about individualisation. We also provide evidence for the claim that we are not simply providing an alternative interpretation of the individualisation thesis, but are exposing the often implicit frameworks that critiques of individualisation draw on. In particular we discuss the ways in which (now traditional) critiques of the individualisation thesis limit our understanding of the relationship between inequality and social change. We are especially critical of the tendency to conflate the argument that the world is an unequal place for young people with the view that this establishes that social processes have not changed.

Individualisation has been understood by many youth researchers as a claim that social structural constraints have a diminishing influence on life chances and that individual choices and personal risk management abilities hence come to play a larger role in shaping outcomes. We would say that this is a misunderstanding that has arisen partly from ambiguities and obscurities in the theory itself, but also to a great extent from a tendency to equate social inequality with the continuity of social processes across time.

In the second half of this chapter we reconstruct individualisation as a concept for thinking about structured inequality. Our claims about individualisation as a concept are multifaceted. On the one hand we show that the individualisation thesis overlaps with a number of other theories that have come to prominence in recent decades, including some surprising synergies with race and post-colonial theorising, and is far less radical than some have suggested. Far from denying social structure, the individualisation thesis provides new insights into the changing relationships between individuals and institutions. On the other we show that, while the concept of individualisation may not be as radical or innovative as some have believed, it provides a useful starting point for conceptualising the changing experience of youth. We suggest that individualisation captures the spreading but unequally faced challenge of 'holding together' the biography in the face of new institutional constraints that threaten to pull it apart. In other words, we argue that instead of denying social inequality the concept of individualisation can be more fruitfully understood as a starting point for investigating how social factors shape patterns of inequality in contemporary conditions. Given our own geographical location and where our own research study has been based, our examples here as elsewhere in the text are often (though not exclusively) Australian, including many taken from the Life Patterns research programme with which we have both been integrally involved. Using the experience of the Life Patterns research participants to provide an empirical grounding for conceptual debates, we conclude the chapter by showing how gendered patterns of employment inequality in Australia, and the contradictions young women in particular are forced to navigate, can be understood as remade through social change.

Understanding Changing Patterns

Some of the most influential sociological theory of the past twenty-five years has argued that older certainties, such as those provided by stable gender roles or the unquestioned centrality and power of the nation state, are losing their hold, and as such the work of shaping the future increasingly becomes the active responsibility of each person (Giddens, 1991; Beck, 1992; Castells, 2000; Archer, 2012). These sociological arguments about changes to individual biographies should not be equated with so-called 'post-modern' positions that emphasise a more radical break with modernity in which new forms of play with representation and identity are emphasised (see for example Lyotard, 1984; Baudrillard, 1983; Jameson, 1991). The impact of this post-modern moment is sometimes overstated, and many authors seen by others as its proponents have actively distanced themselves from the label. It has instead been the theories of a new phase of modernity that have had a more significant and lasting influence on debate in social science broadly and in youth studies. Given the extent to which youth is associated with critical biographical turning points, the sociology of youth is an obvious area of study to put claims about changes to the biography under scrutiny (Leccardi and Ruspini, 2006; Furlong and Cartmel, 2007).

In this context the theory of 'individualisation' has received most attention. Use of the concept of individualisation and related notions such as 'self socialisation' has a long history, particularly within German-speaking sociology. Scholars in this tradition began to introduce the concept into English-language sociology in the late 1980s (Buchmann, 1989; Heinz, 1991, 1992). It has been, however, the engagement with and critiquing of the version of individualisation propounded by Ulrich Beck and his collaborators that has most significantly shaped the direction of research in recent youth studies.

Beck is perhaps most famed in youth research for purportedly proposing a form of individualisation that gives rise to a 'choice biography' (du Bois-Reymond, 1998; Woodman, 2009; Roberts, 2010). This 'choice biography' is contrasted with the 'normal biography' seen to have shaped the life course in the post-war period in much of Europe, Australia and North America. The 'normal biography' type is used to represent the relatively predictable and linear transitions – for example between education and employment and between the family of birth and an adult relationship and family formation – that were shared by most young people and hence standardised or 'normal'. Choice biographies in contrast are seen to emerge in the contemporary Global North as the predictability and assumed permanence of institutional structures around work, living arrangements and relationships are challenged. The weakening of the 'normal biography' is driven by a number of changes visible in the statistics from Australia in the previous chapter, including feminisation of the labour-market, an increased probability of regular career changes or retrenchment, the rise of single parenthood and a growing acceptability of divorce and co-habitation before marriage. The idea of a 'choice biography' is associated with the argument that these changes mean less of the biography appears given and more appears open to, or in need of, conscious decision making.

Many youth scholars have highlighted the argument that an active shaping of biography is required in contemporary conditions that appears in Beck's work (Brannen and Nilsen, 2005; Roberts, 2010). In the book that introduced his version of individualisation to the wider sociological community, Beck alluded to the experience of youth in stating that:

> Increasingly, everyone has to choose between different options, including as to which group or subculture one wants to be identified with ... In this sense, individualization means the variation and differentiation of lifestyles and forms of life, opposing the thinking behind the traditional categories of large-group societies – which is to say, classes, estates, and social stratification. (Beck, 1992: 88)

His work also reveals a tendency towards polemical language in his discussion of concepts in which youth sociologists are heavily invested. An example is the labelling of these 'traditional categories', including class, as 'zombie categories' (Beck, 2002). The idea of choice, and the concurrent questioning of the relevance of 'traditional categories' of stratification, have been central to the way that youth researchers have responded to the individualisation thesis. While many would agree that young people have new opportunities, and hence face the risk of making the 'wrong' decision, the individualisation thesis is widely felt to overemphasise the degree of change in society, and particularly change that is freeing young people from the constraints of social structures such as class (Roberts, 2010). As te Riele puts it, even if he does acknowledge a new risk consciousness and may not actually deny that inequality exists, the concept of choice biography is 'hazardous' because it 'ignores the constraints on the choices available to young people... [and] emphasises choices and rewards, rather than risks and penalties' (2004: 246). Even those who find some value in Beck's individualisation thesis tend to conclude that he has overemphasised agency and hence a 'middle way needs to be found' (Huq, 2006: 33; see also McLeod and Yates, 2006; Nayak and Kehily, 2008). This middle way would, according to many commentators, bridge Beck's theory of agency and the assumed liberation from structures, and traditional theories that emphasise the role of structure and social reproduction, such as those of Bourdieu (on the creation of social distinction) or the Birmingham School (on class-based youth cultures) (Evans, 2002, 2007; Lehmann, 2004; McLeod and Yates, 2006; Threadgold and Nilan, 2009; Threadgold, 2011).

A significant and compelling body of theoretical and empirical work has been amassed to critique claims of individualisation, calling these claims a 'new theoretical orthodoxy' (Brannen and Nilsen, 2002) or 'flavor of the month' (Cohen and Ainley, 2000: 80). These critiques have shown unequivocally that while new possibilities for young lives have been created over recent decades and young people have to make decisions, it is only a relatively small group of privileged young people that really get to make choices about their future (see Jones and Wallace, 1992; Andres et al., 1999; Brannen and Nilsen, 2002, 2005, 2007; Evans, 2002, 2007; Lehmann, 2004; McLeod and Yates, 2006; Roberts, 2010; Skrbis et al., 2011, amongst others). This work has provided substantial evidence that class, gender and race continue to shape young lives. Some have felt compelled to state that it is frustrating to have to make such a seemingly obvious point. Ken Roberts (2003) argues that debates about individualisation are replaying 'tired debates' about choice and constraint in youth sociology. He suggests that it is obvious that young people today, as before, choose within the constraint of structures outside their control. For Roberts (2003: 23) the key task of the sociology of youth is to avoid compounding the common 'fallacy' of individualisation to which 'young people and sometimes sociologists succumb'.

We agree with Roberts that engagements with the concept of individualisation within youth studies are sometimes frustrating, but for different reasons. The reiteration by many youth researchers that inequality continues to exist at times verges on caricature. We believe this tendency derives from an implicit and too simplistic dichotomy between social change and inequality. To put this another way, it is assumed that because inequality is persistent (and because it is also assumed to be the 'same' over time), this is evidence that at least in this sphere no significant social change has occurred or at a minimum that change has been substantially exaggerated. While the individualisation thesis, filtered through the concept of the so-called choice biography, has become one of the most discussed, (mis)interpreted and criticised concepts in youth studies, it is misleading to call the individualisation thesis an orthodoxy because there are few examples of this thesis being strongly and wholeheartedly endorsed. While many cite the concept of individualisation when noting changing patterns of education, employment and relationships in young lives, as we show above a significant number of youth researchers have claimed to 'test' the concept, either empirically or conceptually, and to find it fatally flawed (Andres et al., 1999; Evans, 2002, 2007; Lehmann, 2004; Skrbis et al. 2011).

As we argue in the coming section, we read individualisation not as a theory of agency but of changing social institutions, a theory that can be used, tested or critiqued only through doing the difficult work of showing not only *that* but also *how* social position shapes young lives. This work is too often elided in efforts to disprove a version of the argument that verges on caricature.

Bringing Zombie Categories Back to Life

We draw on the concept of individualisation as a resource for thinking about inequality when others have dismissed it for its apparent failure to account for inequality. Beck and his writing colleagues bear some responsibility for this dismissal and some of the criticisms of his work are well-founded. For many Beck's style of sociology is too wide-ranging, makes broad generalisations and overstatements too easily, and often seems to be contradictory (Atkinson, 2007; Threadgold, 2011; Sørensen and Christiansen, 2013: 135). In particular the scope and the speed with which Beck produces new theoretical claims across a range of fields mean that his work often overlooks nuances of the fields of research, from risk and insurance, to class analysis and even youth studies (see Beck and Beck-Gernsheim, 2009) in which he (often briefly) engages (Sørensen and Christiansen, 2013).

It is clear that Beck's writing not only focuses on but also even exaggerates social change. He readily admits to this, opening his famous *Risk Society* (1992: 9) with the statement that 'this book contains empirically oriented, projective social theory – without any methodological safeguards'. A later book states that '[e]very question concerning the shape of the future must be taken to extremes – not for the stake of being radical, but in order to break down the appearance of natural and eternal self-evidence with which "What-Exists" armours itself against any challenge' (Beck, 2000:10).

Linked to this aim of challenging what seems self-evident, as we previously noted, Beck has called class a 'zombie category' (Beck, 2002). Yet despite speaking of 'living–dead' sociological concepts, a relatively cursory engagement with the substance of his argument makes it difficult to argue that his point is that these divisions no longer matter. It is apparent that he is instead trying to challenge researchers to develop understandings of these social divisions for new times. As he puts it in *Risk Society*, 'class does not disappear just because traditional ways of life fade away … A new chapter in the history of classes is beginning, but we still need to comprehend its historical dynamics' (1992: 99).

He justifies this method on the basis that it can highlight failings in existing conceptual apparatuses, believing that new frames are needed for sociology, and that attempts to understand the current moment and emerging social structure using the dominant sociological concepts of the twentieth century miss too much, including the processes by which social inequality is being produced, because of the assumptions that are embedded in them:

> The purpose of my distinction between a first and a second age of modernity is *not* to introduce a new problematic evolutionary form of periodization based on either–or epochal 'stages', when everything is reversed at the same moment … The main purpose of the distinction … is a twofold one: first, to position the question of new concepts and frame of references and, second, to criticize conventional sociology as an empty-term sociology, a zombie sociology. In a research study at Munich University on 'reflexive modernization' … which I am in charge of, we are conducting long-term research on subjects like these: how does the meaning of 'class' change under the conditions of individualization and globalization? (Beck, 2002: 24, emphasis in original)

In the case of research on class, Beck argues that researchers often fail to capture the complex cross-national and multiply-mediated nature of contemporary inequality. This complexity means most significantly that the particular sets of circumstances facing people ostensibly sharing a class position will show considerable intra-class differentiation (2002: 29–30). Relatedly, this individualisation process weakens the basis for a shared class culture, tending to both dilute and obscure the uniformity of experience on which a shared class consciousness could emerge. Finally, the structural changes he proposes personalise the relationship between class and the state. To begin with there is a shift from class struggle to welfare-state support as an individual right that is relatively taken for granted, and then a shift again to new demands that people must actively do something or risk losing state support. This induces 'broken-down biographies' as it becomes more difficult to perceive of suffering as collective problems and hence 'social problems can be directly turned into psychological dispositions: into guilt feelings, anxieties' (Beck and Beck-Gernsheim, 2002: 24).

We would reiterate that Beck bears some responsibility for the criticisms his work has attracted. His method and the scale and complexity of his theorising, and the way his argument has shifted and developed over time, make significant interpretive demands on the reader. Yet he often appears caught in a 'Catch 22' in the face of some of the critique directed at his work. Ironically, when he does talk (regularly) about patterns of inequality, including class, this is paradoxically seen as further evidence to his critics that he does not think they exist. Atkinson for example says the following:

> The problem is, however, that Beck fails to acknowledge the ways in which some of the key institutions he heralds as *slayers* of class may be hindered in their allotted role by the fact that they are *riddled with class processes themselves*, aggravated further by the fact that he himself, once again falling victim to his own contradictions, indicates that this may be the case. (2007: 360–361, emphasis in original)

In this one sentence Beck is accused of failing to acknowledge that contemporary life is riddled with class processes, and that this is exacerbated by the way he recognises that contemporary life is riddled with class processes!

As we first mentioned in the previous chapter, Stephen Ball (2006) reminds researchers of the necessity and dangers of sociological theory. The social world is complex and our theories should not assume it is more orderly and predictable than it is. Yet for Ball we can and should try to understand this complex world. To do so, he argues, means accepting that social theories, whether developed by Beck or other theorists influential in youth studies like Foucault or Bourdieu, will always be unfinished and necessarily imperfect

(Ball, 2006: 5). As the work of Beck aims to 'reach' beyond the data (Nisbet, 1962) and has developed and changed over time, it is unlikely that all the pieces will fit together neatly. Complexities and apparent inconsistencies in the theories are, for Ball, what allows researchers to be challenged by, and to work in creative ways with, sociological theory.

While youth sociology can and should challenge Beck's concept of individualisation, the field also needs to properly respond to the challenge it puts forward. It is valid to be cautious about the claims of change in his work as even Beck states that he employs exaggeration as a method. The mistake made by many youth researchers and others is to assume that through this exaggeration Beck underplays inequality and hence to interpret evidence of inequality as evidence against the changes he proposes. Researchers who focus on trawling through Beck's work to catch him out for seemingly contradicting himself (see Atkinson, 2007; Roberts, 2010) miss the opportunity to draw on the insights in his work that may provide a starting point for the study of young lives. On these grounds it is possible to return to his writings on the biography and see that it is actually very difficult to dismiss them as a valorising of choice.

The Creation of the Choice Biography

The widespread, and sometimes heated, criticisms of the choice biography within youth studies can be perplexing for researchers trying to follow up on the idea within Beck's texts (Woodman, 2009). The introduction of the concept of 'choice biography' into English-speaking youth studies can be traced back to pieces by the Dutch sociologist Manuela du Bois-Reymond (1995, 1998). Yet the concept is most closely associated with and most often referenced to Ulrich Beck, in part this is because du-Bois Reymond attributes the concept to him. The 'choice biography' tends to be referenced to Beck's most well-known book *Risk Society* (1992). Yet the closest he comes to discussing 'choice biographies' in this book is a passing mention, with citation, to the notion of an 'elective biography' proposed by Katrin Ley (Beck, 1992: 135), a researcher less well known in English-speaking sociology. Beck mentions Ley's (1984) concept in passing a handful of times across his many publications, and does so alongside other descriptions of the contemporary biography such as the 'do-it-yourself biography' and the 'tightrope biography', terms that he uses more often to describe his understanding of the impact of individualisation (1992: 135).

An obvious question is why a concept that plays such a small role in his writing, and taken from another researcher, has been picked out and presented as emblematic. It is unlikely to be a deliberate misrepresentation. Neither do we believe it is the result of rushed scholarship in an era where academics are pushed to produce results ever more quickly. While Beck's style of sociology and his rhetorical flourishes must take some blame, this is not the primary driver. Talburt and Lesko (2012: 4) argue that youth researchers are often emotionally 'invested' in their topic. Many are motivated to bring attention to the impact of inequality in order to play some role in alleviating it. This investment is not one that researchers should shy away from; highlighting continuing inequality is one of the most important contributions that youth studies can make. However, Beck's work appears to challenge some of the central categories researchers have previously used to do this work. Facilitated by an often implicit binary framework for understanding change and inequality, some youth researchers have been invested in quickly dismissing the concept of individualisation on the grounds that it is an implausible claim for the rise of a generalised 'choice biography', a claim that neither Beck, nor Ley or du Bois-Reymond actually make. This misses the real challenge that Beck's work poses for youth studies. In other words, Beck is used as a foil to show that the old divisions do indeed matter (Woodman, 2009). The challenge for youth research is not to show this but to show how they matter.

An immediately obvious oversight of the criticism of Beck for overemphasising choice is that beginning with some of his earliest work to appear in English, often with Beck-Gernsheim, even when referencing Ley's concept of elective biographies, he regularly makes explicit statements that the individualisation he is proposing cannot be thought of in terms of choice:

> The normal biography thus becomes the 'elective biography', the 'do-it-yourself biography'. This does not necessarily happen by choice, neither does it necessarily succeed. The do-it-yourself biography is always a 'risk biography', indeed a 'tightrope biography', a state of permanent (partly overt, partly concealed) endangerment. (Beck and Beck-Gernsheim, 1996: 25)

This means that a key element of the definition of individualisation is omitted in understandings of the concept as the replacement of 'normal' institutionalised and standardised biographical transitions for biographies of choice. Life, for young and old, is at least as shaped by social institutions as ever before. In fact life has never previously been as 'securely bound into networks of guidelines and regulations' as it is now (Beck and Beck-Gernsheim, 2002: 22). Beck and Beck-Gernsheim argue, however, that a significant part of the shift towards second modernity is that today these 'guidelines actually compel the self-organization and self thematization of people's biographies' (Beck and Beck-Gernsheim, 2002: 23).

This does appear to suggest something like an 'enforced' choice biography where contemporary manifestations of the institutions of education and the labour market are not aimed at providing 'docile' employees but encourage and even demand a type of 'entrepreneurial self' (Kelly, 2006; Threadgold and Nilan, 2009). Demands are put on young people to think of themselves as flexible, creative, and not to blame failure on structural conditions but to see this as a result of their own underdeveloped entrepreneurial spirit. However, this Foucault-inspired reading of individualisation is only partial as individualisation is not primarily about the shaping of particular subjectivities but instead is about an institutional change that is translated into individual biographies as the aforementioned state of permanent endangerment:

> … society breaks down into separate functional spheres that are neither interchangeable nor graftable onto one another, people are integrated into society only in their partial aspects as taxpayers, car drivers, students, consumers, voters, patients, producers, fathers, mothers, sisters, pedestrians and so on. Constantly changing between different, partly incompatible logics of action, they are forced to take into their hands that which is in danger of breaking into pieces: their own lives … It becomes filled with incompatibilities, the runes of tradition, the junk of side-effects. (Beck and Beck-Gernsheim, 2002: 23)

While the weakening of biographical ascriptions based on gender, class or race could plausibly open up new opportunities if supported by a strong welfare state providing education and security without obligation, Beck's work has increasingly pointed out that these conditions for ameliorating social divisions are fading rapidly (Beck, 2007). Instead of a new freedom to choose, and in the place of clear collective identifications and role ascriptions passed from the previous generation, Beck proposes a proliferation of institutional rules, guidelines and an actual multiplication of people's 'structured' relations with state and economic institutions.

With several other theorists of late modernity, Beck is less denying the powerful relationships between social structure and individual lives, than asking researchers to question what this structure looks like today and how it impacts on people. In the introductory section to the second half of *Risk Society*, containing the first sustained description of 'his individualisation thesis, this is stated emphatically:

> ... we find that the structure of social inequality in developed countries displays an amazing stability. Research on this clearly indicates that ... inequalities between the major social groups *have not changed* appreciably ... The analysis that follows therefore aims to explain a paradoxical state of affairs ... patterns of social inequality have remained relatively *stable*. Yet at the same time the *living conditions of the population have changed dramatically*. (Beck, 1992: 91, emphasis in original)

In other words, what is at stake is not whether substantial inequalities between groups continue but how in the face of significant change this continuity is achieved.

Holding Lives Together

The notion of holding together different demands and potential incompatibilities is not original to Beck and Beck-Gernsheim (2002) but has a long history in sociological research on race and in post-colonial studies (Nilan, 2012). Beck sometimes, although arguably not regularly enough, acknowledges a debt to Bhaba, Hall, Gilroy and others for their thinking about the postcolonial experience of enforced transculturation, of living across and somehow bridging incompatible worlds (Beck, 2006: 69–70). In theorising the contemporary biography as one shaped by structures that force individuals to 'take into their own hands that which is in danger of breaking into pieces' Beck and Beck-Gernsheim (2002: 23) are echoing the famous statement about black identity in early twentieth-century America when W.E.B. du Bois (1994 [1903]: 2) wrote of 'two souls, two thoughts, two unreconciled strivings; two warring ideals in one dark body, whose dogged strength alone keeps it from being torn asunder'.

   The valance given to this double consciousness has become more complex over the past century. Today scholars drawing on the history of race theorising and postcolonial studies use concepts like 'intersectionality' and 'hybridity' in part to mark the interplay of different social stratifications, but also to suggest that this mixing can become a personal resource for creatively managing a fluid world (Bhabha, 1994; Nilan, 2012: 253). As Nilan (2012: 253) has argued, a limitation to research on hybridity is that it tends to create a boundary between a mainstream 'youth' and 'multicultural' or immigrant young people. As such, 'researchers studiously identify the double consciousness or hybrid "third space" … of immigrant youth in Western countries but never the reverse'.

Along similar lines Rattansi and Pheonix (2005: 118) argue for seeing youth identity in general in terms of hybridity and the combining of seemingly contradictory beliefs. These researchers are not simply stating the truism that all cultures at all times have emerged from hybridising cultural elements from different places, but are suggesting a radical acceleration and intensification of this process between and within different cultures and places. Similarly, individualisation in our reading is an argument for thinking about structural changes, which unevenly and unequally institute this experience of being pulled by contradictory demands and needing to bridge many gaps between expectations, even if also ostensibly being exposed to a greater number of possibilities across society.

All identity in late modern societies necessarily involves a border crossing or mixing of cultures to an extent never before experienced, even if it is in the name of imagining new traditionalisms and essentialisms (Canclini, 1995; Beck, 2006). This does not mean that all young people across the globe and across genders, classes and ethnicities now face the same challenges and opportunities. Far from it. Nayak (2003), in his ethnographic study of racism and class in the lives of young people from a working-class and overwhelmingly 'white' town in the UK, shows how these global flows create a new visibility for whiteness as an ethnicity and challenge its hegemonic status. Despite this, these cultural flows do not institute a new equality and reflective attitude towards race, but an ambivalence about whiteness. Elements of black culture, particularly tied to music and sport, are increasingly valorised as better than 'white' while at the same time reinscribing essentialisms (black people as naturally athletic, rhythmic) and recreating if also misplacing racialised language to devalue the behaviour and culture of what Nayak's participants saw as a new underclass of 'undeveloped' whites within the community.

Individualisation does not mean that the experience of youth is being equalised by the opening up of new choices for all young people. The ideas put forward under the concept of individualisation are suggestive of two forms of inequality that are usefully explored in the context of young lives. Firstly, the contradictions between the demands, rules and guidelines that various institutions and cultural positions make on young people proliferate more in the lives of some than others. We hypothesise that this is unlikely to be the upper-middle class, white young people, often seen as the only ones who can live an individualised biography (see Roberts, 2003). Secondly, some have greater access to resources to successfully avoid or better negotiate these conditions of proliferating institutional and structural demands. An important insight for youth studies in Beck's work, which has often been missed, is that young people need to redefine structure for themselves, not because structures disappear but because contradictions within these structures proliferate.

Researching the Making of Inequality in New Times

Youth research is booming around the world, producing countless valuable insights into the contemporary experience of youth, including from those who frame their studies as criticisms of individualisation or the 'choice biography'. For example, Brannen and Nilsen (2002) have highlighted that many young people don't actively plan for the future. Instead some defer thinking about the future (either out of security or insecurity) and others actively shape their future only in the short term, in relation to a constantly changing environment. Challenging the assumption that linear transitions are necessarily the best for young people, te Riele (2004) has shown that it is not excluded young people who have to get better at choice making but educational institutions that need to better cater for diversity, particularly different learning pathways. Finally, Lehmann (2004) has shown that past experience makes a difference to the career decisions young people make, and that, at least implicitly, class, gender and an awareness of institutional limitations shape the 'choices' that young people make.

While these and other empirical studies of the patterns of youth transitions or aspirations that show class and gender patterns are important for the details they provide on youth inequality, this empirical detail cannot 'falsify' or disprove the broad ranging, complex and speculative idea of individualisation. In fact in our understanding these findings tend more to support individualisation than disprove it. But most significantly, they fail to fully engage with the challenge of understanding how patterns of inequality are being made in the context of rapid change. For example, Lehmann (2004: 387) highlights that 'educational and occupational plans still conform to gender expectations', but only mentions in passing that this is in the context of women's massive gains in higher education participation. Girls now increasingly outnumber boys in higher education in many parts of the world, especially in many if not all the high prestige degrees like law and medicine. This change in the gendered nature of higher education and the ambivalence this would suggest for Lehmann's analysis fade into the background because he has primarily invested in disproving the choice biography.

While simplifications may be unavoidable when engaging with sociological theory care is required in doing so, particularly within works of critique. This is of course not to argue that any sociological theory should be taken on 'wholesale' because critical engagement with approaches is an essential part of our task as social researchers. However, the best basis for using critique to build more powerful and nuanced conceptual resources is to give the strongest account of the work to begin with, otherwise significant critical energy will be directed towards knocking down 'straw people' or in the pursuit of so-called 'red herrings'.

Inequality and a new generation in Australia

In the previous chapter, as one example of the rise of new global transitions regimes, we presented population-level data on the life patterns of contemporary young Australians today compared to young Australians thirty-five years ago (ABS, 2013). To summarise, these statistics highlight substantial change in the experience of youth in Australian. Young people leaving school today in Australia are not only likely to be the most educated generation ever in that country, they will also be among the first where not only completing secondary education but some post-school study is no longer the exception but the norm. While the expansion of higher education began earlier in the twentieth century, long before they were born, this trend has accelerated markedly during their lifetime, particularly for young women. They will also, irrespective of class or gender, likely face periods of causal employment and a series of false starts and changes in direction along the way if they are ever to establish themselves in secure employment and coherent career trajectories (Andres and Wyn, 2010; Cuervo et al., 2013). Between their parents' youth and their own, young people in Australia have seen patterns of cohabitation completely reverse, from almost no couples cohabitating before marriage to most doing so. No doubt facilitating changes in the social acceptance of new types of relationships and living arrangements, young Australians are establishing life patterns in a less religious, but also more religiously and culturally diverse context.

The lives of participants in the Life Patterns research programme have reflected these education, labour market and cultural changes. Evidence of individualisation is clear in their lives. The research participants in general recognised that they will have many jobs and several occupations over their lifetime and that this employment will often be insecure and may not easily provide a stable sense of self. Many of them cannot and do not want to follow the employment trajectories of their parents, with the young women in particular likely to work through their twenties even if studying, and to continue working in patterns different from their mothers. Many of the participants also accept that their lives will not necessarily be lived within a nuclear family, either for the majority of their lives or at all, and that different forms of living are in general more of a possibility for them than it would have appeared to the vast majority of their parents. This does not mean, however, that they reject all that was important to previous generations, or that they would not benefit from some of the securities, particularly job security, that were more widely available a generation ago. For example the participants' hopes for family life mostly followed the conventional pattern of an opposite- sex partner and two children. Individualisation means, however, that this seems much more like a decision that has to be made and actively pursued, rather than a relatively straightforward progression that will simply unfold.

As older, taken-for-granted biographical pathways come under question this does not end biographical norms but embeds them in a new uncertainty. A person often perceives and constructs their actual biography, positively or negatively, as a deviation from a normal biography of career work, life-time marriage and nuclear family that is still seen as a reference point, even if in many respects it no longer matches lived experience (Beck and Lau, 2005; Wyn and Woodman, 2007). This is also the basis on which gendered inequalities may be produced in new ways that are difficult for people to recognise. The lives of the young women in the first cohort of the Life Patterns research programme provide an example here.

As we have seen, young women were the group to most embrace, and arguably benefit from, the Australian government's push through the 1990s and 2000s for increased rates of school completion and universal tertiary education, and they now well outnumber men in higher education (ABS, 2013). Yet with or without post-secondary education many of the men and women in the study who left secondary school in 1991 spent at least a decade churning in and out of jobs, and in casual employment or without a long-term contract after leaving school (Andres and Wyn, 2010). This meant that many of the young women in that cohort were unable to establish themselves in careers that utilised the skills they had been encouraged to 'invest' in before they reached a point where many felt they could no longer delay becoming parents (Andres and Wyn, 2010). This indicates a shift in some of the mechanisms of gender inequality in Australia. In the context of family policies in Australia that are far behind the OECD benchmark (Pocock, 2003), the women in this cohort, now heading towards middle age, have not been provided the structural conditions to have the efforts they have put into education properly recognised and rewarded in the labour market.

Conclusion

Late, and even post-modern, theorists remind us that sociology is the study of a dynamic object. Patterns in social life and social institutions can continue over time while both the processes by which they are maintained and the role they play can change. This does not mean that change is ever total, even, or always rapid, but it does mean that the challenge for sociology is to show not just the continued existence of class, gender or race, but also how they are functioning in today's contexts.

If we look outside of sociology to public discourse, the public intellectuals of the New Right, shock jocks, and many economists and policy makers in the neoliberal tradition emphasise choice and proclaim that class, gender and race are becoming less significant. In wider public discourse, and the institutions in which young people spend time, the ideology of choice is strong. While showing the empirical falsity and ideological foundations of such a view is an important role for the sociology of youth, too often the critique has been aimed inward, towards other sociologists who are not really arguing for the end of structured inequality at all. We feel the danger is that too often simply showing that class or gender still matters, in large part through criticising a caricatured version of individualisation, is seen as a significant theoretical contribution in itself, and as such this limits the analysis in some youth research from fully exploring what class or gender (for example) looks like now, and so in the end detracts from the task of addressing inequality.

In this chapter our aim has been in part to show that parts of the individualisation thesis display a significant overlap with other contemporary sociological theories, including some unexpected resonances with post-colonial theory. Individualisation is hence in this sense less radical in its claims than many assume. We have also shown that the individualisation thesis put forward by Beck and his colleagues is not denying that life is riddled with inequalities that are classed, gendered and raced, but is reminding sociologists not to fall into the trap of assuming that these are produced in the same ways as before or play the same role in people's lives. Our task, with these, as with other social divisions, is to solve these riddles for contemporary times.

This book is not simply an application of the individualisation thesis to thinking about youth. Instead, following the ethos put forward by Stephen Ball, we see the concept of individualisation as providing a valuable (and perhaps provocative) starting point for conceptualising the contemporary experience of youth. The lack of attention in Beck's work to how different people actually respond in everyday life to the broad-scale processes that he proposes are reshaping social life constitutes just one gap in his work. In this chapter we have used the concept of hybridity to begin to fill in some of these blanks and in coming chapters we also draw on other concepts from biographical researchers to understand the impact of social change on everyday life. First, in the next chapter we return to an old but neglected concept in the sociology of youth, that of social generation, to build a conceptual framework specifically for youth studies that we believe can counter this tendency to conflate continuity with inequality.

4

GENERATIONS

In the previous chapter we revisited debates about individualisation to argue that as relations of inequality are not natural but are constantly produced, the dynamics of inequality can change with social change. This can be missed if researchers implicitly link an emphasis on continuity (rather than change) with the analysis of inequality. The analysis of young people's lives is enhanced by frameworks that guard against this conflation. This chapter progresses this argument by proposing that a longstanding but under-utilised concept of 'social generation' can provide such a framework.

Social generations, as opposed to generations of kin, are groupings that share fundamental social conditions during their youth, and in this context shape lasting dispositions and face opportunity structures that distinguish them from generations that have come before (Corsten, 1999; Vincent, 2005: 582). The concept is closely linked to a family of other concepts including 'cohort', referring to an aggregate of people who experience the same life events (such as finishing school) within the same interval (Ryder, 1965: 12), and 'life course', referring to the way individuals' experiences of these events have common elements across their lives (Elder and Pellerin, 1998). While aiming to account for the interlinking of lives with significant others, the life-course approach focuses on the individual, while the concept of cohort is premised on the conditions and institutional events which a group of people born at the same time will share. In practice cohorts tend to be defined by shared year of birth or shared life passage event, for example the birth cohort of 1971, or the Class of 1989, linking social change to population level outcomes and focusing less on subjectivity (Burnett, 2010). The concept of social generation is arguably fuzzier but also richer than these related terms as it bridges the two, highlighting the shifting subjectivities created by young people as a response to social conditions (Burnett, 2010: 47).

We begin the chapter by returning to the early sociological theorising of generations. We argue that the concept of generations proposed by Karl Mannheim (1952 [1923]), the author most associated with developing the sociology of generations in the early twentieth century, continues to provide a valuable framework for thinking about youth. This framework, as we develop it, asks not that researchers document class, gender or other divisions, but that they show how divisions within a generation are created or recreated under changing (and diverse) conditions. Mannheim suggested a generation was broken up into a number of 'generational units' which although sharing the same general conditions would react in different ways based on differences in their social position.

Despite its continuing value, as it has been relatively under-utilised since its emergence in early twentieth-century sociology, the concept of social generations has not received the attention and debate that other concepts in youth studies such as culture and transition have received. Perhaps because of this lack of attention there are several conceptual issues that remain unresolved. We engage with these issues in the second half of the chapter, developing the concept of generations and intra-generational inequalities by drawing on more recent theories of subjectivity, the impact of economic and cultural resources and relational models of social stratification. In particular we use the work of Pierre Bourdieu (1990, 2000a) to understand how inequalities are actively produced in changing conditions using social and cultural capital.

The arguments that follow are often quite abstract because we take the time to engage with the complexity of the arguments presented by Mannheim. This analysis enables us to show that his work cannot be characterised as similar to the relatively crude 'generationalism' in popular discourse and increasingly in policy discourses. Generationalism is a label for generational thinking that assumes that an age group is homogeneous, sharing a set of (usually negative) attitudes and attributes (Davis, 1999). Generationalism minimises the differences between young people and to some extent characterises the functionalist theories of modern youth culture that emerged in the middle of the twentieth century. Our analysis of the conceptualisation of social generations (following Mannheim) holds that the sociology of generations offers an alternative perspective and is a valuable resource for academic youth studies to engage with broader debates about generational change. Our analysis also engages in some detail with Bourdieu, whose work is widely associated with social reproduction, to conceptualise generational change. While we would acknowledge the attempt to use Bourdieu to create a kind of 'middle ground' approach, tempering theories of change with his work on reproduction, our analysis is aimed instead at showing how he can be considered a theorist of generations, integrating his theory of dispositions and inequality with arguments for individualisation as developed in the previous chapter.

We use and develop the concept of generations to provide a conceptual anchor for investigating the complex intertwining of change and continuity in the production of inequality in the lives of contemporary young people. While we give examples, in large part this chapter is focused on theoretical discussion. The following chapters employ the sociology of generations to rethink the major empirical traditions in youth studies, the study of youth transitions and youth cultures, and to rethink empirical research into the temporal horizons of youth experience and the significance of place in young lives. In this chapter we build the foundations for a contemporary sociology of generations.

The Emergence and Marginalisation of the Sociology of Generations

The sociological concept of social generation emerged out of thinking about age and social change in the wake of the First World War. Among others, Francois Mentré (1920), Ortega y Gasset (1961 [1923]) and Karl Mannheim (1952 [1923]) proposed that cohorts of young people could face historical conditions that would make a reliance on older patterns of thought and action difficult if not impossible. The direction of influence is not one way however. These authors recognised the way that a new generation builds subjectivities within changed conditions and reworks ideas and institutions inherited from the previous generation as one of the primarily drivers of history (Edmunds and Turner, 2005: 562). Unlike the crude generationalism that saturates public debate today, with its tendency to discuss generations as if they were a single entity holding an homogeneous value set diametrically opposed to the value set of their parents' generation, these early academic accounts recognised both similarity and difference. While members of a generation are endowed 'with certain general characteristics ... [b]eneath this general sign of identity, individuals of so diverse a temper can exist that, being compelled to live in close contact with one another, inasmuch as they are contemporaries, they often find themselves mutually antipathetic' (Ortega y Gasset, 1961: 15).

The outstanding contribution to the early sociological theorising of generations is Karl Mannheim's essay on the 'Problem of Generations' from 1923. Mannheim's starting point was sociological. He argued that biological age in itself means nothing, but any biological rhythm in human society and even individual lives must be mediated through social factors. Such a rhythm of aging in human affairs is necessary for the existence of generations but not sufficient or even primary (Mannheim, 1952). Unless those sharing the same age also share, at least to some degree a culture and similar set of social institutions, those of the same age group are not likely to have many traits in common.

Mannheim proposed a concept of generation composed of three elements. First, what he called the 'site' of the generation. In other words, a generation is firstly shaped by its temporal-structural location. Simply being born at the same time, or that their youth, adulthood or old age coincide, does not in itself involve a similarity of location; instead it is when a group are positioned within similar institutions and experience the same events at a similar point in the life course (Mannheim, 1952: 297). The significance of the same event, such as a war, revolution or recession, will differ depending on whether it is experienced as a 'decisive' event in youth or in later life superimposed upon earlier experiences.

Second, Mannheim proposed that this generational position will shape subjectivity. A generational location delimits possible modes of feeling, expression and action, and even encourages a tendency towards certain modes of behaviour, but not in a mechanical way (Mannheim, 1952). On this dimension a generation emerges when times change so that older social relations cannot be mechanically reproduced and a creative response on the part of a new generation is demanded. Further distinguishing his concept of generation from simply a succession of birth cohorts, in response to the pressures and possibilities of this temporal location, Mannheim argued that shared orientations or even an explicit shared generational consciousness can emerge. For Mannheim, potentially but not necessarily, the shared position and disposition of members of a generation could lead to a new political movement (of the left or right) that could change society.

Finally and centrally, like Ortega y Gasset, Mannheim did not see a generation as homogeneous. Mannheim conceptualised a generation as broken up into an indefinite number of what he called generational units.

These units are groupings that, although sharing the same generation, 'work up the material of their common experiences in different specific ways' (Mannheim, 1952: 304). These units can emerge, for example, around intra-generational social class divisions (Edmunds and Turner, 2002). Mannheim's concept of a generational unit is on one dimension defined by its differ-ence from the generation that preceded it and on another by differences from other units within the same generation. Although inequality was not Mannheim's major focus, this provides the basis for a framework that explicitly formulates the problem of the active recreation of divisions in the context of social change. Despite this potential, and some interest in the concept of social generation from theorists of political movements (Feuer, 1969), the sociology of generations has remained surprisingly marginal in the sociology of youth. Given our claim for its value, one of our tasks is to show that there were not compelling reasons why the sociology of genera-tions has been marginalised.

A significant cause for the neglect in youth studies of the sociology of generations in the Mannheimian tradition is that the concept of genera-tions has been associated with the crude generationalism implicit in some functionalist sociology (as well as popular discourse). In particular the subcul-tures approach developed out of the Birmingham Centre for Contemporary Cultural Studies (CCCS) in the 1970s, arguably the most influential strand of youth sociology in the second half of the twentieth century and our focus in Chapter 6, was developed explicitly in opposition to the concept of genera-tions (Clarke et al., 2006 [1976]). The subcultures approach was constructed to counter the 'myth' of a new generation, the view that:

> Generation defined them .... Thus, the simple fact of when you were born displaced the more traditional category of class as a more potent index of social position; and the prewar chasm between the classes was translated into a mere 'gap' between the generations. (Clarke et al., 2006: 14)

Proponents of the Birmingham School set out to contest claims for a main-stream youth culture that was alienated from the culture of adults (due to the expansion of schooling and changes in the labour market that created a sepa-rate 'adolescents society') (Coleman, 1961; Musgrove, 1964). For the writers in the CCCS, these theories of youth culture held the nefarious ideological position that age and generation were what mattered (Murdock and McCron, 2006) and that youth culture was 'incipiently classless' (Clarke et al., 2006: 8).

Clarke and his colleagues (2006), in their opening chapter to *Resistance through Rituals*, the key theoretical statement on youth from the Birmingham School, challenged the view that a general youth culture existed at all. They argued that claiming the primacy of such a shared culture misleadingly 'suggests that all the things which youth got into … were more significant than the different kinds of youth groups, or the differences in their social class composition' (Clarke et al., 2006: 8). More recently Roberts (2007) and Pollock (2008) have made similar criticisms of recent efforts to revive the sociology of generations in youth studies, with Pollock (2008: 479) suggesting it is guilty of 'elevating historical context to the highest order of priority'. There is a basis for these criticisms, old and new, but they are misplaced if they are directed at the sociology of generations itself. Influential mid-twentieth century accounts of the institutional creation of a separate youth culture, such as Coleman's (1961) account of the 'adolescent society', undoubtedly put greater emphasis on the similarities between young people and less on inequalities that may connect them with their parents. Yet, as acknowledged at points in *Resistance through Rituals*, this framework of implicit generationalism in the work of Coleman and Musgrove was neither an explicit nor developed theory of generations in the tradition of Mannheim (Murdock and McCron, 2006; see also Jones and Wallace, 1992).

Like Weber, Mannheim (1952 [1923]) proposed a theory of social change and the basis of political action, in part in reaction to an over-simplistic and over-determined class-based model of change in Marxist historical materialism (Edmunds and Turner, 2002: 4). As such, it is unsurprising that Mannheim's work was not taken up by scholars working with an approach to youth heavily indebted to new readings of Marx's theories, such as Clarke and colleagues (2006) and others who applied themselves to the task of seeing class resistance in youth rituals (Hall and Jefferson, 2006). It is equally clear however that Mannheim did not completely deny class or other social divisions in his quest to create a sociology of knowledge, and of politics, based on the way that culture, structure, change and age interact.

We agree with Mannheim that generational factors do not explain the whole dynamic of history. Mannheim criticised the social theories of his day, including theories of race, 'national spirit' and class, as well as even earlier theories of generation for 'one-sidedness: they all single out just one factor as the sole determinant in historical development' (Mannheim, 1952: 312). Drawing on this insight the sociology of generations does not aim to replace the study of class, youth culture, transition or gender, but provides a conceptual layer or a filter that links social change and youth and through which the primary divisions of class, gender or race take on a particular hue for people of particular ages at particular times.

While the primary target of the Birmingham School was functionalist accounts of a general youth culture that were felt to be underplaying the ongoing relevance of class inequality, the proponents of a subcultures approach also acknowledged a second risk for youth researchers – an opposite fault: 'the tendency to adopt a static or circular view of history and so rob the... period of its historical specificity' (Clarke et al., 2006: 10). Despite some interest in Mannheim's work by CCCS affiliates (Murdock and McCron, 2006), who also recognised the danger of underplaying generational processes, there has been a lack of attention regarding the sociological lineage of generation from Mannheim. Mannheim was not the direct target of the Birmingham School's well justified challenge to the implicit generationalism in functionalist sociology of youth in the mid-twentieth century. Yet his work on generations, which had only been translated into English less than two decades before the emergence of the subcultures approach and was finally beginning to gain some traction, largely disappears from the mainstream of youth studies of transitions and culture in the wake of the CCS critique of generationalism. As a result a conceptual tool that is highly valuable for avoiding the danger of robbing the present of its specificity was largely lost to youth studies.

In recognising that sociology should concern itself with structure, culture and history, Clarke and colleagues echoed another highly influential sociologist of the mid-twentieth century, also renowned for his critique of functionalist sociology and his studies of new patterns of social conflict, C. Wright Mills. Unlike the CCCS, Mills (1959) draws heavily on Mannheim's theories of society and knowledge to build his argument for the promise of the 'sociological imagination' to link the biography to structure in history: a promise that the sociology of youth, facilitated by the right conceptual tools, can play an important role in fulfilling.

As an undervalued legacy the sociology of generations has not received the same attention as some lines of sociological thinking, such as concepts like class, gender or race (Pilcher, 1994; Burnett, 2010: 42). As we saw in the previous chapter, this does not mean that debates about these other concepts have been settled! Our primary aim in the rest of this chapter, and which we take up again at various points in the chapters that follow, is to explore the strengths and acknowledge the ambiguities of a social generations approach. Where possible we put forward solutions to the questions that arise. Mannheim's approach was developed in an essay-length piece of writing conducted nine decades ago. As such, questions about how to conceptualise what a generation shares with each other, how a generation differs from others and how to conceptualise the intra-generational differences between generational units require further elaboration. We cannot aim to give definitive answers to these questions but we do state a position drawing on the theories of subjectivity and stratification put forward by Pierre Bourdieu.

For Mannheim the transmission of common cultural heritage is reflexive and precarious (Edmunds and Turner, 2002: 5) and cultural change will mean that successive cohorts will regularly have to rework cultural elements to make them their own. This seems to put him in tension with Bourdieu's famous theory of social reproduction driven by a seemingly less reflexive transmission of cultural knowhow and dispositions. However, if Mannheim and Bourdieu's concepts are linked with the conceptualisation of the relationship between continuity, change and inequality we proposed in the previous chapter then new resonances between the two emerge. We develop these resonances in the following discussion.

What is a Generation?

Mannheim has a nuanced understanding of the subjective dimension of a generation. On the one hand a generational location sets a negative delimitation, providing a multiple but limited range of possible 'modes of thought, experience, feeling and action'. On the other it has a positive expression: '[i]nherent in a positive sense in every location is a tendency pointing towards certain definite modes of behavior, feeling and thought' (Mannheim, 1952: 291). Mannheim (1952) also states that these concrete locations within a generation provide the mechanism within shared lived experience by which an abstract set of generational challenges are filtered into different concrete experiences for members of different generational units. Yet this nuanced understanding, which hints towards later models of the co-constitution of social structure and social action, is to some extent overshadowed when Mannheim links his sociology of generations to his larger project of building a sociology of knowledge and social change through political movements. His work on generations is centrally focused on understanding how collectives could coalesce around new ideas to become political actors, a relatively small subset of wider generational experience. While departing from an analysis driven by structural materialism, Mannheim's theorising of generations inherited central aspects of his vision of political change from Marx, aiming to theorise how 'conscious' collectives could emerge. Mannheim, while aware of non-conscious dimensions of generational 'experience and feeling' was interested primarily in how a generational grouping conscious of itself as such could emerge and, like a 'class for itself', reshape society. For Mannheim, it was this consciousness that made a cohort a real 'generation for themselves' (Edmunds and Turner, 2002).

Recently writers have developed notions of modes of feeling, experience and action among young people that de-emphasise the significance of an explicit generational consciousness. For example, several recent studies from the UK have explored the way young people struggle to recreate for new times modes of masculinity with heavy affective investment in the face of social change, and particularly the decline of mining and trade occupations, that remove the previous basis for these modes of existence (Nayak, 2003; Walkerdine and Jiménez, 2012). Drawing on a wider sociological critique of the extent to which highly consequential social action is obscured if the focus of theorising is conscious action, Eyerman and Turner (1998: 93) define a generation by its common 'habitus', including emotions, attitudes and embodied practices, of which members are not necessarily aware.

Eyerman and Turner (1998) take this concept of habitus from Bourdieu (1977, 1998a), who conceptualises social action as being driven primarily by the socially based dispositions developed within each individual's social milieu, which are not totally deterministic but nor are they strictly rational and conscious. Bourdieu says:

> [Social agents] are not like *subjects* faced with an object (or even less, a problem) that will be constituted as such by an intellectual act of cognition; they are, as it is said, absorbed in their affairs (one could also say in their 'doing') they are present at the coming moment, the doing, the deed ... which is not posed as an object of thought, a possible aimed for in a project, but which is inscribed in the present of the game. (1998a: 80, emphasis in original)

This way of relating to the future does not draw on explicit rational plans or conscious deliberation (as in the understanding of the 'choice biography'). Instead 'social agents have "strategies" which only rarely have a true strategic intention as a principle' (Bourdieu 1998a: 81) Bourdieu argues that social life is best understood using the metaphor of a sporting contest for which actors have been trained to play particular positions. He writes of 'pre-perceptive anticipations', which is like a feel for the game: 'it is to have a sense of the history of the game. While the bad player is always off tempo, always too early or too late, the good player is the one who *anticipates*, who is ahead of the game …. Because she has the immanent tendencies of the game in her body, in an incorporated state: she embodies the game' (1998a: 80–1, emphasis in original).

Bourdieu has been critiqued by social scientists and by many youth researchers for developing an overly deterministic model of both the socialisation of the individual and of social reproduction. In other words, Bourdieu is criticised for having a circular model of the way structure is embedded in cultural beliefs and dispositions (the habitus) that then remake the same structural patterns across generations (Jenkins, 1992). This seems to make the concept of habitus antithetical to the concept of social generations. The habitus, seemingly inherited through the process of socialisation in the family, appears to adjust young people to the place already assigned to them by social processes, being endowed with particular cultural knowhow and social connections that tend to reproduce a position in the social hierarchy of inequality across the generations.

Bourdieu used the notion of habitus in some of the studies in the middle period of his career, such as *Reproduction* (Bourdieu and Passeron, 1979) and *Distinction* (Bourdieu, 1984), primarily to explore sociological problems concerned with social reproduction within a French culture that claimed to be meritocratic. Yet the way that the concept of habitus was developed makes it very difficult to see the concept itself as inherently deterministic, as a number of youth researchers among others have argued (McNay, 1999; Bennett, 2007; Threadgold, 2011; Roberts, 2012). Many have argued that Bourdieu did not see the habitus as akin to an automaton, but as a bounded creative principle of acting that can fail, is not necessarily coherent, and can create unforeseen actions in changing settings (Wacquant, 2014).

Action is the contact between an actor endowed with certain cognitive styles and practical knowhow and a 'pregnant world', and the fit between the two 'spans the gamut from felicitous to strained, smooth to rough, fertile to futile' (Wacquant, 2014: 5). This means that the habitus will look different in different contexts and needs to be studied in its actual formation (Wacquant, 2014: 6). It also means that if this formation occurs in the context of change, or across social fields with heterogeneous, inconsistent or changing rules, the type of habitus formed might be plural (Lahire, 2011). This is the type of setting we described in the previous chapter as the context for contemporary youth.

Bourdieu's first theorisations of the habitus were empirically grounded in fieldwork in colonial Algeria. Scholars in postcolonial studies have followed others in criticising Bourdieu for an over-determined view of society that ignores colonialism and underplays ethnic difference and the postcolonial experience (Said, 1989; Connell, 2007). The common tendency towards dualistic accounts of precolonial and modern societies slips into some of Bourdieu's theoretical treatises. It can also probably be said that, as a significant portion of his work was focused on understanding class reproduction within mid twentieth-century France, his framework needs to be redeveloped for transnational contexts. The critiques however seem to overstate these limitations (Threadgold, 2011: 384). Concepts, such as the habitus, accused of universalising the experience of the Metropole of the Global North (cf. Connell, 2007: 28), began as conceptual research tools designed to understand the experience of colonialism and the rapid change this created.

While Bourdieu's early ethnographic work was carried out as an employee of the French colonial apparatus in Algeria as part of his military service, it is clear he was not a defender of colonialism. He strongly criticised the modernisation theories of the day that saw social progress in the colonial project (Go, 2013: 55) and argued that the modernist view obscured the 'systematic examination of the influence such transformations have on the system of social relations and dispositions' (Bourdieu, 1979: 30).

He used the notion of a habitus that persisted over time to provide an alternative explanation for what a colonial mindset saw as economic irrationality or some mysterious cultural difference in Algerian tribespeople. This enabled him to distance himself from the racism that underpinned colonialism (Bourdieu, 1962, 2000b). While emphasising this persistence, he went out of his way to state that this habitus was not static, nor necessarily unified:

> The very logic of the colonial situation has produced a new type of men and women … who carry within themselves all the contraries … [T]he opposition between the traditionalist peasant and the modern peasant no longer has any more than a heuristic value and only defines the extreme poles of a continuum of behaviors and attitudes separated by an infinity of infinitesimal differences …. [t]his multi-faceted reality holds out traps for hurried or prejudiced minds. In all realms of existence, at all levels of experience,

one finds the same successive or simultaneous contradictions, the same ambiguities. The patterns of behavior and the economic ethos imported by colonization coexist inside of each subject with the patterns and ethos inherited from ancestral tradition. (Bourdieu and Sayad, 2004 [1964]: 463–4)

In his early ethnographic and statistical work in Algeria, Bourdieu appears to be proposing a similar idea to the theories of double consciousness, and later hybridity, that we discussed in the previous chapter and which have been so central to thinking about race, migration and the post-colonial experience both in sociology and in youth studies. The habitus may theoretically stay the same as the world changes, but such cases were rare in colonial Algeria, particularly for the younger generation and what emerged instead was a hybridised mixing of new dispositions and elements of 'tradition'.

In some of his last work, written in the context of globalisation and 'neoliberal' economic reforms, Bourdieu returned to the task of theorising a hybridised habitus but now applying similar ideas to late twentieth-century France. In *Weight of the World*, his earlier interest in the question of mismatch between habitus and field, the suffering this brings and the possibilities it also opens for creative action become a central theme of his analysis of life in late modern France (Bourdieu et al., 1999; see also Lahire, 2003; Adkins, 2004). In his very last work Bourdieu refers to his own habitus as 'cleft' due to an educational trajectory out of step with his peasant upbringing. He describes his own dispositions as 'inhabited by tensions and contradictions', 'ambivalent', and formed by a 'coincidence of contraries' (Bourdieu, 2008: 100).

Bourdieu's own biography was uncommon for his generation in France, but he does suggest that in times of rearrangement of social structures, such as we have claimed as shaping the current generation of young people, a non-unitary habitus can form. He agrees with many others that uncertainty has become the central and 'modal' condition of contemporary life across social classes, genders and racial divisions (Bourdieu, 2000a). In describing the habitus in this environment, Bourdieu uses very similar terms to Beck and Beck-Gernsheim's (2002: 24) discussion of the 'tight-rope', 'risk' and 'do-it yourself' biography. The concept of individualisation suggests a mechanism by which a cleft habitus of 'tensions' and 'contraries' could arise and arguably become common among a new generation – a generational habitus developed by people living in a world infused and shaped by an awareness of rapid change and in which, to varying extents, people must manage a proliferation of contradictory rules and guidelines.

Intriguingly, given that as we have shown in the previous chapter youth studies scholars tend to see Beck, similarly to Mannheim, as a theorist of change and reflexivity and as such opposed on these fundamental questions to Bourdieu, Beck has also hinted recently towards shared ground with Bourdieu in terms of the basis of social action. While conceding that the type of deep empirical studies that Bourdieu undertook are needed to explore the lived experience of the 'world risk society', Beck has proposed that this research should proceed on the basis of investigating the practical reason or 'habitus' by which people act (Beck, 2009: 207). He is critical of Bourdieu at points in his writing, but it appears to be the habitus as a relatively unitary set of dispositions, as proposed in books like *Reproduction* (Bourdieu and Passeron, 1979), that Beck has in mind when he critiques the possibility that from knowing someone's class position during childhood and youth 'it is possible to determine their 'outlook, relations, family position, social and political ideas or identity' (Beck, 1992: 131). Like the concept of class, it seems that Beck does not want to jettison Bourdieu's notion of action based on dispositions, but is challenging researchers to rework elements of this model for contemporary conditions (Beck, 2002: 33). It seems that Bourdieu was attempting to do this himself in his later works.

Combining the ideas of these thinkers who are often seen as opposed provides grounds for understanding the significance, nuances and implications of the changes that have impacted on those born in recent decades. Their experiences of school, further education and employment in the 1990s and 2000s constitute a set of generational conditions that would lead to split dispositions. For many young people, whether or not they share a relative position in the relational structure of social positions with their parents, there will be a lack of fit between their parents' biographical experience and their own.

A non-unitary set of dispositions could for example be created from a young man with a family situation where the primary employed adult had left school in their early teens and worked in manual employment but where he instead stays on in education (whether he wants to or not) and takes up work in the service sector of the economy. This would on the one hand suggest a type of choice biography, an opportunity for reflection, an inner dialogue over options to decide between dispositions pulling in different directions and even to reflexively question those dispositions (Lahire, 2011; Archer, 2012). Yet these pulls in different directions are far from experienced to the same extent and for a growing percentage of young people institutional structures do not provide the kind of consistency and predictability to allow this type of slow reflective thinking to happen. In the face of educational credentialism, the intensifying challenges of gaining secure employment (not necessarily neatly articulating with education), and other expectations connected to social identities of various kinds that face this generation, many young people will likely need to fall back, creatively, on their dispositions, their 'feel for the game', no matter how poor this 'feel' may be for the situation they face or how contradictory the pull of their various dispositions. As we argued in the last chapter, not all young people will face the same level of contradiction in the structural conditions they must navigate, and not all will be equally resourced to do so. Despite rapid change, it will be the young people facing the most contradictions and with the least resources who will face the greatest risk of displaying the wrong disposition in the wrong context.

Intergenerational Relationships

Goodwin and O'Connor (2009: 23) point to a limitation with the concept of generations if it ignores the interconnection, as well as the conflict, between generations. Even in Mannheim's (1952: 301) early formulation he addresses the relationship between the young and old, and one of the central sociological problems of generation is the nature of this interaction (1952: 301). Mannheim does suggest that even if sharing many aspects of their social positions, if a parent or teacher is part of a different social generation then educating and supporting a young person will come with formidable challenges. The new generation faces a different set of experiences and challenges from those faced by the previous generation at a similar life point, and will develop a different orientation to these challenges. As Mannheim (1952: 301) notes however, '[t]his tension appears incapable of solution except for one compensating factor: not only does the teacher educate his pupil, but the pupil educates his teacher too. Generations are in a state of constant interaction'.

It is not only young people who are impacted by social change. That young people around the world live in different generational conditions to their parents does not mean that change somehow does not impact on older generations, or that the main social antagonisms will be intergenerational. In particular it does not mean that the values of today's young generations around the world will be radically alien to those of their parents. Dunham (1998) uses the concept of generational units to show how many young people in the 1960s inherited an abstract political disposition from their parents, such as progressive or conservative, but had to rework this for new times. Despite being part of a common shared history, shaped by the counter culture, civil rights and the Vietnam war, the 60s generation was not homogeneous (Edmunds and Turner, 2005: 567), including different factions on the anti-war left, anti-Communist youth groupings, and the intellectual beginnings of the New Right (Klatch, 1999; Edmunds and Turner, 2002: 5). The positions that young people take on political and other issues will be influenced by their past, their social and geographic location and by other generations. Cultural capital can be inherited but, particularly in times of change, it will have to be creatively put to use, and even well-resourced parents and young people may be torn about how to invest resources in the reproduction of social stratification (Devine, 2004).

Following Eyerman and Turner (1998) and Edmunds and Turner (2002), we have developed Bourdieu's concepts to enable us to think about generations in dispositional terms and to link this to class stratification. We have not however had to stretch Bourdieu's ideas far. Even in one of his works most explicitly focused on reproduction he points to generational struggles interacting with 'cultural capital' in processes of stratification. In his study of the reproduction of social 'distinctions' within French culture (Bourdieu, 1984), he follows his general model by treating generations as socially constructed by the conflict over economic and cultural 'capital' within fields. These struggles can be intergenerational, as younger participants struggle to impose a new set of lifestyles and tastes within a field. Aspirations once seen as the central stakes in the field can be challenged by new entrants who manage to reconstruct those stakes as no longer relevant (Bourdieu, 1993: 99). They can also be intra-generational as particular people utilise social, cultural and economic capital to reproduce a social position across the generations even as the social world changes; some are better equipped with resources attached to social position and inherited from parents to take advantage of the possibilities afforded by change in the rules configuring a field or to lay claim to emerging fields where the rules of the game are ill-defined (Bourdieu, 1984: 357–8).

Bourdieu gives as an example the rise of new culture industries in France, in which new rules of taste and consumption were constructed mixing pop and high culture in novel ways. For Bourdieu (1984: 357) these 'new occupations are the natural refuge of all those who have not obtained from the educational system the qualifications that would have enabled them to claim the established positions their original social positions promised them; and also those who have not obtained from their qualifications all they felt entitled to expect'. These young people had the dispositions and cultural capital to occupy and define these new occupations. So while Bourdieu does theorise the way that social position is reproduced across time, this is a relational and abstract concept of reproduction. While some young people may do so, Bourdieu is not suggesting that they necessarily literally end up doing the same thing as their parents.

The notion of a generational habitus provides a tool for thinking about the subjective, embodied and affective dimension of generations, and generational units, which moves beyond Mannheim's focus on a conscious sense of belonging to a political generation. Young people play a role in responding to and shaping the social conditions they face, and in reproducing distinctions within and between generations across time in changing conditions, by deploying the cultural knowledge and social capital with which they are endowed in new conditions. The material and cultural resources available to young people and the dispositions they form will vary by generational unit. There may be marginal groups that are most exposed to newly emerging challenges, or miss out on the new opportunities created (Woodman and Wyn, 2013), and there can be groups within a generation that appear highly political when other members of the generation do not (Edmunds and Turner, 2005: 575).

The value of habitus, and linking the generational experience of youth to the unfolding life course, is that it reminds researchers that this constant reworking of dispositions will be on the basis of the cognitive styles, inclinations, and habits that were previously established by this and previous generations. The reproduction of social divisions is created through activity, not necessarily or even primarily conscious, against a backdrop of changing conditions. In a later definition of the habitus Bourdieu states that '[d]ispositions are subject to a sort of permanent revision' (2000a: 161), but that this revision is never a radical escape because it must work on the premises established by previous experience. When the world is changing quickly, social actors do not have the luxury of reflexively shaping their attitudes from scratch, and particularly if the rules of the game become more inconsistent across settings, 'agents often have trouble holding together dispositions' (2000a: 161). For many of today's young generation it is likely that these ongoing adaptations will not be the reworking of a unitary habitus but of a messy set of dispositions, the 'coincidence of contraries' that Bourdieu found both in himself and his participants in Algeria.

When does a Generation Emerge?

A further question concerns the value and possibility of specifying when a generation emerges and its temporal span. Identifying significant shifts in the experience of youth is clearly at the heart of a generational approach. Yet there is no straightforward rule for articulating the temporal and spatial boundaries of generations. While some popular accounts have developed the concept of generations into a universal theory of consistent generational change following a predetermined pattern (Howe and Strauss, 1997), building such schemes is not in the lineage of the sociology of generations we are developing here. As Mannheim (1952: 286) argues, '[i]t is a complete misconception to suppose, as do most investigators, that a real problem of generations exists only in so far as the rhythm of generations ... can be established'. Whether and when new generational conditions and subjectivities emerge depend 'entirely on the trigger action of social and cultural processes' (Mannheim, 1952: 310). The sociology of generations is developed on the basis that any biological rhythm of generational replacement must work through the medium of social institutions and events, as social change is not linear or of a uniform speed, nor homogeneous in its impacts across space.

Hence we do not advocate that youth researchers should follow the lead of Strauss and Howe and others and start building typologies of generations across time. It is highly unlikely that key criteria for precision about what makes a generation, let alone some precise date when a new generation starts, could be agreed upon. The divisions between generations or generational units will necessarily have an heuristic quality; the tensions that shaped the experience of young people in previous eras and other places will not necessary disappear but could weaken, or become secondary, or come to play a secondary role in different times and places.

However, a robust sociology of generations requires empirical evidence to indicate the timing and nature of changes that shape the experience of youth. Mannheim does not address this issue and nor does he describe in any detail the material conditions of the generational locations that shape the generation and generational units he discusses (Cohen, 1999:185). The work that has followed Mannheim has also tended to be limited by describing the conditions of a generation primarily in political terms (cf. Feuer, 1969; Dunham, 1998). While we are also aiming to develop the concept of social generations, we look to better use this framework to locate young people, and in the case of our research young Australians, within the material conditions of their lives.

Using this generations framework we argue that a set of changes, some with their genesis four decades ago but accelerating in Australia from the 1990s, have reshaped the experience of youth, creating new generational conditions beginning with those cohorts that left secondary school in the early 1990s that are continuing to be worked through by the cohorts leaving school today. We will build this case in the coming chapters. Although broken up to some degree by their relationship to the digital revolution which we discuss in Chapter 7, we would point out that young people today share conditions that were experienced by those who were finishing school in the early 1990s. As such we believe it is possible to speak of a long and continuing generation in Australia that we have labelled the post–1970s generation (i.e. inclusive of the popular media labels of generations X and Y).

The patterns of extended periods of education, precarious connection to the labour market, insecure contract conditions and related changes in patterns of home ownership and family formation, visible in the population data we presented in the previous chapter, are the results of these cohorts having faced a weak youth labour market and credential inflation, coupled with social changes that have meant that the types of adulthood available to their parents are not available to them. This does not mean that new opportunities and challenges are equally shared among all of Australia's young people; the opportunities of a generation are not equally distributed. It does however mean that a study of inequality will need to identify differences within and between generations. In the coming chapter, as we compare this notion of generations to currently influential metaphors of youth as a transition to adulthood, we show that many of the Life Patterns participants share in an abstract way many values with their parents' generation, but they have to conceptualise and realise them in new ways, and this has been much harder for some than others, leading not only to a 'new youth' (Leccardi and Ruspini, 2006) but also to a 'new adulthood' (Dwyer and Wyn, 2001) and the creation of new forms of inequality.

Conclusion

In arguing that the legacy of the sociology of generations has been underutilised in the sociology of youth, our interest is not primarily to engage in debates about the timing of generational change, the year or particular event by which a new generation emerges, or to set up typologies of different generations over history. We are interested in the use of this concept to investigate a changing world with complex processes of change and continuity in which new opportunities emerge and old divisions have to be actively reinforced, or even made anew. Using the concept of (non-homogeneous and internally stratified) social generations in youth studies as a filter for thinking about class, as with gender, race or other social divisions, in the context of social change, provides a valuable conceptual tool for rethinking the relationship between change and inequality.

We have attempted to develop Mannheim's concept using the notion of a generational habitus. Habitus is experience embodied in the views, feelings and dispositions to act that make up an 'actor'. All biographies at all times likely include some conflicting experiences and exposure to conflicting ways of understanding the world. Hence a 'habitus' will at times face conditions at later points in time and in other spheres of life unlike those in which it was produced. Bourdieu and others have contributed the outlines of a 'dispositional' model of action that can be made consistent with recent theories of individualisation. This enables youth researchers to take a step closer to theorising the making of inequality for a new generation.

A youth studies that uses an orientation from the sociology of generations does not necessitate abandoning existing approaches or research techniques. The methods and research questions of the Life Patterns research programme are consistent with other studies in both the transitions and cultures traditions that are central to youth research, tracking young people through social institutions including but not limited to school and work, and using qualitative methods to attend to participants' understanding of their own lives. In the coming chapters we discuss the transitions and cultures approach to youth sociology, the two dominant contemporary frameworks for understanding youth, in light of the generational approach we have built in this chapter. By sensitising our understandings of the data available in the Life Patterns research programme using the concept of generations and a modified understanding of generational units, we are able to approach questions of continuity and change in the context of transitions and cultures in an alternative way. The challenge and promise of youth research is to trace the way the possibilities available to young people in general are remade over time, as it is on this basis that it is possible to trace how patterns of equality are made, through processes that can shift over time, or at the very least need to be actively maintained.

5
TRANSITIONS

Transition is an enduring and pivotal concept in youth studies. Along with studies of youth culture, which we take up in detail in the coming chapter, studies of 'youth transitions' make up a large part of contemporary youth studies. It seems commonsensical to think of youth as a period of transition and a phase of the life cycle, yet this seemingly obvious reality is also potentially one of the most controversial influences on youth research as well as on government policy aimed at young people. In this chapter we review the way in which changes in the context and experience of youth and young adulthood have been understood by a range of theorists through the lens of transitions. We explore the contribution that a transitions approach makes to understanding change, continuity and inequalities. Transitions-focused research has played a significant role in identifying 'transition regimes' (du Bois-Reymond and Stauber, 2005: 63). Transition regimes, which we first discussed in Chapter 2 when introducing the concept of a global transition regime, are institutional processes, such as education systems, labour markets and welfare systems. Their discourses and practices shape the meaning and experience of youth through institutional transition points and statuses, such as the completion of secondary education or the entry into full-time employment (Mizen, 2004).

Despite this contribution, limitations inherent in this concept mean that many studies of transition do not account for the possibility that not only patterns of transition *through* but the very meaning and experience *of* both adulthood and youth can change. At the risk of over-simplifying our argument, in this chapter we interrogate the concept of the transition to adulthood, aiming to acknowledge the value of studying trajectories but also challenge the developmental foundations of the metaphor of transitions itself as applied to youth studies. We argue this positions youth as a stage, phase and space through which ideal trajectories to adulthood may be forged. Although few youth researchers working with a sociological framework would not endorse that youth is a *social* category, the metaphor of transition limits our capacity to understand the full extent to which youth is a relational concept. All too often youth researchers tracking transitions understand youth transitions as a pathway to a fixed destination; the sociology of generations attunes research-ers to the way this endpoint, adulthood, is not fixed. As we explore below, transitions regimes do not just shape transitions to adulthood, they also forge distinctive social generations in which the meaning of youth and adulthood itself is transformed.

We see the potential for rethinking the (diverse) body of work that under-stands youth as a 'transition' within a project of understanding how social change impacts on successive generations of young people. In part, this generational approach involves advocating for a reflexive sociology of generations. Many academic and media commentators on sociological questions about youth were born some decades before the young people whose lives they analyse. We conclude the chapter by suggesting that this makes an explicit sociology of generations important as a counter to implicit generationalism, encouraging reflexivity and discouraging research that implicitly judges younger people and their actions on (older) researchers' experiences of, or nostalgic reconstructions of, their own youth and how they remember their transition to adulthood.

Youth Transitions and Development

The concept of transitions achieved prominence in the youth studies litera-ture in the 1980s in policy-oriented youth research that explored the social implications of the failure of youth labour markets in developed countries. Employment transitions research does have a history dating back earlier than this period, but earlier work was largely psychological, focusing on the for-mation of vocational identity (Evans and Furlong, 1997). Sociological studies were conducted before the 1980s but this work also tended to focus on vocational identity, investigating processes of role allocation and socialisation (Roberts, 1968; Ashton and Field, 1976).

These studies, psychological and sociological, were informed by theories of the formation of adult identity of the time. The precedent for characterising youth as the period of transition to adulthood was set in the psychological theory of development proposed by G. Stanley Hall (1904). Hall coined the term 'adolescence' to describe a distinctive phase of psychological develop-ment, characterised by stormy and stressful relationships and risky behaviour. During the 1950s and 1960s a range of theorists (including Piaget, 1954, and Erikson, 1965, 1968) expanded on Hall's ideas of adolescent psychological development. They built on Freud's notion of the developmental and transi-tional stages of the psyche, from infancy through to maturity, to propose that youth represented a distinctive, universal and essential life stage of uncertainty and experimentation during which particular developmental tasks must be mastered to ensure the transition to a healthy, stable, rational adulthood and adult roles. It is evident in the way that these theories were used in the 1950s that even then some youth researchers were ambivalent about the extent to which developmental theories were capable of generating a nuanced under-standing of youth. This is strikingly evident in the study of young Australians in Sydney, undertaken in 1952, by W.F. Connell and colleagues (Connell et al., 1957). The book identifies the hopes and anxieties for the emerging colony (Sydney) and for its young people, and thus provides an insight into research that focuses on both social and individual transitions. The researchers frame the project as addressing the tasks of education in a period of significant social change following the Second World War.

Throughout the 1980s young people's transitions to adult statuses, par-ticularly as workers, became a major policy challenge for reasons clearly beyond the individual young person's personal development and capacity to find the right niche in the division of labour. As full-time employment and stable career opportunities for young people in economies based on manufacturing and primary industries became increasingly scarce, educa-tion became a refuge from unemployment and a means of gaining the credentials to compete for jobs in new knowledge, service and high-skill economies (Furlong, 2013; ILO, 2013). As has been widely noted, one of the effects of this development was the magnification of youth as a period of preparation and waiting for adult life. For example, youth transitions were widely described as extended in research and policy documents and policy-oriented research (FYA, 2013), and characterised as arrested (Côté, 2000) or as evidence of an emerging (but not fully-developed) form of adulthood (Arnett, 2004; Bynner, 2005).

While largely focused on school to work transitions, the burgeoning field of sociological youth transitions research over the past three decades has also expanded its scope to acknowledge the relevance of other markers of transition. Working under the broad banner of transitions research, youth studies scholars have developed studies of household transitions (Jones, 1995; Heath, 2009), youth offending and drug careers (Barry, 2006; Webster et al., 2006) and motherhood (Thomson et al., 2009), and have identified growing complexity and diversity within transitions experience (MacDonald et al., 2001). Sociological transitions research has also focused on documenting the speed of transitions across these spheres for young people of different class backgrounds, ethnicities or gender, in other words tracing patterns of inequality, showing that the opportunities to shape this transition, including its speed and linearity and the adult positions people come to occupy, are stratified (Roberts, 1997; Andres et al., 1999; Cieslik and Pollock, 2002; Evans, 2002; Lehmann, 2004).

The growth in sociological understandings of transitions has played an important role in countering the continuing dominance of developmental-psychological and now neurological understandings of youth. As Furlong's account of the history of youth studies points out, the developmental theories that underpinned this focus on youth development have strengthened again in recent times with the advances in digital imaging technologies (Furlong, 2013). These technologies have enabled neuroscientists to produce images of young people's brains, finding evidence that some areas of the frontal lobe cortex are not fully developed until the mid-to-late twenties.

Many youth researchers explicitly challenge these developmental assumptions. For example, Bessant (2008) has questioned the interpretation that this means that young people don't reach adulthood until this point, seeing this argument as reductionist, essentialist, overly simplistic and biologically determined (see Males, 2009; Seaton, 2012, for a more extended discussion of biological reductionism). Showing the way that transitions are socially institutionalised is important for showing that youth is more than biology. However, in fundamental dimensions the concept of transitions in sociological research also continues to parallel substantial aspects of these developmental psychological understandings of youth in social terms.

The concept of 'emerging adulthood' (Arnett, 2004) is used to argue that social change has meant the transition to adulthood has become an increasingly drawn-out process in which young people can explore identity possibilities. As such it is a relatively optimistic take on contemporary transitions, as young people are understood 'to move into adult responsibilities gradually, at their own pace' (Arnett, 2004: 7). Others are less optimistic, seeing instead an 'arrested adulthood' as many young people adapt to having a delayed transition forced upon them (Côté, 2000; Bynner, 2005). Others point out that transitions are not only extended but for many are also non-linear and otherwise messy, using concepts such as reversible, 'yo-yo' transitions, and non-linear transitions (te Riele, 2004; Biggart and Walther, 2006; du Bois-Reymond and te Poel, 2006). While few go as far as using the concept of 'moratorium' (Arnett, 2004: 7), the language of false starts, challenges and non-linearity before reaching apparently more stable, if unequal adult roles echoes the metaphors of youth as adolescence developed by Hall and Erikson. A sense of experimentation, storm and stress and moratorium continues to shape these understandings of youth, even if it is now translated into sociological terms and stable adulthoods are seen as deferred further into people's third decade of life.

The metaphor of transitions to adulthood

Whether or not it maintains an implicit link to psychological theories of development, there is empirical evidence to support this conceptualisation of extended and messy youth transitions, and to show that some young people suffer from either being forced into too rapid transitions or instead have to live through the uncertainty of extended transitions. Over the last quarter of a century a robust body of research has developed that documents, describes and analyses young people's lives during the so-called transition years (from age 15 through to 25–30). While much of this research reports on rates of progress against institutional markers of 'adulthood' (educational attainment, employment, relationship and residential status for example), a considerable amount focuses on young people's experiences. An example here is recent research on young adults' lives during their years of post-secondary education, which reveals that young people experience considerable stress and pressure during these years, associated with financial hardship and the stress of keeping a balance across the competing spaces of work, study and relationships (Slade et al., 2009). These findings lend weight to the idea that the period of life between leaving secondary school and finding a secure, full-time job and stable accommodation takes longer than it used to, and places a significant proportion of young people under financial, social and psychological pressure. The emerging information about the deterioration of mental health during the post-secondary education years can be taken to reinforce the view that youth is a vulnerable and risky transitional space that extends well into people's third decade.

Yet there is a significant problem with conceptualising youth in this way as a messy, extended, but bounded phase of transition. Tracking the lives of people through their twenties, thirties and into their forties, the Life Patterns research programme has found that mental health does not improve once young adults reach their mid-thirties (Wyn et al., 2014), as the task of managing different complexities creates new pressures and sources of stress. Precarious work, non-standard working hours, an ongoing engagement with education ('life-long learning') and the pressure of managing the competing demands of work and family life, particularly for women, contribute to chronic stress, reflected in an overall drop in self-assessed mental health between the ages of 28 and 38 among participants in our study. This finding lends weight to the idea that such 'storm and stress' are not a 'transitional' experience, at least for many people born after the 1970s.

One of the ways in which the work that theory does can be made explicit is through a consideration of their metaphorical elements (Furlong, 2009). Transition is a spatial and temporal metaphor, alluding to trajectories through a defined space in time (Cuervo and Wyn, 2014). In youth studies, this meta-phor has been widely expressed as pathways and journeys. Although these trajectories could be mapped against transition points in relation to a variety of dimensions, including wellbeing and civic participation, and researchers are increasingly discussing a larger number of such transitions broadly con-ceived (MacDonald et al., 2001), transitions research almost by necessity of its metaphor relies on the notion of trajectory to an end point.

The critiques of the notion of individualisation that we discussed in Chapter 3 have largely emerged from researchers associated with transitions research (Evans, 2002; Lehmann, 2004). The overly simplistic understanding of continuity and change that has facilitated the 'choice biography' critique of Beck's theory is in part built on the metaphor of transitions. The metaphorical four dimensional box of space and time that is the transitional phase of youth may contain a greater diversity of pathways and false starts, and may have even been stretched somewhat by social change, but the box itself and its dimensions remain largely unchanged because these are placed outside of empirical and conceptual consideration. This is not because change has not occurred, but because the metaphor of transi-tions itself draws researchers away from being able to properly conceptualise this change. The conclusion of youth understood as a transitional state, adulthood, is largely taken for granted as an endpoint of youth pathways and provides the implicit benchmark on which unequal outcomes become meaningful and are shown to be reproduced across the generations.

The insights that come from longitudinal research into the early years of adulthood (i.e between the ages of 30 and 40) are important because they enable youth researchers to glimpse the continuities between youth and adulthood, highlighting the limitations with this spatial metaphor of youth transitions. Although many have critiqued the assumptions about adulthood as a point of arrival that are embedded in a youth transitions approach (see for example, Lesko, 1996; Blatterer, 2007), few youth researchers have explored what people experience during the years of early adulthood (although there are exceptions such as Henderson et al., 2007; Silva, 2012). Research on those who have 'transitioned' into adulthood suggests that assumptions about the nature of contemporary youth transitions may be based on a lack of information about the world into which young people are transitioning. In particular, a transitions approach may contribute to underestimating the continuities between youth and adulthood for current generations, or the extent to which the lines between youth and adulthood are at best blurred.

Despite the dominance of the transitions metaphor in contemporary youth studies, a time-space of youth in which messy changes occur on the way to an end point of adulthood, the field is replete with research that employs alternatives to the metaphor of transitions. For example, the *Inventing Adulthoods* study explores the changing nature of adulthood in the UK in the early 2000s (Thomson et al., 2004; Henderson et al., 2007). This study, based on longitudinal research, analyses how young people seek out ways to be competent and achieve recognition in different areas of their lives, including in education, employment, families and civic life. Importantly, this research highlights the active work that young people do to create a sense of security and belonging, in the context of increasingly fragmented and unreliable institutional processes. Similar to the concept of individualisation as the juggling of life between various incompatible institutional demands, this is an example of looking between the spaces of transition markers (Hall et al., 2009). As we show in the coming section, this analysis is mirrored in the experience of the Life Patterns participants.

Transition Regimes and the Making of a Generation

The idea of a 'new adulthood' represents our approach to understanding the changing nature of the nexus between youth and adulthood and its intersection with generation (Wyn et al., 2008). The idea of a new adulthood gives expression to the idea that youth studies must go beyond debates about changing transitions to better understand the relationship between youth and adulthood. As highlighted by the experiences of Life Patterns participants, a social generational approach can articulate this connection in ways that are not obvious when working with the transitions metaphor. In this section we argue that the lines between youth and adulthood are increasingly difficult to define, and the fluidity and complexity that have been associated with the idea of an extended period of youth are, we suggest, now a *characteristic* of many adult lives for this generation – not a precursor to it. The new adulthood is not best understood as the result of changing transitions, but the way that a new generation has been forged.

A lens that is attentive to the making of generational conditions can highlight how transitions policies shape young lives. This critique of the temporal-spatial metaphor is especially relevant in the context of youth policy as the notion of youth as a life stage or the space through which young people move and then exit, preferably as efficiently and normatively as possible, aligns with policy agendas that cannot easily acknowledge the larger changes in the experience of youth and adulthood that have been instituted, in part, by educational and economic policies themselves (France, 2007; Wierenga et al., 2013). This makes it unlikely that youth policy will abandon its reliance on the concept of transition in the near future. A focus on identifying 'at-risk' young people whose messy transitions are putting their futures in jeopardy allows policy makers to downplay the role of structural change and policy decisions in changing the types of adulthood that are available. Critical youth sociology should, however, highlight just this.

Many of the factors that have reshaped youth are the unintended consequences of education and labour market policies, in particular the transition regimes we have identified both in this chapter and Chapter 2. While some of the consequences may not have been envisioned, many of the factors that have reshaped young lives were deliberately brought about by policy makers. The lives of the post-1970s generation in Australia are shaped by global factors, but filtered through Australian government policy. As with much of the world, including Europe, North America, and New Zealand, Australia has experienced a raft of new policies that reshaped the experience of youth in the past thirty years (Furlong and Cartmel, 1997; Mizen, 2004; Leccardi and Ruspini, 2006; Andres and Wyn, 2010; Nairn et al., 2012). These policies were shaped by new economic realities, such as the beginnings of a shift away from primary production and manufacturing towards the service sector and knowledge industries as the foundation of the economy.

The Organisation for Economic Co-operation and Development (OECD) pressed on member countries the view that the emerging new economic order would require new 'flexible' attitudes to working and training, including dedicating more time to education and recognising that education and training may need to be a life-long endeavour (OECD, 1996). The changes made to policy were aimed at encouraging young people, supported by their parents, to invest in their own education to successfully negotiate the labour market by building the human capital needed for newly emerging industries. This occurred alongside a concurrent 'deregulating' of the labour market, or at least re-regulating to give more flexibility over labour utilisation to employers, with the view that this was the only way to maintain a competitive economy in the face of increasingly global competition (Woodman and Wyn, 2013: 266).

Decentralised and enterprise level as opposed to industry-wide bargaining over conditions was legislated in Australia in the early 1990s, and employer associations have pushed hard to reduce security of tenure and to have greater flexibility over labour utilisation in the years since (Woodman and Wyn, 2013). This change is visible in contract arrangements, as we showed in Chapter 2; 'casual' or insecure contracts have more than doubled in Australia since 1982, with almost half (48 per cent) of young employees now working on the basis of one of these insecure contracts (ABS, 2008). Despite some periods of rebalancing towards employees with the ebbs and flows of political power and the position of the government of the day, the pattern is forwards towards increasingly precarious conditions of work, particularly for those newly entering the labour market and without qualifications (Furlong and Kelly, 2005; Standing, 2011).

Research and policy interest in the impact of insecure work have tended to focus on older employees and families, not young workers, again highlighting that this insecurity is not limited to youth. While fewer young employees are parents, and this focus on the impact of work on 'family life' is understandable, the youth labour market has been one of the most affected by the growth of insecure work. Industries likely to employee young people, such as hospitality and retail, have been at the vanguard of less secure conditions and increasingly non-standard hours of work (Furlong and Kelly, 2005; Price et al., 2011: 3). These conditions are shaping the lives of our Life Patterns participants. There are fewer jobs that provide security available, but the overwhelming majority of both cohorts of the Life Patterns participants place a high priority on having employment security (Cuervo et al., 2013). While the Life Patterns participants have told us in interviews that they do not aspire to emulate in all aspects the career trajectories of their parents, there is no reason to believe that the new generation of workers no longer value a sense of security and some feeling of control over their work patterns (Woodman, 2013). Yet they are a core of the new and insecure labour market.

Writing about similar changes in the UK, Mizen (2004) contrasts the way that youth is articulated within currently dominant 'monetarist' economic policies compared to the 'Keynesian' policies that shaped the meaning of youth for those born in the post-World War Two baby boom. The Keynesian state was a welfare state, with a commitment to providing free schooling, full employment and strong citizenship rights. The 'monetarist' policies that have come to prominence alongside new global financial flows, the rise of powerful multinationals and fierce competition for investment, are part of a new relationship forged between the state and the economy. By reducing income support to the unemployed, cutting payment rates or instituting new exclusions, withdrawing support from public education and reframing even higher education as vocational training, these policies have emphasised economic and in particular market goals over social goals (Mizen, 2002).

The dominance of the economy, and global market forces, has not however led to a withering of the state, or the ability of the state to shape youth outcomes (Kelly, 2001). On the one hand the youth policies that have emerged in the post-Keynesian era have relied more heavily than before on the category of age as a mechanism for withdrawing the responsibility of the state for ensuring young people's economic or social livelihoods. On the other hand the surveillance of and intervention in young people's lives in education, in health status and employment have expanded, not diminished (Wyn and Woodman, 2006: 499). The experience of youth is made by the way that youth − and youth transitions − are imagined in different institutions and by the state in general. Yet more so than ever these understandings of youth operate inconsistently, and so make inconsistent demands on young people. Young people can be de jure or de facto treated as an adult in some spheres, such as the criminal justice system, while being denied this in other spheres, such as being forced to 'earn or learn' to receive government welfare support and being denied full 'adult' rates of unemployment benefits until they are into their 20s.

The ways that young people have responded to the new opportunities that expanded education and a post-industrial economy have delivered, and even more so to the new risks and inconsistent rules for success, have been instrumental in bringing about a generational shift in dispositions and patterns of living. For example, as we mentioned in Chapter 3 interviews with both cohorts of the Life Patterns participants revealed that, in general, they realise that, relative to their parents, there are in one sense more possibilities for intimate relationships beyond the nuclear family, particularly given the rise in co-habitation before or even instead of marriage, but also relationships are now more explicitly recognised as liable to break down and in need of being actively built and maintained. This maintenance takes place in the context in which both men and women accept, and some may even celebrate, that their future will likely include numerous jobs, many with limited security of tenure. Finding the time to build relationships comes with new challenges as people must respond in a flexible way to the time demands of the contemporary capitalist world of 'flexible' work. In this context, many of the Life Patterns participants are concerned with balance; a greater amount of active effort is required to co-ordinate work and intimate relationships (Wyn and Woodman, 2007). While the particular aspects to be juggled changed over time, particularly as children arrived, there was for the first cohort of the Life Patterns study no clear break, or clear criteria, that separated their lives as young people and their arrival as adults. If adulthood is defined as stability in work and relationships, for many this never eventuated.

In contrast to the claims of some of the 'generationalism' in popular discourse, there is no evidence that our participants have developed a radically alien or opposed set of values to their parents in how they imagine their adulthood. The focus on balance, for example work–life balance, is far from unique to the young, and is widespread among older generations (Pocock et al., 2012), yet the Life Patterns participants have been concerned about balance, beginning from their late teens but never 'resolving', in a particular way that suggests a generational shift. For their parents it was likely that it was when they had established themselves within workplace hierarchies and started families, and were in the so-called 'rush hour of life' that concerns about work and time for family come to prominence. Members of the post-1970s generation have recognised, either from personal experience or seeing that of others, that precarious employment is the new norm, and that periods with a tenuous link to employment, or even unemployment, may be part of their lives. Yet at the same time the contemporary social milieu will make increasing demands on young (and older) people to 'actively' take up what the market has to offer to invest energy and identity in work, even if that work seems mundane and no guarantees of tenure, or even regular hours of work, are given. The 'on-call' nature of employment, from the casual service worker asked to take up extra shifts at the last moment to the young knowledge worker who is constantly connected to work email through their smart phone, means that work increasingly bleeds into other spheres of life (Gregg, 2011).

The prioritising of balance among Life Patterns participants is more than a case of them following the longstanding pattern of young people using leisure to make life meaningful in the context of mundane work in which they are not invested (Hebdige, 1979: 53). In general, they hold a more ambiguous idea of balance that often means putting more resources and energy into all spheres of life, and trying to maintain a sense of control and security by seeing these investments and their personal resources as their means of dealing with a continuing sense of insecurity. Some look to avoid investing their identity in paid work, but many feel compelled to do so while struggling to invest time and energy in other spheres, including leisure activities and relationships, in the knowledge that employment demands can impact negatively on relationships and give fewer guarantees on which economic wellbeing or an identity can be secured (Sennett, 2006). It is not that balance was not important to the Baby Boomers but now is, rather that an intense outlay of activity in multiple spheres aimed at 'achieving' a balance in new conditions is demanded of people from a young age (Woodman, 2004).

As we noted in the previous chapter, the sociology of generations is primarily concerned with three aspects. Firstly, the structural conditions a generation faces. Secondly, the way that young people respond to, and contribute to shaping, these generational conditions. Finally, and significantly for conceptualising the relationship between change and inequality, it is concerned with identifying divisions or 'units' within a generation. In the above section we have already teased out some elements of these conditions and responses which provide a foundation for thinking about these inequalities. In this context of diminished job security, and new challenges as well as opportunities for building relationships, this picture of the making of the post-1970s generation is also one of intra-generation inequality. As we saw in Chapter 3, the women in the Life Patterns study have been more likely than the men to respond to the incentives or even demands for extending the personal investment in education, yet are given relatively poor institutional support to balance the demands of work and parenthood (Pocock, 2003; Andres and Wyn, 2010; Cuervo et al., 2012).

Further, many of the young men and women in Life Patterns have not seen the benefits promised to them as the Australian economy was liberalised. Despite persistent stereotypes of an overly ambitious generation, the study

participants have held modest hopes for income, employment and relationship security. Yet the reality of intensifying work and education demands and
a tendency for workplaces, or educational institutions, to pay scant regard
to demands in other spheres of life has made achieving these aims difficult
(Blatterer, 2007; Gerson, 2010). It was only a small percentage of the young
men and a handful of young women in the Life Patterns study that had actually been able to realise the benefits that were promised to flow to them from
a 'liberalised' monetarist economy. In a context in which education has been
encouraged but has also come increasingly to be understood as a personal
investment, education has become even more valuable a resource in contemporary Australia, but one that many find difficult to convert into economic
success unless they also have access to networks to convert credentials into
job opportunities (Andres and Wyn, 2010).

Following the framework for thinking about generational dispositions we
developed in the previous chapter, the divisions within this generation can
also be seen in the contradictions of structure and the 'contraries' of habitus that our participants face. A number of the working–class young men in
our study have found themselves in 'service' sector jobs involving emotional
labour as the manufacturing sector disappears (see also Roberts, 2013). These
men must mix the demands of traditional masculinity tied to class or ethnic
background with 'service' dispositions developed through their employment.
Some of these working–class young men will at the same time be trying to
study at university, even if it is rarely in the most prestigious institutions, and
may still also be trying to find the time to remain part of their local football
club and its culture. At the other end of the class spectrum, many young people from the highest class backgrounds have also found themselves in lower
end service work, such as retail or hospitality, for a period of their lives and
working as 'equals' with people from a mix of class backgrounds. But for
those who are simply undertaking a period of work experience, or working
to earn extra spending money while they are finishing a professional degree
at university, the contradictions of 'service' work with the dispositions they
develop at school, in university and in the family will be relatively easy to
manage.

In this section we have argued that the current generation of young
Australians should not be seen as radically opposed in their values to those
of their parents, but neither are the changes that have occurred insignificant. Many of the norms of adulthood continue to exist, passed on from
their parents' generation, and particularly values around hard work and
building security, providing for a family and contributing to community

show continuity. Yet the conditions for their achievement are weakening and the meaning of these values is being reshaped sometimes in ambiguous and almost contradictory ways. For example, many of our participants seek security through flexibility, and balance through an intensive investment of energy in employment, study, leisure and relationships at the same time. It is difficult to understand these changes using a metaphor of transition to adulthood, either delayed or non-linear.

As financial independence, marriage and home ownership become shakier foundations for a notion of adulthood, new understandings are being developed, and the need for this reworking of meaning also appears to be classed. Based on interviews with 93 working-class young Americans, Silva (2012) suggests that this group is redefining adulthood in non-material terms as psychological development and as the resilience built through surviving tough times. Likewise, many of the Life Patterns participants are not giving up on the idea of security but are reconceptualising it as a personal achievement embedded in a flexible skill set and attitude, preparing for and to some extent embracing uncertainty and change as an alternative way of feeling 'secure', but one tied to a clashing search for security also in solid, long-term personal relationships and a search for balance.

In the face of new ways of thinking about adulthood, Blatterer (2007: 113) points to a 'normative lag' between the vision of adulthood held by the newer and older generations that can lead to struggles for recognition. As government policy treats young people as adults in some circumstances and not others, so can colleagues, teachers and others with whom young people interact vary in whether they recognise a claim to be treated as an adult. Blatterer's (2007: 101) participants in his small interview study in Australia hence found themselves caught between adulthoods, one that they may feel authentically to make them mature and another based on ways of acting adult expected of them by others and recognised in various settings in which they act. The tensions identified by Blatterer (2007) and Silva (2012) are the kinds of ambivalences theorists of individualisation have suggested characterise our contemporary, liquid, age (Bauman, 2000; Beck and Beck-Gernsheim, 2002).

If individualisation is understood, as we have argued, as a theory of the management of 'contraries' or contradictions, then it is difficult to conceive of its effects as primarily experienced by those young people with the most resources. Research on the most marginalised young people (for example young homeless people) provides an understanding of how those in a generation who have least have to work the hardest to mobilise the resources and perform subjectivities that enable them to belong to their generation. This is alluded to by Kelly (2006) through the concept of the entrepreneurial self that is the object of neoliberal policies. He argues that those who do not perform the reflexive, entrepreneurial subjectivity required of their generation are categorised as being 'at risk'. Farrugia and Watson (2011) show how this works. They recognise how young people experiencing homelessness work at the task of creating identities of individual responsibility and reflexivity that enable them to negotiate the insecurity and instability of their lives. Farrugia and Watson (2011) and MacLean (2011) (who explores the experiences of young people who use inhalants such as glue and paint) reveal the ways in which these marginalised young people struggle to perform the identities of their generation, despite having minimal resources to do so. For example, young homeless people (researched by Farrugia (2011) and Watson (2011) in separate studies) articulated a strongly individualised understanding of their circumstances, and understood that they were 'responsible' for managing their way out of homelessness. While lacking the material and cultural capital of peers who have homes, these young people nonetheless attempted to draw on their available resources (which in the case of young homeless women included intimate relationships) to have stability and security (epitomised by having a place to live). In many ways it is these young people who are at the sharp edge of the individualising tendencies embedded in their generational condition.

Research from the South also raises questions about the use of a transitions metaphor in understanding inequalities between young people (Nilan, 2012; Everatt, 2013). For example Everatt (2013), writing about young people in the province of Guateng in South Africa, argues that there are considerable challenges in applying a transitional perspective to developing countries in which significant proportions of young people are neither in education nor employment and in which inequalities are increasing. As global transition regimes become increasingly significant, and are used to measure progress against policy and institutional indicators, the young people in South Africa referred to by Everatt will be categorised as NEET (not in education, employment or training), the historical, economic and social structural and cultural conditions of their lives made less discernible.

As increasing proportions of the world's young people, with varying degrees of incentive and coercion, engage in education they are also engaged in global transition regimes as youth labour markets and the demand for skills are reshaped by globalisation (Brown et al., 2011; ILO, 2013). New demands to cope with new uncertainties will emerge around the world, in particular ways and unequally for different groups, including for the large proportions of young people who remain outside the institutions of education and formal employment. Researchers, such as Feixa and Cangas (2005) who analyse the changing meaning of youth in Mexico and Chile, and Everatt (2013) who analyses the social construction of youth in South Africa, reveal the ways in which young people mobilise the resources available to them to navigate these uncertainties. Everatt's research reinforces the conclusions drawn by Farrugia and Watson: those who are most disadvantaged are positioned to work the hardest to manage the fragmenting, isolating and individualising processes reshaping the lives of young people around the world.

Documenting transition pathways (for example on a global scale: see ILO, 2013) and doing so on a national scale (see Foundation for Young Australians, 2013) remains an important source of data on the status of youth, and provides important profiling information that enables researchers and policy makers to grasp patterns of institutional engagement. While researching these patterns and identifying the critical turning points in young lives will remain important, understanding youth through the metaphor of transitions, no matter how broadly defined, retains a tendency to assume the idea of a set starting and end point. Studying the turning points and institutionalised movements between various educational and employment engagements, relationships and civil statuses, and housing situations, can alternatively be supported by a social generational lens. This generational approach recognises not so much delayed or complex transitions as the way that the meaning of youth and adulthood (in relation to each other) is being redefined for and by contemporary young people, in different ways in a variety of places, and will no doubt change again in the future. This allows us to highlight the impacts of transitions regimes and the consequences of these regimes being both a driver of social change and yet based on policy assumptions out of step with the reality of social change.

As we continue to study the intersections of various turning points in young lives against the backdrop of change in different parts of the world, the metaphor of transition to adulthood as it is currently understood becomes difficult to sustain as a foundation for youth studies. It is not so much the case that the transition to adulthood has been delayed or extended, or even is no longer possible. Instead, the Life Patterns participants suggest that for their generation we can no longer understand youth as experimentation leading to a stable adult identity. The 'new youth' (Leccardi and Ruspini, 2006) involves messy and incremental steps into a 'new adulthood' that itself is increasingly defined by a precariousness and relative instability (Wyn and Woodman, 2006).

Research and Reflexivity

While advocating for the benefits of adding a generational framing to studies of young people's lives, we are not meaning to suggest the replacement of one orthodoxy with another, but arguing for a reflexive youth sociology that pays attention to the work that theories do and the ways in which they constitute the subjects of research. As Talburt and Lesko point out, youth is constructed through a historical process of shifting assemblages of rationalities, technologies, practices, institutions and individuals (2012: 5). These shifting assemblages are also related to economic, political and social transitions, driven by processes occurring within and across national boundaries. The point is to interrogate the logics that these processes create and to resist embedding orthodoxies. This argument is especially relevant to the policy-oriented research that constitutes much youth sociology; research that aims to 'make a difference' but too often instead consolidates the dynamics of exclusion and marginalisation and the creation of 'truths' about youth (Kelly, 2006).

As we have seen in this chapter, the Life Patterns participants are actively trying to create, and often necessarily redefine, security in the conditions they face. We also suggested that it is in these conditions that new claims to adulthood are made and contested (Blatterer, 2007). This problem of recognition points to the value of a sociology of generations as a lens for thinking about young people's lives, both as a contribution to public and policy discussions about youth and as a conceptual framework in academic sociology. A generational framework, focused as it is on the social, historical and political nexus that shapes the experience of youth, helps avoid the danger of reading the experience of contemporary young people through the lens formed by the experiences of being young for the researcher, politician or media pundit. A significant proportion of the discussion about youth transitions falls within this category. The transitions that were not delayed, or alternatively too fast or messy, but seen as 'just right' were those made by the young people born in the post-World War Two baby boom (Woodman, 2013). This 'golden era' of youth transitions, even if somewhat imaginary (Goodwin and O'Connor, 2005), is the implicit and possibly unconscious norm against which transitions to adulthood are often judged and found wanting. Not only does this misrepresent the experiences of movement between statuses in education, employment, and relationships that are possible for young people today, it also functions to covertly transform patterns of generational change into symptoms of failing transitions to a vision of adulthood that remains static.

Conceptual frames that encourage reflexivity about generational conditions, while also pointing out that a generation is not homogeneous, minimise
the likelihood that the lives of young people participating in research will be
implicitly evaluated in terms of a researcher's memories of youth and adulthood and normatively judged based on relative distance from an 'historical
artefact', a product of a particular set of economic, social and industrial conditions that may no longer exist (Wyn and Woodman, 2006: 511). Attending
to inequalities in material and cultural resources that enable young people to
create security (and be counted as adult), and the ways in which the most and
least resourced respond to these challenges, can help us understand the divisions and inequality in 'transition' patterns in the contemporary world.

Conclusion

This chapter has discussed the emergence of the highly influential and arguably dominant youth transitions approach in youth studies. We identify the
resonances that the idea of youth transitions has with developmentally-based
theories of youth that were forged initially in the early 1900s, and then further elaborated mid-century. These theories focused on the problematic
nature of youth development, which particularly in times of social change
might involve young people slipping into the dysfunctional or deviant behaviours, identities or youth cultures (which we discuss in the coming chapter)
that were inimical to development into normative adulthood. The notion
of youth transitions that emerged in the 1980s took a more sociological
approach, focusing on transition through the institutions of education and
employment. However, this approach also focused on problematic and at-risk
transitions to adulthood, represented in the failure to progress through insti-
tutionally-defined stages of education and into employment. Both rest on the
idea of normative transitional stages and assume adult status as the end point.
Even research explicitly aiming to identify and hence challenge the continu-
ance of inequalities makes these same assumptions, tending to reinforce the
categories of mainstream and at-risk.

While the tendency to emphasise education and employment above all
other aspects of life has lessened within academic transitions research, working within a framework defined by the concept of transition continues to
make it difficult to avoid reifying adulthood as the transition destination.
Our discussion highlights the metaphorical nature of transitions, and invites

youth researchers to engage in a deeper analysis of what this metaphor offers analysis. We would point out that the metaphor of transition positions youth as a stage, phase and space through which ideal trajectories to adulthood may be forged.

However, we would also acknowledge that the identification of transitions through institutional pathways provides important insights on both a local and global scale. Transitions research provides relevant information about the status of young people in institutionally-sanctioned trajectories and the dominant patterns of institutional engagement. By drawing instead on the concepts of social generations and generational units we do not mean to be seen as advocating a new orthodoxy. We would however advocate a reflexive youth sociology that pays attention to the work that theories do and the ways in which they constitute the subjects of research. This means recognising the situated, cultural and relational aspects of young people's lives at the same time as recognising institutional processes of control and progression. The context of significant global social transformations, such as the rise of the 'Asian Century', brings new patterns of transition, informed by new economic realities and aspirations.

The task of building a more nuanced approach to youth transitions is in part complicated by the nexus between youth studies and youth policy. As we illustrated at the outset of this chapter the idea of transitions 'makes sense', and has in part achieved a dominant position in youth studies over the last quarter of a century because of the take-up of this metaphor by policy makers. While transitions approaches identify inequalities in outcomes as well as gaps in the rate of progression against institutional markers, they are less effective in identifying the processes behind these outcomes. They are hence also less effective for the goal of intervening in these processes, in identifying programmes and practices that would address the chronic inequalities amongst groups of young people. By definition, transition regimes are institutionally defined – so they reveal problems but they do not generate rich enough data to address those problems. We would suggest that it is timely to recognise the work that alternative metaphors, including generations, can do for youth research.

6

CULTURES

In Chapter 4 we argued that the sociology of generations has been marginalised in part because of the association of the term 'generations' with functionalist studies of youth culture from the mid-twentieth century. This association was in large part cemented by the work of scholars attached to the Birmingham Centre for Contemporary Cultural Studies (CCCS) in their well-founded critiques of these mid-century functionalist accounts of youth culture. Along with the transitions approach discussed in the previous chapter, youth cultures research is one of the most influential strands of contemporary youth studies, building on the concept of subcultures developed by this group.

The prefix 'sub' in the subcultural approach is used to denote a close coupling of cultural practices and social stratification, particularly by class. The American sociologist of gang formation, Albert Cohen, recognised that '[e]very society is internally differentiated into numerous sub-groups, each with ways of thinking and doing that are in some respects peculiarly its own ... and that one can scarcely help acquiring if [one] is a fully-fledged participant' (Cohen, 1956: 12). The CCCS drew on this definition to link the concept of subculture explicitly and primarily to class, conceptualising sub-cultures not primarily as subsets of general youth cultures but of class cultures.

Like the concept of individualisation discussed in Chapter 3, the centrality of subcultures to youth cultures research does not mean that the approach has become an orthodoxy, but that significant debates about youth focus on this concept. It is both subject to heavy critique and defended. In the 1990s and 2000s a series of so-called 'post-subculture' concepts were proposed, such as neo-tribalism, lifestyle or scene, which shared the aim of challenging this close coupling between youth and class. Drawing on theories of social change, post-subcultural approaches propose that older (class-based) identifications are less relevant as a foundation for cultural preferences and practices. Instead, researchers argued that complex constellations of relatively ephemeral identifications with different lifestyle forms define young people's identities (Redhead, 1990; Bennett, 1999; Muggleton, 2000; Hesmondhalgh, 2005; Miles, 2000). Others have come forward to defend the subcultures concept from these criticisms, reiterating the centrality of investigating social class to understand young people's cultural forms (Blackman, 2005; MacDonald and Marsh, 2005; Shildrick and MacDonald, 2006). As such the relationship between youth cultural forms and inequality has generated some of the most important ongoing debates in the sociology of youth.

We argue that this impasse is again linked to the tendency in youth research to associate social change with a weakening of the impact of socially structured inequality. It is not the case that writers associated with the post-subcultures approach deny inequality, most are explicit that it continues to shape cultural practices. Instead they make a powerful case that culture has a greater degree of autonomy from social structure than was previously acknowledged and that social change has impacted on youth cultural forms. Yet these alternatives to subculture, while not denying inequality, have largely not been able to capture both the fluidity of cultural engagements and that inequality (Griffin, 2011). Against the backdrop of the subcultures debate we argue for the value of taking a biographical approach to understanding youth cultures and analysing the interaction between different investments across fields, including education, work and cultural practices (Henderson et al., 2007). While the generational conditions shaping the lives of young people today may permit multiple concurrent cultural identifications to a greater extent than before, the construction and reshaping of cultural forms and the identities linked to them are based as much on the challenge of holding together competing tensions experienced in everyday life, the resources for which are unevenly distributed.

Concepts of Subculture

The cultures track of youth research has its roots in the early twentieth-century American sociology of 'deviance'. This work aimed to counter influential assumptions that gang involvement was a sign of psychological inadequacy, showing instead that youth gangs were collective responses for survival and 'fun' to provide a sense of coherence in the face of a 'disorganised' social structure (Thrasher, 1927; Whyte, 1943). Drawing on this work, Albert Cohen (1956) developed and popularised the concept of subculture (Blackman, 2005). Cohen built on the early gang research of researchers like Thrasher and White attached to the 'Chicago School' while also drawing on and critiquing the functionalist and utilitarian 'strain' theories that saw youth gangs as an 'illegitimate' means of achieving 'legitimate' norms of success through consumption of goods valued by mainstream society but denied to some groups (Merton, 1938). Cohen saw gangs as the result of a rapid transformation of 'group standards' of morality within a particular sub-group of society which would be 'created, re-created and modified wherever individuals sense in one another like needs, generated by like circumstances, not shared generally in the lager social system' (Cohen, 1956: 65).

The subcultures approach came to dominate youth cultures research with the Birmingham School. As we showed in Chapter 4, the CCCS, similarly to Albert Cohen, developed the concept of subculture to challenge a dominant alternative. Like Cohen, the Birmingham School were challenging psychological theories of deviant youth culture, but the CCCS also wanted to challenge the then influential mid-century sociological argument that a mainstream youth culture marked out young people, in general, from the generation before. They saw proposals of a general youth culture as a politically suspect disavowal of class. The Birmingham School argued instead that youth cultural forms were differentiated along lines that tied them to larger class cultural divisions based on the class positions inherited from their parents. The model of class that informed the CCCS alternative was neo-Marxist, based on the view that in modern societies the most fundamental groups are the social classes, and the major cultural configurations will be 'class cultures' (Clarke et al., 2006: 6). Subcultures are subsets within one of the larger class-based cultural groups (Clarke et al., 2006).

The CCCS model was informed by Althusser's (1971) theory that ideology works subconsciously and seductively through the practices of everyday life, and by Gramsci's (1971) concept of hegemony. Rather than brute economic coercion, class inequality is sustained through alliances and compromises that maintain a relative naturalness around the current economic and political system. Some working-class cultures could be read as a symbolic resistance to this hegemony.

As well as these neo-Marxist philosophies, and Albert Cohen's work on gang 'subculture', two other Cohens provided the impetus for the CCCS approach. Even more than Stanley Cohen's famous (1972) study of the 'moral panic' about the youth subcultures of the 'mods' and the 'rockers', it was Phil Cohen's (1999) study of working-class men responding to a changing London East End that provided an applied neo-Marxist model of class conflict in action (Blackman, 2005). Phil Cohen combined an understanding that subcultures were formed in relation to the mainstream culture (as recognised in previous American writing on subcultures) with the argument that they were also formed in relation to the class culture of their parents. The cultural response to their social circumstances could be read not as the pursuit of illegitimate means towards mainstream goals, but as a bricolage of representational elements to symbolically or 'magically' overcome the impacts of structural change marginalising the type of working-class communities that their parents' generation had built (Cohen, 1999: 57).

Throughout the 1970s and 1980s members associated with the CCCS developed Cohen's framework to produce theoretically driven, neo-Marxist interpretations of young people's cultural practices. The context of intergenerational transmission of class position in a changing environment set the scene for young people to create 'mythical' cultural solutions to ongoing structural marginalisation. The argument was that while there would be more than one constellation of ideas, even within the dominant class, and other groups would find ways to express their culture and challenge the cultural hegemony, this would be from a structurally subordinate position. Unless the solutions created became more than just symbolic, 'magical' solutions that covered over contradictions, they would in the end fail as resistance. It was in this tradition that Willis (1977) famously studied the emergence of subcultures of resistance to school, which ultimately reproduced class positions.

The Birmingham School shared a general orientation towards a neo-Marxist interpretation of culture but it was not an homogeneous approach. Even in *Resistance through Rituals*, the book most associated with the subcultural approach, early efforts to improve the general approach were included. McRobbie and Garber (1976) and Powell and Clarke (1976) for example highlight a tendency to marginalise girls' cultural forms and ignore the often oppressive experience of women both in male-dominated youth subcultural groups and in school. Following on from this early identification of gender blindness in the study of subcultures, there was a push to attend to young women's cultural forms, both in the private sphere of the bedroom and in the street and club (McRobbie, 1978; Griffin, 1985). Still drawing on structural theories, these studies showed that young women were not building their lives in relation to the same class constraints as the young men; at the very least these class relations for young women were significantly mediated by the patriarchal form of society, which shaped cultural products like magazines, leisure opportunities and the future expectations of young women (Sharpe, 1976; McRobbie, 1978).

As the Birmingham approach to subcultures developed over time, the focus shifted towards the content of the youth styles themselves as much as the collective class experience at the base of these styles. Hebdige (1979), for example, while remaining broadly with a subcultures approach by theorising culture as a response to social position, focused on punk and other musical and fashion-based subcultures primarily as styles in themselves. Hebdige investigated the history of punk as a style that, while a working-class and predominantly white movement, hybridised different cultural elements across classes and ethnic groups, drawing in particular on Rasta and reggae influences. The reason these styles could be seen as class resistance, and authentic subcultures worthy of sociological attention, was the shock they aimed to provoke, which provided a symbolic interruption of the hegemonic status quo, even as they were quickly co-opted by entrepreneurs for commercial ends. While Hebdige reiterated the importance identified by earlier subcultural scholars of the class basis, and hence the ultimate futility of a stylistic invocation of meaning to paper over structural contradictions, his writing presaged a coming interest in the pluralistic, fluid and quickly changing associations of youth in style cultures across race and class boundaries that would come to characterise newer approaches that broke with the subcultural framework.

Post-subcultures

Others, writing from the 1980s through to today, have argued that the subcultures framework is either fatally flawed conceptually or has been rendered redundant by social change. These authors are usually grouped together under the term 'post-subcultures' (Redhead, 1990). Gary Clarke questioned the easy equation of creative consumption with class-based resistance:

> The fundamental problem with Cohenite subcultural analysis is that it takes the card-carrying members of spectacular subcultures

as its starting point and then teleologically works backward to uncover the class situation and detect the specific set of contradictions which produced corresponding styles. (1990: 83)

This meant that confrontational and spectacular male working–class cultures were read through the lens of theories that gave priority to class, leading the researchers to seek evidence of 'resistance' to class relations. This approach tended to make the world more predictable and ordered than it was by overlooking cultural practices that did not fit with the theoretical framework. For example, punk may have been used by an 'authentic' working-class section of young punks as a 'magical' solution to their structural position, yet many of the stylistic elements that Hebdige (1979) investigated had their genesis not with the working class but with a middle–class 'art school' creativity. If this is understood, it makes the dichotomy between authentic (stylistic) class 'resisters' and a later emerging group of 'style imitators' hard to maintain (Clarke, 1990 [1981]: 83). Extending this point, Muggleton (2000) challenged the close coupling between class and culture seen to bind creativity to intergenerational class relations. For Muggleton, the links between class and culture were often exaggerated by the CCCS analysts, and he argued that if proper attention were paid to the empirical reality of youth cultural forms, these could not so easily be mapped on to class structure.

While agreeing that the CCCS may have exaggerated the class homogeneity of style cultures in the 1970s, other post-subculturalist theorists place a greater emphasis on social change making such homogeneity even less likely today. One basis for this critique is the growing recognition of hybrid identities and identity politics, and through this the recognition that it is increasingly unsustainable to claim that the politics of race or gender were subordinate to class politics (Rattansi and Pheonix, 2005; Nayak, 2003; Huq, 2006). A second basis is the widespread influence of new general sociological theories, which spread in the later part of the twentieth century, emphasising an acceleration of social change (Harvey, 1989; Bauman, 2000; Laidi, 2001; Rosa, 2013). For some theorists this rapid change was fragmenting subjectivity, so it was less meaningful to talk of an 'individual' with a single identity that persisted over time (Maffesoli, 1996; Baudrillard, 2002).

These ideas formed the basis of a concerted challenge to the foundations of the subcultural approach. While agreeing with the subcultural approach that stylistic resistance will ultimately fail as resistance, newer approaches challenged whether collective identifications with 'signs', through fashion for example, even if they have the potential to shock or draw attention, were likely to have more than the most momentary of subversive effect. This is not primarily because even 'authentic' subcultural forms that resist social expectations are eventually 'incorporated' as marketable commodities, as Hebdige (1979: 92) highlighted, but because the foundations that could make cultural styles original, authentic and meaningful over time no longer exist (Muggleton, 1997: 196). Instead of subcultures, particular individuals construct consumer lifestyles (Miles, 2000) by picking and mixing from a 'supermarket of style' (Polhemus, 1997). For Steve Redhead, a post-subcultural approach was needed because of social change to capture a shifting nexus between social positioning, youth cultural forms and identity that had emerged in the rapid changes in the decades following the development of the CCCS approach to subcultures, making this earlier framework redundant (Redhead, 1990).

Arguably the most influential alternative to subcultures has developed out of the work of French sociologist Michel Maffesoli (1996), who theorises that the contemporary social world facilitates different forms of association. Instead of the relatively stable commitment to subcultural identity theorised in the work of the CCCS, Maffesoli argues that these neo-tribal senses of belonging have strong emotional valence but messier forms and less continuity. He also suggests that rather than a concrete group existing through time, these tribes exist primarily as a 'state of mind' or 'ambience' expressed through lifestyle forms (1996: 98). While not concrete subcultures, this 'state of mind' at the basis of a sense of tribal belonging is more than individual. It requires enactment in events that create a temporary and site-specific shared affective experience, an 'ambience' that creates a collective. Regularly reinforcing this sense of collective belonging with emotionally-rich shared experiences is central, and what ties neo-tribes to the traditional meaning of tribe and non-modern elements of solidarity (Maffesoli, 1996: 6).

The newness of these tribal forms is that these 'tribal experiences' are not as members of a 'traditional' ongoing collective who share fundamental elements of their identity. They are necessarily temporary and multiple connections to a sense of collectivity that occur in the context of and against other forces that push towards atomisation rather than building solidarity in the traditional sense (Maffesoli, 1996). Ben Malbon (1999) discusses the rave culture of the 1990s in these terms, highlighting the importance of the 'oceanic experience' of the dance club. This experience is one of losing the self in the shared flow and rhythm of the music. While Malbon argues sharing this experience is important, a relative homogeneity of identity – based on class, ethnicity or anything else – between dancers is not needed, and a conscious aware-ness of it may even detract from this type of oceanic experience (Malbon, 1999: 186).

Within youth studies the concept of neo-tribe developed from Maffesoli's work was popularised by Bennett (1999). He used the term to argue that young people have multiple identifications that are temporary, or at least shift over time, and as such an 'individual' can play a role in constituting several groups rather than identifying with a single pre-existing group that provides a dominating centre to their identity. As such, a young person may engage in and enjoy cultural forms of a particular type, such as a particular music genre or fashion style, at times and in some contexts but not others (Bennett, 1999). Along similar lines, Redhead argues that a style community is not a 'pre-constituted community to be represented' but instead something that emerges when, temporarily, 'disparate groups … have been yoked together' (Redhead, 1990: 86–7). This way of understanding cultural engagement is very different from seeing youth cultural forms as a collective way of life of particular subgroups within a subordinate larger class grouping (Bennett, 1999; Luckman, 2003; Cummings, 2006). While the class basis of youth subcultures may have been an exaggeration even in the 1970s, for these authors contemporary conditions make older (class-based) identifications increasingly less relevant as a cultural foundation, and more ephemeral iden-tifications with music and fashion scenes have increased salience.

Continuity and Change in Cultures Research

Despite these criticisms, some youth sociologists have defended the sub-stance of the subcultural legacy. Acknowledging the critique that the CCCS approach had too narrow a focus on the 'spectacular' cultural prac-tices of white, working-class men, these authors argue that post-subcultural approaches overemphasise the fluidity and playfulness of identity associations that are possible, and through a focus on everyday life and consumption have sidelined larger political questions (Blackman, 2005). As such, while they argue that post-subcultural theory may be of relevance for some aspects of contemporary youth cultural practice, and in relation to dance music culture in particular, this is only the case for a small minority. Social inequality, and in particular class relations, continue to shape engagement (Hollands, 2002; Hodkinson, 2002; Blackman, 2005; Hesmondhalgh, 2005; Shildrick and

MacDonald, 2006). Hodkinson (2002) for example uses his insider research with 'Goth' culture to argue that participants exhibit qualities of collective and stylistic fixity that adhere more closely to conventional subcultural readings.

The ethnographic studies conducted by Hollands on the night-time economy in Newcastle in the north of England highlight the way that cultural engagements continue to be shaped by economic inequalities. Hollands (2002: 168) found that forms of engagement were divided between the 'disadvantaged, the insecure and the privileged'. A relatively small group of wealthy and professional young people drives the demand for high-end, exclusive venues in which they are 'protected' from other sections of society by the cost of entry or drinks and by security staff. Those in less secure and less well renumerated employment, such as the growing lower end of the service economy, support a 'mainstream' of clubs and pubs that allow a temporary 'escape'. Finally there is an unemployed section of young people dependent on welfare and the informal economy who find little available for them in the mainstream nightlife, who are fighting against creeping exclusion from city-centre nightlife and other young people, both the insecure and the privileged, who treat them with 'sheer contempt' (Hollands, 2002: 166).

Empirical evidence shows conclusively that class, gender and race continue to shape youth cultural forms, even when particular musical styles become part of 'popular culture', such as the way black and white, rich and poor, male and female, engage differently with the global spread of hip hop or Bhangra (Nayak, 2003; Huq, 2006). A shared conclusion of many based on these empirical studies and related conceptual critique is that while the CCCS approach had obvious failings that needed to be addressed, the post-subcultural turn has abandoned a focus on social structure to the profound detriment of youth studies. For these authors a re-engagement with social structure is needed to again make the cultural implications of class, ethnic and gender divisions central to youth cultures research (Huq, 2006: 24; Nayak, 2003; Blackman, 2005; Shildrick and MacDonald, 2006).

In these debates about the relative utility of post-subcultural or subcultural concepts a homology is visible with the debates about individualisation discussed in Chapter 3. The criticisms of the post-subcultural moment in youth cultures research closely follow the contours of debates about the 'choice biography'. Blackman's challenge to what he calls 'post-modern' cultural theory is based on its claim of radical social change. He included authors like Bennett and Muggleton in the criticism that this approach 'reduces "real" subculture to surface signifiers without authenticity where identity is determined by choice'

(Blackman, 2005: 15). Shildrick and MacDonald argue that 'the overriding conclusion of [recent] studies of less flamboyant, less stylistically spectacular youth is that the sorts of free cultural *choice* described by more post-modern, post-subcultural perspectives tend to be reserved for the more privileged sections of dominant cultural groups' (2006: 133, emphasis in original).

These responses in defence of the legacy of the subcultural approach follow the same template as the response youth studies scholars have made to individualisation. They largely dismiss newer approaches by tying them to a valorisation of choice and a perceived lack of attention to class, which is attributed to an overemphasis on the extent of social change that has occurred. As with critiques of individualisation, claims that social structuring has weakened and choice has been set free can then quite easily be shown to be empirically false. Again, as with criticisms of individualisation, these responses to the post-subcultural turn have some basis. Post-subcultural approaches have exaggerated the failings of the subcultural approach and in building alternatives have appeared to emphasise choice. Muggleton (2000: 167) for example provides a self-description of his research as a study of 'postmodern subculturalists' who represent the 'culturally adventurous of all classes', paradoxically seeking out socially shared practices to express individualistic sensibilities. Yet by dismissing this work too easily as a valorisation of choice youth studies researchers again risk missing the substance of the challenge that is being raised.

Muggleton's aim is not primarily to deny the influence of social structure but instead to affirm the (partial) autonomy of culture. Explicitly invoking Max Weber's study of religious belief and its role in the foundation of capitalism, Muggleton (2000: 28) justifies a focus on elements of culture independent from class as an explicitly and self-consciously 'one-sided view' as a corrective for the tendency for this to be played down in the youth subcultures literature. He is clear that class is important:

> I am not denying that material factors … and changes in the class structure … are implicated in the development of subcultures. I want, however, to demonstrate that subcultures can also be explained by reference to changes in cultural belief systems that have an autonomous, although interactive, relationship to socioeconomic factors. (Muggleton, 2000: 28)

Bennett (1999) and Miles (2000) are also explicit that they are not denying structural inequality. They instead use neo-tribe and lifestyle respectively as concepts to demark a relative and ongoing expansion of the autonomy of style from class position, particularly class position based on the relationship to production processes. Miles (2000: 1) opens his study of lifestyle by recognising that young people's lives vary according to 'variations in class, gender and education', but argues that 'although class continues to play an important role in the construction of identities, that role is not so all-powerful as to *determine* young people's lifestyles' (Miles, 2000: 17, emphasis in original). For Bennett, while social inequalities of all kinds, including economic, are very real and continue to have profound consequences for young people, they are less 'rigidly defined or experienced' than the defenders of subcultural analysis seem to propose (Bennett, 2005: 256). By not acknowledging these claims, or at the very least disclaimers, about structured inequality the defenders of subcultures have made dismissing the post-subcultural moment for valorising choice and denying structured inequality too easy. As is the case with critiques of the individualisation thesis, in this area youth scholars are at risk of ignoring the substance of the challenge for theorising the link between inequality and youth culture that critiques of the subcultural approach are raising.

Yet, in turn, as Hesmondhalgh (2005) points out, elements of the criticisms of 'subcultures' as a concept also appear overstated in relation to some of the research that is included under the banner of subcultures. In theorising the relationship between music and subcultures, Paul Willis (1978) for example emphasises the way his young working-class participants had to work creatively to create connections between pop music and their own lives. Hesmondhalgh (2005: 31) points out that this analysis does not seem to focus on structure at the expense of social action.

Understanding the relationship between social change, division and politics was unquestionably one of the aims of the CCCS approach. As Clarke and colleagues conclude in their introduction to *Resistance through Rituals* (Clarke et al., 2006: 44–5):

> Cultures are the range of socially-organized and patterned responses to [the] basic social and material conditions. Though cultures form, for each group, a set of traditions – lines of action inherited from the past – they must always be collectively constructed anew in each generation.

This approach is nuanced, on the one hand highlighting the inequality between youth that was tied to continuity with the parent culture yet on the other the purpose of the conceptual apparatus they developed and the empirical examples they explored was to highlight the importance of change for understanding inequality and resistance. Phil Cohen's interest in the East End district of London was in the changes taking place there. The fall of traditional industries, immigration and a shift to high-rise living arrangements were weakening extended-kin and neighbourhood-based solidarities. Work in the skilled trades that had employed young people's parents had disappeared, replaced with poor quality unskilled work on the one hand and more highly credentialed work that the next generation had little chance of obtaining (Cohen, 1999).

In this sense the East End was a laboratory for social changes that were soon to spread widely across the UK and other nations, including many we have characterised as defining the lives of the post-1970s generation in Australia. Cohen saw the subcultures in the East End as an attempt to 'retrieve some of the socially cohesive elements destroyed in their parent culture, and to combine these with elements selected from other class fractions' to manage a tension between new ideologies of consumption and the traditional working-class frugality of their parents' generation (Cohen, 1999: 57).

While acutely keen to take a long view, connecting new cultural forms to class dynamics with a long history, Clarke and colleagues (2006: 10) also noted the need to be wary of going too far in this direction and hence of robbing 'the period of its historical specificity', and that 'wider socio-economic change can fragment, unhinge and dislocate [a class culture's] intricate mechanisms and defences' (Clarke et al., 2006: 23). The reconstruction of classed cultural forms is constantly occurring and at times the changes are rapid. The post-subcultural critiques have powerfully argued that this is the case in the decades since the early work of the CCCS in the 1970s.

In the end the editors of *Resistance through Rituals* eventually reached some common ground with their critics, echoing many elements of the theories of social change discussed in Chapter 3. A new introduction to a 2006 edition of the book acknowledges that the speed and scope of changes since the 1970s raised challenges for their perspective, while still seeing value in the legacy. Hall and Jefferson call for a 'double-sidedness', namely 'acknowledging the new without losing what may still be serviceable in the old' (Hall and Jefferson, 2006: xii). Intriguingly, this new introduction also supports our contention that reacting to the implicit generationalism of functionalist accounts of youth culture led them to an undeveloped theory of generations. They note that the centrality of social generations in Cohen's work on youth subcultures in East London was overlooked as they developed this work into their subcultures approach:

> It should not be forgotten, however (although we did at the time), that Phil Cohen's seminal early essay, which talked about sub-cultures as 'magical resolutions' of class contradictions, also saw subcultures as generationally specific symbolic systems. (Hall and Jefferson, 2006: xvii)

This small aside acknowledges one of the most significant limitations of the subcultures approach. It is not that the early subcultural theorists refused to recognise change, or that they failed to recognise fluidity or multiple forms of belongings, or even that their work did not recognise that youth subcultures were in a symbolic dialogue with the parental generation as well as the class conditions they faced. To a degree at least, subcultures research has recognised all this. However, in addition to the lack of attention to gender and race that has now been well highlighted, they subordinated generational questions to questions of class cultural continuity over time. By giving relatively scant attention to the everyday lives of young people in their changing times, ulti-mately the subcultural analyses by scholars attached to the CCCS did not, despite intentions, really investigate the processes by which class inequality was reproduced over time but took this for granted. For the Birmingham School complexity was ultimately, and theoretically, reducible to the funda-mental division between capitalists and workers that continued across time and which provided the raw material around which cultures are formed. Their interest was not in how divisions were remade; this could be taken for granted as the class division itself was the driver of change and the focus shifted to asking how the young working class (at least the young white men) coped with change and continued to resist.

As such the CCCS scholars were interested in the small pockets of youth rep-resenting 'authentic' class resistance to capital. These were groups that 'appear only at particular historical moments: they become visible, are identified and labelled (either by themselves or by others): they command the stage of public attention for a time' (Clarke et al., 2006: 7). The concerns of, and the stylistic response of, distinct youth cultural forms like the mods and rockers, skinheads and teddy boys, distinguished them not only from the broad intergenerational working-class culture but also from more 'ordinary' working-class youth. As such, the scholars in the CCCS are explicit that subcultural theory is not a theory of working-class youth as a whole, as the 'great majority of working-class youth never enters a tight or coherent subculture at all. Individuals may, in their personal life-careers, move into or out of one, or indeed several, such subcultures' (Clarke et al., 2006: 9).

In part by drawing on a Weberian perspective, asking that both other social stratifications and culture itself be given at least a degree of independence from class, the post-subcultural approach is also challenging this tendency to make what Gary Clarke called the 'dangerous assumption' that all members of an authentic subculture are from a corresponding class location, instead of doing the work to show what this class location looks like for different young people (Clarke, 1990: 83). Yet at the same time, while raising important questions of subcultural approaches, it remains unclear whether the alternative conceptual resources that post-subcultural scholars have put forward for understanding contemporary youth cultural forms are able to show us how inequality is produced (Griffin, 2011). This is captured in Hesmondhalgh's response to Bennett's theorising of neo-tribes: '[w]e need to know how boundaries are constituted, not simply that they are fuzzier than various writers have assumed' (Hesmondhalgh, 2005: 24).

Generational Change, Cultures and Divisions

Hesmondhalgh's (2005) point about the need for a theory of the constitution of divisions mirrors the theme running throughout this book. We are arguing that youth studies needs concepts that support investigations of how social division, across multiple dimensions including class, gender, race, sexuality, disability and geographic location, is being made today, in the context of social conditions that differ from those that impacted on the lives of young people in previous generations. In Chapter 4 we proposed that the concept of generational units may be a starting point for doing so. There we showed that Mannheim's concept to recognise both the diversity within a generation and the impact of social position makes clear that the sociology of generations should not be seen as necessarily opposed to class analysis, including the work of the CCCS.

Mannheim defined generational units as concrete groupings, shaped by factors such as class. His definition overlaps in some respects with the way the concept of different youth subcultures has been used to understand continuity and change. Indeed Edmunds and Turner (2002: 5) in their development of the sociology of generations use the concept of generational units to think about youth subcultures. Amongst the young British working class of the 1970s and 1980s, a minority were actively engaging in political acts in the face of an apolitical mainstream. For Edmunds and Turner (2002) the mods, rockers and punks analysed within the subcultures approach are examples of generational units creating and exhibiting distinctive lifestyles in response to their generational conditions. The critiques of subcultures on the basis of young people's fluid and multiple belongings, however, also highlight limitations with the concept of generational units. If generational units are understood as concrete groups, the post-subcultural critique of subcultures can again apply. Both post-subcultural and post-colonial scholarship have shown that young people can have many belongings and identities and that empirically they clearly belong to multiple cultural and political configurations concurrently, across class, gender and ethnic divisions (Bennett, 2000; Huq, 2006).

Another approach to studying youth cultural relations is to focus on everyday life. Young people cannot easily be considered as members of one culture, let alone one subculture or generational unit, and their participation in social and cultural groups will be only one aspect of their lives. Shildrick and MacDonald (2006: 127) along with Hodkinson (2012) have argued that post-subcultural studies are limited by a fixation with the spectacular specifics of the stylistic art of the few, a limitation these studies share with the earlier studies of subculture in the CCCS tradition. A focus on visible and spectacular youth cultural styles limits the ability of researchers to understand youth cultural practices in their broader structural context. Deciding in advance that it is these spectacular styles that define the elements of youth culture that are important has impacted on both subcultural and post-subcultural approaches to the study of youth. It has led newer 'post-subculture' approaches to underplay the structural impacts of inequality on consumption, while for earlier subcultural approaches it facilitated theoretical leaps that assumed social constraints had a fundamental continuity over time without properly attending to how this continuity was created.

Over three decades some youth researchers have argued forcefully that a preoccupation with the most spectacular, or trouble-making, or excluded young people or types of youth cultural practices means that comparatively little research focuses on 'ordinary' youth experience (Jenkins, 1983; Griffin, 1985; Coles, 1986; Clarke, 1990; Miles, 2000: 104; MacDonald, 2011; Roberts, 2011). For example, Paul Willis's famous ethnography of the cultural processes by which young working-class people end up in working-class jobs focuses on the differences between the working-class 'lads' and the studious 'ear'oles', giving no attention to those in between, despite these 'semi ear'oles' being discussed by his participants (Willis, 1977: 15).

Others also highlight that all young people, including Willis's (1977) lads, will be 'ordinary' in many aspects of their lives and 'spectacular' in other ways that may happen to bring them to the attention of researchers, authorities or the popular media (Jenkins, 1983; Thomson and Taylor, 2005; Hodkinson, 2012). In the previous chapter we drew on Blatterer (2007) to discuss struggles for recognition as an 'adult' in the context of generational change. Similarly, and linking research on youth transitions to studies of youth culture, no matter how a young person feels about it, their engagement in one sphere, for example leisure or their family life, may be treated as a concern by researchers or policy makers, while their engagement in another sphere, for example at their work and their employment conditions, is not (Jenkins, 1983).

There have always been justifiable reasons to attend to the spectacular elements of youth cultures and to look to identify within confrontational style the 'spectacular symptoms of a wider and more generally submerged dissent' (Hebdige, 1979: 80). Yet much of the significance of youth cultural practices to young people may involve more mundane practices of belonging that are common across youth cultures, and these practices can only be fully understood in the context of the full breadth and depth of young people's lives. Youth cultures researchers do not have to abandon particular areas of focus, but a strong case has been made that studies of dance, music, style and consumption are most insightful when embedded in a study of the multiple dimensions of young lives (Nayak, 2003: 177).

Miles (2000) champions an approach based on exploring youth 'lifestyles' which broadens the frame of reference. Relative to subculture, the concept of lifestyle directs attention away from culture as collective 'meaning' and toward individual practice. A turn to individual consumption opened up opportunities for feminist analyses of youth subcultures, especially in the 1980s, because historically identity was not as closely tied to position in the paid economy for young women as it was for young men (McRobbie and Garber, 1976; Sharpe, 1976). Nonetheless, for young women as well as young men, by the 1980s identity was increasingly built around consumption (Bauman, 2000). Thus, Miles (2000) argues that through individual consumption choices in everyday life young people are investing in building identities in contemporary consumer societies, which gives identity greater autonomy from relations of production.

While identity based on consumption can be fickle and unfulfilling, Miles (2000) also argues that the ability to appropriate and reinterpret global social forms for local cultural formations provides an anchor for creating a sense of identity and meaning in a rapidly changing world. The appearance of greater fragmentation in cultural engagements, he argues, should be understood as examples of flexibility and adaptability in youth lifestyles, which paradoxically allows lifestyle to play a primary role as a provider of stability and coherence in a world of flux (Miles, 2000: 159). However, he also argues that in the end this creativity, because it is so often based on purchasable consumer items, comes at a heavy cost. The contemporary spread of mass consumption coupled with a greater differentiation of available products means that the consumer lifestyle offers young people an 'island' to escape to that also turns out to be a prison:

> On this island, young people can feel safe from the ravages of the cruel seas (of rapid social change and inequality) that surround them … They cannot, however, escape from that island, nor from the tentacles of consumerism. And it is in this sense that consumption fails to provide young people with the service they demand of it … Consumer lifestyles cannot provide a genuine escape from the ravages of individualization. (Miles, 2000: 145)

Here Miles presents an argument that resonates with our discussion of the increasing expectation on young people to act like a circus performer (the juggler, tightrope walker or acrobat) trying to defy the social forces that risk pulling their biographies apart (Beck and Beck-Gernsheim, 2002). His notion of lifestyles, however, has two limitations. Firstly, as Bennett (2011: 500) highlights, consumption should not be conflated with consumerism as youth cultural consumption is not only built around goods purchased or purchasable. They can, and often are, instead appropriated and created in a 'DIY' fashion. Secondly, given the way that young people have to juggle different demands, including, as Miles acknowledges, over and above the demands tied to consumer expectations, it is difficult to see the consumer lifestyle as an 'island' separated from work, education, employment and non-purchasable cultural practices undertaken with other people.

As we have argued throughout this book, we need to understand how young people combine and juggle different demands and engagements, and this means avoiding the temptation to privilege any one area of life as central or as an island separate from others. We have suggested that youth is characterised by a growing challenge to hold together the biography. A 'biographical approach', which focuses on everyday cultural practices in the context of young people's other engagements, provides a productive framework for conceptualising their cultural practices. Following Henderson and colleagues (2007), we use 'biographical' to indicate a holistic treatment of young people's lives. This approach enables the analysis of how different elements of life interact, and how 'investment in one area (say work) is likely to be matched by disinvestment (or less investment) in other areas (say family commitments) [and that the] different biographical fields that are in play depend on the young person's social location' (Henderson et al., 2007: 13). Biographical research aims to investigate the experiences and outlooks of individuals in the context of their everyday lives, framed within their broader historical context.

A biographical focus is not inimical to some of the concepts that have been put forward as part of the post-subcultures approach. It has some affinities with the notion of lifestyle broadened beyond consumption and also with Maffesoli's work on neo-tribes. While the use of neo-tribe in youth sociology has focused, like the subcultures approach, on music, dance and style groupings, Maffesoli's (1996) concept of new tribalism was developed to represent general social conditions that were much more than this. The idea of the new tribalism was intended to capture the continual switching between different roles and affects or 'treads of reciprocity' in people's lives, including examples such as small professional associations, religious practices, and even jogging. The tribal life is a creation based on the face-to-face relationships and 'minuscule facts that make up everyday life' (Maffesoli, 1996: 81).

A biographical approach is also not fundamentally opposed to a number of ideas linked to the subcultural approach. While most subcultures research does not take a biographical approach, elements of such an approach are visible in Cohen's (1999) foundational essay on young people in London's East End which attends not just to subcultural style but to new living and family arrangements. A focus on the biography is also closely linked to arguments in feminist-inspired youth sociology for better attending to everyday life to understand the cultural lives of young women, particularly as made by Angela McRobbie beginning with her time at the CCCS (McRobbie and Garber, 1976; McRobbie, 1991). Another member attached to the Birmingham School, Brian Roberts, and author of one of the very few methodological chapters in *Resistance through Rituals* (Roberts, 2006 [1976]) went on to be a key figure in developing the biographical approach we are describing here (Roberts, 2002). Roberts (2002: 5) provides a link between the biographical approach and the study of social and generational change, arguing that the appeal of the approach is the possibility of working up from individual accounts of life experience, contextualising within their contemporary cultural and structural settings, and through this aiming for a new understanding of the impact of major social change. Taking a biographical approach to investigating young people's cultural practices is a way of working across the division between the cultures and transitions strands of youth research. There are semi-regular calls to better bridge these two strands of youth research (Hollands, 2002; Nayak, 2003: 33; Shildrick and MacDonald, 2006; Furlong et al., 2011; Geldens et al., 2011). While the division between the two strands is very real, much of the youth research that tends to have a lasting influence, like Willis's (1977) study of learning to labour, does not fit clearly within one camp or the other, and studies that aim to work across the transitions and cultures approach are becoming more common, particularly in the growing number of qualitative studies of 'ordinary' young people and their work and education engagements (see McLeod and Yates, 2006; Henderson et al., 2007; Wierenga, 2009; Roberts, 2011).

The creation of a theoretical and methodological 'middle-ground' between cultures and transitions research (Woodman, 2009; Coffey and Farrugia, 2014) is unsurprising considering the general view of the relative strengths and limitations of the two strands of youth research. Firstly there is a view, which is evident in the debates about post-subcultures we have discussed in this chapter, that recent cultures research may be well equipped theoretically, and with its use of qualitative and ethnographic methods, to investigate the creative manner in which young people shape cultural forms. Secondly there is a widespread view that while transitions research may be more limited in understanding 'agency', evidence on labour market and educational 'structures' is important for seeing how this agency is 'bounded' (Evans, 2002, 2007).

While understandable, attempting to bridge this division by giving an equal focus to both structure *and* agency, can only progress analysis so far as it is too simple. Our engagement with the cultures strand of youth research in this chapter has highlighted the ongoing struggle by researchers within this tradition to analyse the changing nature of youth without oversimplifying the relationship between young people's actions and the cultural and structural factors within which these actions are enmeshed (Woodman, 2009). The concept of 'bounded agency', on the other hand, seems to represent a truism, begging the question of what an agency that was unbounded could possibly mean, as this would seemingly require constantly revisable choice without consequence, pushing the meaning of agency to breaking point. This concept seemingly avoids engaging with the highly influential frameworks for thinking about structure and action as in a co-constitutive relationship (Bourdieu, 1979; Giddens, 1984), as well as stronger critiques that theorise the subject as not an actor but the continually reproduced outcome of structured but contingent and uncertain social practices (Foucault, 1982; Butler, 1990). Even in critical realist accounts (Archer, 2003) or rational choice approaches (Coleman, 1990) that retain the structure/agency dualism, agency and agents' projects are only meaningful in the context of enabling and constraining structures that stand in the way of or facilitate these projects.

If agency is theorised as bounded by structure then it forecloses conceptualisations of agency as acquired or enabled by these structures, and hence agency tends to be operationalised in a simplistic way as either what researchers think is 'good' (as Coffey and Farrugia, 2014 argue) or whatever is left over after culture and structure have been accounted for (as France, 2007, points out). As we argue throughout this book, this type of thinking encourages a tendency to over-identify the processes of inequality with enduring 'social structures', and by definition, to downplay the extent to which the processes by which inequality is produced change.

Taking a biographical approach provides a way of exploring these dynamics that avoids sharp dualisms and also goes beyond recognising the 'contradictory intersections of identities' (Rattansi and Phoenix, 2005) by which individual action is pushed and pulled. A biographical approach is also about embedding research accounts in an understanding of the institutional reshaping of young people's everyday lives. Due to the structural complexities and multiple contradictions that are driving the process of individualisation, analyses that start with the shared social-structural position of a group of young people and work up to discover their shared lifestyle or vice versa are likely to be inconclusive, or to force the evidence into a theoretical straightjacket. As we highlighted in Chapter 3, individualisation is however fundamentally an institutional process, shaping the biography as a 'latent side effect' of government or organisational decisions that change the labour market and education. As Beck (1992: 132) argues, '[i]nstitutional determinations and interventions are (implicitly) also determinations of and interventions in human biographies'. Layering the biographical approach with the concept of generations, we are arguing that to understand generational divisions as shaped by class, gender or race, research may need to start with the biography of individuals. This is not to avoid larger questions of political economy through committing to some kind of methodological individualism, but as a starting point to investigate how the institutional shaping of the conditions of everyday life in the context of individualisation impact on the possibilities and constraints young people face, including their cultural engagements.

As we showed in Chapter 5, for the Life Patterns participants, like the young people studied by Phil Cohen (1999) and the CCCS group (Hall and Jefferson, 2006), leisure plays a key part in their lives. We argued that this needs to be understood in the context of their multiple other engagements in work, school and care that are in turn shaped by institutional change in the labour market and education. Precarious employment and educational investments, opaque rules and guidelines on how to achieve security or success, and on how much effort is required to do so, take time and energy away from leisure engagements while paradoxically making them more important. If our characterisation of the contradictions facing the current generation of young people is accurate, cultural forms and collective practices may be squeezed by the biographical work of managing the demands of everyday life – of navigating fragmenting social structures to hold together contradictory social demands – and at the same time vital to constructing a sense of consistency across the different areas of their lives. The time and energy for cultural practices have to be found, and this task will be easier for some than others.

A biographical approach can also involve the study of specific groups, scenes or tribes, even spectacular ones, but locates this analysis within the seemingly more mundane and everyday practices of research participants (Kahn–Harris, 2007; Hodkinson, 2012: 568). The future of youth cultures research focused on particular cultural forms is likely to necessitate a greater focus on 'multi–sited' research that follows these cultural forms across time and space and also follows the young people involved through their multiple, and potentially complex and contradictory, engagements with work, study and leisure. By doing so cultures research may avoid the pitfalls of focusing on consumption, either mundane or spectacular, in isolation.

Blurring Boundaries

One of these pitfalls in youth studies is to see superficial similarities (often tied to consumption) across age groups as evidence of a dissolution of boundaries between ages and generations. Recently, in separate work, two sociologists better known for their work on crime have turned to theorising the widely recognised growth in the diversity of lifestyles and the acceptance of this diversity across different stages of the life course (Hayward, 2013; Levin, 2013). While Levin (2013) discusses the increasing variability in the timing of when people have children or finish study, both he and Hayward (2013) focus largely on consumption patterns and 'lifestyle' practices to substantiate their claims for a 'dissolution' of aged-based boundaries. Hayward (2013: 527) suggests there has been a bidirectional muddying of the distinction between youth and adulthood, on the one hand an 'infantilisation' or increasing immaturity of adults and on the other an 'adultification', or a premature aging, of children, for example the sexualisation of young girls through pop culture. He calls the result 'generational mulch', where the norm is now for cultural experiences to be interchangeable across generations (Hayward, 2012: 215).

While we would agree that the boundaries between youth and adulthood are indeed messy, this does not necessarily lead to generational mulch. Other recent research from those more firmly versed in the youth cultures research tradition, and increasingly taking a biographical approach, provides a comparatively nuanced account of this blurring (Bennett, 2006, 2012; Haenfler, 2010; Hodkinson, 2011; Bennett and Hodkinson, 2012; Holland, 2012). Like Haywood and Levin, these scholars recognise that the music, dance and styles that matter to people in youth continue to matter, at least for some, as they head through middle to old age. These authors, however, investigate this continuing involvement in light of other investments and demands and the impact of an aging body. The crucial insight that this allows is that generations matter and that the first experience of 'fresh contact' (Mannheim, 1952 [1923]: 293) with a cultural form for younger people will be different from the 'same' experience at a different point in life, particularly if this is after several decades of involvement.

As such this continuing engagement is not the dissolution of age-based or generational boundaries for two reasons. Firstly, in music for example, continuing development of new genres and subgenres tends to be driven by those making 'fresh contract' with cultural forms; they are produced and consumed by the young. This early contact is often particularly significant for people, such that it is unsurprising to find that those who invest particularly strongly in a cultural form as young people continue to have some investment over time, not because age and generation no longer matter but because they do (Bennett, 2006). Secondly, as well as assuming a static vision of adulthood, this claim of infantilisation assumes but never proves that other 'adult' commitments are incompatible with cultural practices and consumption patterns. Bennett and Hodkinson (2012) argue that continued 'youth' culture involvements do not necessarily or even usually mean an 'infantialisation' where adult commitments are delayed. This does not mean that mixing commitments is straightforward, but that it needs to be understood in terms of other investments, '[c]ritical here is an understanding of how the identities and lifestyles constructed by "post-youth" individuals may often need to include the accommodation of new demands' (2012: 4). While some will be able to negotiate direct participation, for many others demands of care or employment, or even bodily changes, may mean that some forms of direct participation are impossible or very difficult, but a general sensibility tied to punk, straightedge, Goth or rave can continue over time and become embodied in new ways (Bennett, 2006; Hodkinson, 2011; Gregory, 2012; Haenfler, 2012; Holland, 2012).

While this research on aging in 'youth' cultures points to the intersection of youth and generation, contemporary research is showing that the priorities of adulthood and no-doubt old age are changing as the so-called 'Baby-Boomer' generation ages. While they are changing their priorities over the life course, and their youth looked different from the youth of the current generation, Boomers remain impacted by membership of their generation and of the particular intersections of individual biography and historical circumstances that continue to frame their lives. The meaning of both youth and adulthood can be reshaped by a new social generation (Andres and Wyn, 2010). Just as they are creating new meanings of youth and young adulthood today, it is possible, or even likely, that when they reach middle age, today's young people may not have the same middle-aged lives as their parents.

If we are to understand the motivations of scene participants and the role of cultural practices in their lives, attending to the spectacular specifics of their practices is important, but so is seeing this in the context of more ordinary practices that may be shared across cultural forms and how these practices fit with the 'biography'. In the coming chapter we provide an extended example, drawn from the Life Patterns research programme, of what this approach means in practice. As we show, it is not necessarily only older participants who find that other demands get in the way of some cultural practices, or that they have to make difficult decisions about involvement, such as rejecting particular kinds of work or employment to continue direct participation.

We argue that temporal pressures on cultural practices can be just as significant for the current generation of young people, but have taken on a new generational dimension as the nature of the youth labour market and patterns of education have changed.

Conclusion

This chapter has explored contemporary debates about the relative value of theorising youth cultures on a neo-Marxist subcultural basis. As with debates about individualisation within youth studies broadly, the critiques of the subcultures approach that emerged through the 1980s through to the present have coalesced around the relationship between social change, social structure and identity. By the late 1980s, both conceptual critique and changing social conditions had suggested that the traditional class basis for subcultures had, if not diminished, at least become far more complex. This fragmentation and complexity have been the starting point for newer post-subcultural conceptualisations of neo-tribes and scenes.

We note that within these debates about youth cultures, there has also been a tendency to link social change with greater freedom from constraints and to see evidence of inequality as evidence that claims of social change are an overstatement. The debate has been slanted by a position that understands defending the significance of inequality to mean defending the value of the concept of subcultures. As with the concept of individualisation, we have interpreted the post-subcultural turn not as a denial of structured inequality but as a challenge to trace the impact of unequal resources, and of relations of class in the context of the seemingly more fragmentary but still profoundly powerful set of social structures in contemporary modernity.

Yet the post-subcultures approach has not been especially successful in furthering an understanding of inequality in the lives of young people. An alternative is to focus on youth cultures through a generational framework. It is difficult to think of real existing groups as a subculture, subset or 'unit' of a single larger culture, either of class or generation. Instead we suggest that youth researchers will need to move beyond this type of categorisation of particular young people or particular youth practices. Instead, the challenge will be to understand identity, shared cultural practices and resistance in the context of the different tensions that unequally pull contemporary young people in different directions and which they must negotiate. As an alternative for theorising the impact of inequality on the opportunities for, and hindrances to, engaging in group-based cultural forms, including the impact of class, gender and other divisions, we would advocate a biographical approach.

Biographical research of the 'ordinary' possibilities that are opened and the constraints that are imposed upon young people today, in the conditions facing this generation will build a picture of which young people are most advantaged and what it means today to be excluded from the possibilities available to other members of the generation. This will provide a context for theorising about why some actions can appear spectacular or problematic, the role of cultural practices in young people's identities, and how the politics of young people's practices should be understood.

7

TIME

Temporal questions were foundational to sociology. As we discussed in the opening to Chapter 2, social change often provides the impetus to sociological theorising. The trinity of Durkheim, Marx and Weber focused on the emergence of new industrial social forms and the impact of this on solidarity, inequality and identity. In different ways they explored the way this 'modernity', despite the suffering it caused, also created new capacities for shaping a better society in the future (Wagner, 2001; Adam, 2009). Interest in such temporal questions, particularly concerning continuity and change, has remained part of the sociological imagination in the intervening decades. The explicit theorising of the temporal dimensions of society has, however, waxed and waned over time. From the 1990s, linked to the constellation of social changes we have discussed throughout this book, sociology has again been experiencing a boom in such theorising (Bergmann, 1992: 82; Hassan and Purser, 2007).

The sociology of youth is by definition a field concerned with time and change, irrespective of the peaks and troughs in interest among social researchers in general. Those who see youth as a period of psycho-social development, a transition, or a relational social institution constructed around age share a reliance on tropes of time, whatever their other disagreements may be. As we saw in the last chapter, in cultures research the temporal duration of cultural forms has been one of the central dimensions separating subcultural from post-subcultural approaches. Within the neo-tribal perspective young people are increasingly oriented towards the present, with fleeting if also intense cultural engagements instead of long-term commitments and solidarities (Maffesoli, 1996: 75).

In Chapter 5 we discussed the transitions perspective showing that questions containing temporal elements also characterise this field of sociological youth research. Concerned as it is with the timing of transitions, arguments for slowed transitions, either 'arrested' (Côté, 2000) or in a more positive take 'extended' through the third decade of life (Arnett, 2004), compete with arguments for the increasingly complex mixing of statuses and reversible transitions (te Riele, 2004; Valentine and Skelton, 2007; Worth, 2009). The subjective dimension of transitions, how young people imagine their future and their ability to control it, has been one of the most investigated questions in recent years. Researchers in this area have asked whether there are new opportunities or demands for planning or whether instead young people's temporal horizons are shrinking ever closer to the present (du Bois-Reymond, 1998; Brannen and Nilsen, 2002; Pais, 2003; Leccardi, 2007; Brooks and Everett, 2008). This interest in temporal orientation is in large part driven by debates about the choice biography we discussed in Chapter 3 (see for example Brannen and Nilsen, 2002, 2007; Lehmann, 2004).

Adding a generations lens to the conceptual apparatus of youth studies can provide another layer to researchers' understanding of the temporal structures that shape young people's lives. We will argue that this provides an alternative framework for researching young people's temporal orientations. The conceptual approaches developed in this book are relevant if they aid our understanding of 'ordinary' everyday life for young people. By shifting from a theory of generational consciousness to a habitus shaped by discontinuities and contradictions in cultural transmission, we focus on the way that diverse generational conditions and subjectivities concurrently develop in the 'everyday' practices, ordinary and not so ordinary, undertaken with others. This has the potential to provide new understandings of the interaction of economic structural change and the experience of being young that have been obscured by the dominance of, and division between, research on young people's cultural practices on the one hand and transitions research on the other (Furlong et al., 2011).

Developing this biographical and generation framework, we turn in this chapter to a question of time that is largely neglected by youth research, investigating the impact of changes in the youth labour market, particularly the movement towards a 24/7 economy and 'temporary' or insecure labour contracts, on the temporal structures of everyday life. This movement towards a 24/7 economy is one of the more significant changes marking the lives of today's young people as different from those of their parents (Hassan and Purser, 2007). We argue that one of the effects of these labour market conditions is to weaken the institutionalised coordination between lives by creating complex and idiosyncratic personal schedules, creating new demands on individuals to coordinate their time with significant others (Shove, 2009). We open the chapter by showing that the time structures of late modernity, often characterised on the broad scale as 'time-space distanciation' (Giddens, 1990), the push towards 'timeless time' (Castells, 2000) or simply as 'acceleration' (Rosa, 2013), can also be conceptualised as changes in the time structures of everyday life. We illustrate this with the example of the Life Patterns participants for whom these changes have led to new challenges of coordination, of synchronising schedules with others in the face of individualised (variable) timetables. The inability to schedule time together with close friends appears to impact negatively on many young lives, despite the rise of new types of virtual connectivity facilitated by the digital revolution. We finish the chapter by arguing that the new forms of time-based inequality tied to the problem of synchronisation impact on the way that young people and their networks of significant others can use the passing of time to build resources, enjoy the present, and shape the future.

Social Change and Synchronisation

A core component of the biographical approach we discussed in the previous chapter is that engagement in one field such as work or education is likely to have impacts across others, including home life or leisure (Henderson et al., 2007: 30). There are compelling reasons for exploring the temporal structuring of these different investments as they are lived out. Elizabeth Shove (2009) makes the seemingly obvious but consequential point that these investments are temporal; social practices take time. Many prominent social theories of the past four decades have also proposed that the temporal-spatial ordering of everyday practices is central to social reproduction (Bourdieu, 1977; de Certeau, 1984; Giddens, 1984; Lefebvre, 2004). It is through shared practices in time that people develop the dispositions by which they negotiate and shape their world (Bourdieu, 1998a; Thrift and May, 2001) and maintain a secure sense of themselves that allows them to act (Giddens, 1984). Hence it is through these shared practices that new social forms can emerge and through which existing forms can be extended over time. Nobert Elias (1992) speaks of the tempo of our time within his general model of 'figuration', the networks of human independence by which social formations are built. The tempo of any social figuration is for Elias the 'manifestation of the multitude of intertwining chains of interdependence which run through every single social function that people have to perform' (2000: 379).

Recent theorists have proposed that the temporal structures of contemporary societies are changing rapidly, with potentially significant consequences for these shared practices. For example, the German sociologist Hartmut Rosa (2013) argues that the speed of social change is accelerating, driven by three factors. The first factor is the quickening pace of technological development and a related increase in the pace at which older technology is superseded. The second factor, enabled by this technological development, is social change, particularly a greater cultural and economic pressure towards accelerated growth in production and consumption. Social change is both structural and cultural, including the impact of social movements or the spread of cultural forms across space. For Rosa these two spheres, in which stability in one can potentially act as a break on change in the other, are in contemporary times encouraging and advancing change in each other (see also Archer, 2012: 56–7). These first two factors lead to the third change, creating a feeling of being unanchored in time. Demands to adapt to a global economy and compulsions to greater consumption lead to an increased pace of everyday life (Rosa, 2013).

For Rosa (2013: 277–88) the temporal effects of social acceleration are manifold and contradictory. A pertinent contradiction for our focus in this chapter is that keeping up with the speed of change seems to create, both individually and collectively, greater amounts of certain types of rigidity. The temporal structures embedded in routines are both constraining and enabling (Giddens, 1984). While many feel trapped by routines, these also provide a sense of security and predictability (Ehn and Löfgren, 2009: 110) and are necessary for meaningful social connection. Arlie Hochschild (1997) makes a similar point, arguing that the pressure for efficiencies through routinisation has escaped the bounds of the factory. Taylorist work principles, now often disavowed by employers, have bled into other spheres of life, such as the organisation of family life, which are reorganised for maximal 'efficiency' as this appears to be the only way to cope. Even if the ends of this efficiency are opaque, and often perplexing, this nonetheless feel like a compulsion

(Hochschild, 1997). Rosa's point is related but somewhat different, arguing that everyday life itself becomes more routinely flexible to support the flexibility demanded by the economy (Rosa, 2013: 171).

The increasingly 'fluid' structure of contemporary life has been one of the central concerns of contemporary social theory (Bauman, 2007a; Rosa, 2013). This 'liquid modernity' however does not refer to a lack of structure. In late modernity power is exercised through 'flexibility' and shifting the insecurity of change onto others (Bauman, 2007). Manuel Castells (2000: 282–3) puts the reversal of a pattern that defined the mid-twentieth-century experience of work in the Global North, which he calls 'standard employment', towards a new pattern he calls the 'the individualization of labor in the labor process' as a central dynamic in the shift towards a 'network society'. As well as identifying the lack of job security, the end of a social contract of employment security for loyalty to an employer, and the greater need for geographical mobility for many employees, Castells (2000: 283) identifies 'flexi-time' as one of four elements of this individualisation.

While the impact of work conditions on the lives of workers is one of the earliest concerns of the social sciences (Engels, 1993 [1845]), recent scholarship has focused on the impact of 'flexible' employment regimes and the associated rise, or return, of precarious work in the Global North (Pocock, 2004; Campbell, 2004; Standing, 2011). In Chapters 3 and 4 we discussed the impact of this type of work, particularly on young people, such as the impact of poor employment security on starting a family. In this chapter we focus in detail on the temporal aspects of these 'flexible' employment regimes, non-standard or 'unsocial' hours of employment and their impacts on other spheres of young people's lives. Empirical research suggests that for some fluidity is translated into flexibility. For example, for an employer the temporary contract allows them to remove the 'standards' of entitlement, tenure and work patterns won by labour movements throughout the nineteenth and twentieth centuries (Hinrichs et al., 1991) and hence utilise labour in a more 'flexible' way. For the employee, however, this fluidity is often experienced as precariousness (Rogers and Rogers, 1989; Watson et al., 2003; Standing, 2011). One of the more significant elements of precarious work for the employed is a lack of control over hours of engagement (Campbell, 2004).

Australia is at the vanguard of the move towards 'flexible' time in employment patterns, although other countries are following in a similar direction. The 'standard' pattern of employment during the full-time daytime hours of Monday to Friday is in decline in Australia (ABS, 2009a). In large part this is because Australian employers use temporary contracts at one of the highest rates in the OECD (Campbell, 2004). The type of work patterns that characterise contemporary employment is likely to have an impact that bleeds into other spheres of life, including domestic life and leisure time. The notion of 'unsocial hours' has long been used by labour-market researchers to highlight that not all hours of leisure are equal and people tend to want to spend their 'free' time with significant others (Bittman, 2005: 59–60). Leisure time on a Tuesday morning is not the same as on a Saturday evening. This is partly due to cultural patterns of when collective activity takes place but is also due to structural factors – to the extent that the institution of employment still maintains some tendency towards Monday–Friday daytime patterns of work, leisure time on a Tuesday morning more than on a Saturday will be difficult to spend with others and hence potentially more likely to be spent on solitary pursuits. Changes away from standard hours mean the long debate about unsociable hours is taking on a new urgency.

As everyday life is becoming more fragmented into multiple and unpredictable tasks (Bauman, 2007b), and particularly as greater fluidity has been institutionalised into employment patterns, it is increasingly difficult to coordinate lives with significant others (Southerton, 2006; Woodman, 2012; Dixon et al., 2013). The scholarship of British sociologist Dale Southerton (2006, 2009) provides an example of this. Using time diaries completed by people living in 1937 and time-use interviews with a group of adults conducted in 2000, Southerton found that personal coordination of schedules with others was regularly discussed as a challenge by his modern-day participants but such concerns are almost absent in the data collected in 1937.

In this earlier period synchronisation between lives was provided by fixed institutional timetables and the material conditions of life. Scheduling in one sense was less of an option but it was also less necessary in 1937. Paid and unpaid work provided a relatively fixed structure to the day. For example, diarists in 1937 wrote of eating lunch at the same time every day with children returning from school and husbands from work. Southerton's (2009) diarists from 1937 also noted routinely allocated meals with others beyond the nuclear family, such as lunch with the neighbours every Sunday. By the start of the new century these types of routinised shared practices of eating had almost vanished; his contemporary participants reported finding this too difficult to organise.

Research investigating the rise in 'unsocial' hours has not attended to youth, instead investigating the impact of unsocial hours and the challenge of scheduling primarily on middle-aged employees, particularly those with children (see for example Symes, 1999; Presser, 2004; Bittman, 2005). Yet there is evidence that the need to negotiate the impact of individualised employment patterns is felt acutely by young people. Not only in the popular imagination but also in academic youth research, commentators often link 'youth' with a greater access to leisure time than is available to any other group, with suggestions that this access may be extending as the transition to adulthood occurs later (Arnett, 2004). For Arnett (2004: 9) paid employment in the late teens and twenties will for most young people be subordinated to leisure, with paid work's primary role being to support their leisure activities. It is true that young people tend to have more leisure than those in the so-called 'rush hour' of life, but not less than all other age groups. Time-use data collected by the Australian Bureau of Statistics do suggest that young people aged 15–25 have more leisure time than the 25–34 age bracket and the 35–44 age bracket, primarily due to childcare responsibilities, but by the 45–54 bracket older adults' leisure time is again increasing, and young people have less leisure time than the 54–64 bracket and the brackets older than this (ABS, 2006).

With the social changes we discussed in Chapter 3 the conditions for an individualisation of temporal schedules are clear. Despite many modifications to the structuring of young lives, while in secondary school the temporal rhythms of young people's days continue to be largely shaped by the shared institutional timetable set by schooling, which structures time, including leisure time, with friends (Christensen and James, 2001). After secondary school, most will enter some types or mix of post-school study and most will have some form of paid work. Their individual lives will become structured by study timetables that vary from one person to the next, and that vary across semesters. While a substantial number of secondary students work in Australia (Stokes and Wyn, 2007), the rate increases significantly among tertiary students. Whether or not they are also studying, these young workers in their early years after secondary school are much more likely than their parents at the same age to be employed on a 'casual contract' and embedded in the 24/7 economy, where work rosters can also change from week to week and often involve night-time work. These casual contracts facilitate irregular patterns of work as employers can vary work patterns with little notice.

Young people find themselves in the vanguard of the ranks of this new kind of 'flexible' worker (Furlong and Kelly, 2005; Price et al., 2011: 3). They are most likely to work in the retail and hospitality sectors that have been frontrunners in the emergence of new work patterns and the move towards

24/7 operations (Furlong and Kelly, 2005). As extended hours of operation become the norm in these sectors, work hours for each staff member are significantly more likely to fall beyond the 'standard' Monday to Friday, 9–5 pattern. This was borne out in a 2009 survey of working time patterns by the Australian Bureau of Statistics (2010) that showed young people aged 20–24 were the most likely group to have irregular, evening, or split shifts of work, with rates decreasing with age.

Among the Life Patterns participants in the second cohort, now aged in their mid-20s, non-standard patterns of work are very common (Woodman, 2012, 2013). Over 70 per cent of the cohort work either in the evenings, at weekends or on public holidays. Even excluding those participants who are still studying, the rate stays at 65 per cent (Woodman, 2013: 422–3). In 2008 we interviewed 50 members of the second cohort of Life Patterns participants, aged 19–20 at the time, about the impact of these work patterns on their relationships with significant others. In particular these participants discussed the impact of non-standard hours and variability in their work patterns on their relationships. Their experiences suggested that it was at least as often employers as employees who controlled work patterns under flexible contracts. Many of the Life Patterns participants had found it difficult to schedule regular periods of time together with their close friends, or with the acquaintances they would most like to develop into closer friendships (Woodman, 2012).

It is longstanding common sense that young people's friendships change over their late teens and early 20s, 'drifting apart' after finishing secondary school and moving on to new engagements and interests. The reasons, however, given in interviews by the Life Patterns participants for changes in their friendships were suggestive of new factors that have emerged from the recent changes. Many of the participants had started a course or job that put them on an incompatible timetable with a pre-existing group of friends. If a number of people in a friendship group do the same, then there is no longer a standard timetable or rhythm into which to fit shared time. In line with the reconstruction of the concept of individualisation we are using, this is not due to their freedom to choose how to use their time or a freeing of temporal schedules from social shaping, but instead that these temporal structures are partial to particular spheres, more variable and contradictory and hence potentially individualising. The particular combination of schedules that shapes each person's life has become more varied. These patterns mean that the particular pattern of engagement for each young person is more likely to vary over time and there will be more variability between people's schedules. Personal timetables hence become less standardised and the accumulative effect across lives is a more considerable collective desynchronisation (Woodman, 2012: 1086).

The impact of these de-standardised temporal schedules on relationships varied based on the relationship type and the resources the participant could access. The Life Patterns participants who participated in this part of the study were less likely to feel that time with parents had been impacted on by their temporal schedules (Woodman, 2012: 1087). This may be due to them valuing time with family less than with peers at this point in their lives. It may be instead that as time in education has for many young people extended, in Australia it is now more common than three decades ago for people to live in the family home into their 20s and beyond (ABS, 2013). As such, young people may be getting to spend more time with their parents through sharing a residence, even if their schedules do not necessarily align and the regular family meal appears to be becoming rarer (Southerton, 2009; Dixon et al., 2013).

It was primarily close friendships that the interview participants felt were being negatively impacted on by their schedules. Not all participants, however, reported this experience. As the statistics we presented above in this section show, a little under a third of the participants still worked standard hours. Of course, given that many of their friends were likely to work non-standard hours, the challenge of coordinating schedules to spend time together was likely to confront those still employed under the 'standard' as well. A small group, who had financial support from their family, and who were able to draw on their embedded cultural capital to negotiate with their employers, had substantial autonomy over their work times. This includes the ability to decline shifts when a manager asked them to undertake extra work or to adjust their hours of work with short notice, as well as to request and receive extended periods away from work, for example around the exam period if they were studying or for major holidays (Woodman, 2012: 1085).

Given that temporal individualisation is a type of collective de-synchonisation, the impact of personal control over time on social experience is likely to be highly mediated by whether significant others also have similar levels of control. While we have not specifically investigated this question, there is some evidence in the stories recounted by the Life Patterns participants from higher socio-economic backgrounds that suggests they tend to have social networks comprised of people with a similar level of relative control over the variability in their work schedules (Woodman, 2012: 1085). Employment for these participants, even if ostensibly based on a casual contract with no long-term guarantees and few real workplace rights or power, was likely to extend their networks and give them useful work experience while not having a substantially negative impact on relations outside of work.

With high rates of youth unemployment and underemployment around the world, some young people face the problem of too much time and far from enough money (although 'active' labour market programmes can mean that the unemployed sometimes have very little free time or control over their time). Most, however, continue to work, and the conditions of this work are changing. Of course for many workers in precarious labour markets around the world the major impact of this type of work is material, namely poverty and financial insecurity. Another neglected element of these work conditions is this temporal element, which is impacting on the lives of the participants. These Life Patterns findings suggest that apart from a privileged minority, changes to the youth labour market in Australia have not given younger people more flexibility over their work time but have resulted in a desynchronisation of everyday life.

While fewer young people today might expect the standard work arrangements that were available to their parents, and may seek out low skilled part-time work to facilitate full-time study, this does not mean that they want 'precarious' work. At the same time, while work patterns and expectations have changed, the importance of friends is unlikely to have diminished and may even have grown (Spencer and Pahl, 2006) as particular transition events associated with youth become more complex (Collins and van Dulmen, 2006). Finding time with close friends and significant others is both an intrinsic good for many young people and provides a resource to face the uncertainties of late modern life. It is these friendships in particular that have been put under pressure by unsocial hours. Given that our generational framework orients us towards the potential for young people to reshape forms of sociality, particularly in the context of the digital revolution, it is also important to ask how social change may be allowing these young people to experiment with new types of connections before passing too strong a judgement on the larger impact of these work changes.

Sociality and the Digital Revolution

As the meaning of friendship can shift across time and place, scepticism should be directed at any unequivocal claims about a general decline in connectedness or 'friendliness', or overly nostalgic claims about relationships in the past (Spencer and Pahl, 2006; Allan, 2008). A social desynchronisation caused by increasingly individual temporal schedules does not necessarily mean that young people's relationships are suffering in an overall sense. Mixing education and employment, particularly given the recent changes in tenure patterns, has the potential to expand the number of friends a young person has (Wang et al., 2010). Shorter average tenure, and hence potentially more places of employment, combined with variable shift patterns, make it likely that young people will work with a greater number of colleagues than their parents did, both now and across the life course (Woodman, 2013: 420).

Potentially of even greater significance is that new types of friendships are being created. Sociological thinking about the synchronisation of practices (Southerton, 2006; Shove, 2009; Rosa, 2013) is based on an assumption that physical co-presence is highly valued. Given the acceleration of technological change in the digital realm, particularly as this interacts with other changes, there is evidence to support those who suggest a digital 'revolution' which could challenge this assumption about the value of co-presence (Rosa, 2013: 44). More modes of communication are available than ever before, such as the internet and the mobile phone, fostering relations between 'absent' others (Giddens, 1990: 18). New types of sociality both online and offline are now available for groups whose use of public space was previously highly curtailed. Not only same-sex attracted young people and disabled young people but also the one half of the youth population who are young women have had new possibilities for engagement with public 'space' opened by the rise of online networks (Kenyon et al., 2002). Young people, in general, are trending towards a constant connection to these networks, such as Facebook, through their smart phones, and these new technologies have the obvious potential to reshape the temporal-spatial dimensions of social relations (Buckingham, 2006; Ito and Okabe, 2006; Lasén, 2006). Thus physical mobility, i.e. going to where others are, and co-presence are not necessary for some types of interaction.

However, the evidence so far does not suggest this digital revolution has caused a weakening of the importance of embodied sociality and long-term relationships. Instead, the digital revolution and other social 'accelerations' (Rosa, 2013) have embedded the search for belonging in a new set of institutionalised challenges and possibilities. Younger, and older, people still regularly seek out shared time to be physically co-present with others, driven by what has been called a 'compulsion for proximity' (Boden and Molotch, 1994;

Urry, 2002). Summarising empirical work on mobility and co-presence, John Urry has concluded that 'social life often appears to involve variously organised "tight social worlds", of rich, thick co-presence, where trust is an ongoing accomplishment' (2002: 261). Urry argues that sustaining relationships appears to rely on at least intermittently seeing and sensing the other person through physical co-presence. The communication possible through co-presence is more than words. It includes expressions, gestures, body language, status, voice intonation, pregnant silences, past histories, turn-taking practices and eye contact, all of which are important for building trust and a sense of security, and this is still difficult to replicate through mediated communication (Urry, 2002).

Importantly, research into young people's use of digital technology also suggests that there is significant continuity between online and offline worlds. Friends on social networking sites such as Facebook overwhelmingly tend to be friends, or at least acquaintances, from the offline world, with relationships originally made at school, university, playing sport, in a band, or at work (Boyd and Ellison, 2008; Robards and Bennett, 2011: 307). In other words, this research suggests the primary role of online social networking for most people is not to make new friends but to maintain another source of contact with offline friends with whom it may be hard to keep in touch otherwise. It is also important to recognise that virtual technologies can potentially facilitate more face-to-face sociality. For example, mobile telephones – particularly now that they are linked to online social media and their event scheduling functions – have the potential to allow people to make last-minute adjustments to coordinate their schedules, and hence may make a positive contribution as 'coordinating devices' to overcoming temporal individualisation.

Communications technology also has the potential to create an opposite effect, taking away from face-to-face sociality irrespective of a preference for online or offline interaction. While providing new ways of maintaining social connection these technologies also facilitate the bleeding of paid employment into 'non-work' time, with email and mobile telephones facilitating an 'on-call' attitude towards work, at the expense of other relationships (Gregg, 2011: 155–6). As such, digital communication technologies may amplify the types of desynchronisation we have discussed above, and are best theorised as both increasingly necessary to function in a world full of individualised rhythms and timetables and at the same time as a contributor to this individualisation.

The rise of online sociality points to broader questions about the spatial-temporal dimensions of young people's sociality and how these dimensions contribute to the creation of inequality. In Chapter 6 we discussed recent proposals that sociality in general, and young people's relationships in particular, are increasingly neo-tribal in form (Maffesoli, 1996; Bennett, 1999), fitting with many popular takes on the 'digital generation' as young people are sometimes labelled (Tapscott, 1998). In the previous chapter we showed how a key platform of the post-subcultural position is that contemporary cultural engagements tend to be present-centred and relatively ephemeral, if nonetheless powerfully experienced, commitments. As we saw, one response to the post-subcultural move has been to question how fleeting these engagements really are (Shildrick and MacDonald, 2006). The study of group belonging and new online social media, which would seem an ideal platform for relatively ephemeral engagements, is increasingly leading even researchers associated with the post-subcultures position to an ambivalent position on the degree to which fluidity with identification is possible in the digital age (Robards and Bennett, 2011: 305).

Robards and Bennett's (2011) interview study of young people from Australia's Gold Coast and their use of social media finds value in the concept of neo-tribes because their participants conceptualised belonging as multiple and valued the experiences of co-present embodied interaction. The participants used Facebook to construct a narrative piecing together their various senses of belonging, identity and friendships developed over time, primarily offline (Robards and Bennett, 2011: 312). As arguably the major proponent within youth studies of neo-tribes as a concept however, it is interesting that on the basis of this study of young people's use of social networks Bennett, and his co-author, significantly depart from Maffesoli's (1996) original concept of modern tribes. As their data reinforced the importance of continuity of engagement over time, Robards and Bennett (2011: 314) make a conciliatory point, arguing that 'there would appear to be a critical problem with Maffesoli's theorization of neo-tribe, notably in its unerring conviction that neo-tribal associations result only in temporal bondings characterized by short-lived bursts of sociality'.

Ben Malbon (1999), another scholar broadly supportive of the tribal concept of youth sociality, makes a similar criticism. While drawing on Maffesoli's emphasis on sociality as affective to describe the 'oceanic' experience of clubbing, Malbon argues that Maffesoli's theorisation lacks proper empirical contextualisation and hence seems to present belonging as almost completely open and automatic, and so 'fails to evoke the demanding *practical* and *stylistic* requirements and competencies that many of these communities demand, and through which many of them are constituted' (Malbon, 1999: 26, emphasis in original).

A sense of familiarity, shared identity and belonging that is built over time appears to remain important even in online interactions (Hodkinson and Lincoln, 2008). For example, in his study of participants in Goth culture online Hodkinson (2003) found that while the internet is potentially a site for new neo-tribal fluidity, in practice it often reinforces tight boundaries between groups and provides a means to intensify a sense of belonging and to reinforce these boundaries over time. Maffesoli's theorising of new tribal sociality does not properly account for the way that practices of sociality require competencies that are developed over time, which in turn can give groups a degree of inertia over time. Because sociability takes time and coordination, and the resources to do this are unevenly distributed, the individualisation of temporal schedules is implicated in the creation of inequalities, bringing together many of the themes of the previous chapters.

Time, Youth Cultures and Inequality

Arguably the most famous post-Birmingham School rethinking of the intersection of youth cultural forms and inequality is Sarah Thornton's (1996) study of club cultures in the UK. In this research she elaborates on a key concept from Bourdieu's oeuvre, 'cultural capital', and the role it plays in creating and justifying social distinctions (Bourdieu, 1984). Adding a focus on subcultural forms to Bourdieu's focus on popular and high culture, Thornton proposes that contemporary cultural forms, in not only high but also subculture, are riddled with processes of distinction making. Theorising multiple 'subcultural' modes of valuing, Thornton argues that belonging to groups is structured by micro practices of distinction that maintain some degree of autonomy from mainstream valuations. As such, there are multiple subcultural capitals by which hierarchies of belonging, both society wide and subculture specific, are constituted.

Her fieldwork with young clubbers showed that they used representations of what they viewed as less 'authentic' activities of other young people to develop a sense of the superiority attached to their subcultural engagements. Thornton (1996: 163) argues that her framework avoids the binary between resistance or submission which she identifies in the subcultures work in the CCCS tradition. On one level many youth cultures legitimately proclaim and aspire to a more egalitarian and democratic world, as evidenced through efforts to create seemingly more open cultural spaces outside of the mainstream and its demands to consume in particular ways (Thornton, 1996; Bennett, 2011). On another, how-ever, the 'mainstream' which Thornton's participants defined themselves against was not only represented as a capitalist-driven and superficial pop culture, but was also used as a synonym for working-class, or feminine, culture (Thornton, 1996: 166). In other words, Thornton argues that a purported celebration of difference can easily shift from an embryonic form of resistance to an expres-sion and recreation of the status quo of power relations, and not only through incorporation of its once confrontational 'style' into the market.

Subcultural belonging in Thornton's model is predicated on possessing the right forms of culture in the eyes of members of that cultural community. Some of these can be worn or purchased, an outfit or the right record or book, and some must be embodied. Thornton (1996: 114) suggests that an example of this practice is the exam-like quality of entry to some clubbing events. Entry requires studying the look and preparing the body to meet that desired look. There is also the risk of trying too hard, of being picked out as an imposter or inauthentic (Thornton, 1996: 12).

Thornton makes significant progress beyond debates about subcultures or post-subcultures, but appears to still underplay the degree to which subcultural capital must be embodied. She seems to suggest that it may often be possible to acquire subcultural capital by simply studying and then reproducing the 'look' (Malbon, 1999: 64). In part this is because Thornton draws selectively on Bourdieu, taking elements of his concept of cultural capital but failing to link this form of capital to the 'habitus', its embodiment and its essential tem-porality. Using Bourdieu's framework, which we introduced in Chapter 4, the cultural capital to undertake this subcultural 'exam' cannot simply be mim-icked but needs to be embedded in bodily dispositions sedimented over time. The factor that most distinguishes Bourdieu's (1986: 244) concept of cultural capital from other forms of capital, including economic and social capital, is that it presupposes embodiment and a particular temporal cost:

> [I]t implies a labor of inculcation and assimilation, costs time, time which must be invested personally by the investor. Like the acqui-sition of a muscular physique or a suntan, it cannot be done at second hand (so that all effects of delegation are ruled out).

Chris Driver's (2011) study of young men involved in the hardcore scene in Australia provides an example of how the creation of subcultural capital is an embodied process (as such unfolding in time) with others, a kind of practical pedagogy. Among his interviewees, connections to hardcore and other scene participants are forged through physicality. Their 'perceptions of "authentic" membership are very much bound up in one's *embodiment* of specific kinds of knowledge and understanding' (Driver, 2011: 979, emphasis in original). His participants were reluctant to comment on fashion or 'style', emphasising instead the competent practices of engaging with the music at live gigs, such as 'slam dancing', a high contact form of social interaction in an enclosed space, as a primary marker of authenticity.

The 'right' way to engage in cultural practices is taught and learned, not through training focused on the rote learning of the right representations but through embodied learning (Bourdieu, 1998a; Malbon, 1999; Shilling and Mellor, 2007; Driver, 2011). Sharing of these practices, over time, is what can bind individuals into a group and is also central to the creation of distinction. While the shaping of the body and the inculcation of this form of capital are often implicit, work on the body does not have to be. Explicit efforts to reflexively refashion the body over time in a way valued by particular youth cultural communities are important for many young people, even if they have ambivalent feelings about and can even critique the representations that shape these efforts (Coffey, 2013). The point is that while this work to develop cultural or subcultural capital does not necessarily have to be completely unconscious, it is not only or primarily about 'study' and preparing the exterior of the body as a symbolic surface (like a canvas), but action over time that reshapes the physicality of the body and its dispositions.

The Life Pattern participants, interviewed about their work patterns, spoke not only about finding time with friends but also the quality of this time and the type of activities they could undertake. A particular young person who is not engaged in work or study on a Tuesday daytime, to return to our example from earlier, facilitated by the connecting potential of social media and mobile technology which we also discuss above, is more likely than ever before to be able to find at least an acquaintance who also has leisure time at the same 'odd' hour. The flipside to this is that time off on a Saturday evening or Sunday daytime, the times when many shared activities that demand a physical presence (from organised sport to a music gig) tend to be scheduled, is less likely to also be time off for significant others with whom a young person may want to undertake these activities (Woodman, 2012).

Even when that free time does overlap, it might be difficult to use it for the types of pedagogies of practice described here. The temporal individualisation proposed in this chapter has the potential to desynchronise not only the schedules of people's lives but also the related 'rhythms' of the flow between different types of investments, including the energy a person has available to dedicate to a particular pursuit. Variable patterns of work or study can mean that the peaks and troughs in people's energy are put out of synch with those of significant others, from the course of a day to a calendar year. If a group of friends have overlapping 'free' time, those who have not worked that day or are currently on holiday leave are likely to have more energy for social activity than others who have just left work or class, or worked or studied for an upcoming exam late into the evening before (Woodman, 2013: 424–5). Both for good and ill, creating experiences of belonging or distinction, Bourdieu's focus on 'practice' reminds social researchers that cultural capital is embodied and 'takes time to accumulate' (Bourdieu, 1986: 241). It is not only the duration of time available for investing in cultural capital, subcultural or otherwise, that can make a difference to young people's lives, but also the way that schedules and rhythms overlap to allow these pedagogies of practice to take place.

The Present, Past and Future

So far in this chapter we have focused on the way that the temporal structures of young people's lives have been reshaped by changes in the labour market and by patterns of mixing work and study. As we noted in opening this chapter, the temporal structuring of everyday life has not previously been a focus of youth research. Alongside and linked to the discussion of the timing of youth transitions, and debates about the duration of commitments to cultural forms, the other temporal question that has been influential in recent youth research has been the time horizons of young people's planning (Brannen and Nilsen, 2002; Anderson et al., 2005; Brooks and Everett, 2008; Devadason, 2008). By highlighting the networks of sociality, including those made up of family and friends, that young people are embedded within, the focus on everyday life we have pursued in this chapter can provide new insights into how young people plan and the inequality related to this.

While tracing young people's aspirations has been an ongoing concern of academic youth researchers, particularly among educational psychologists, the recent explosion of research in sociological youth studies has emerged as one strand of the debates about individualisation discussed in Chapter 3. Julia Brannen and Ann Nilsen (2002, 2005, 2007) in particular have built an influential argument that few young people are able to plan for their longer-term future and they have used this to challenge the validity of the individualisa-tion thesis. While Brannen and Nilsen use an absence of planning to critique the individualisation thesis, others have instead referenced Beck's work on individualisation as evidence that planning is increasingly difficult (Oinonen, 2003: 129; Leccardi, 2006: 16). As such, while the choice biography read-ing of Beck's work has dominated youth sociology, his theorisation has also been used to argue for institutional constraint in relation to young people's temporal orientation (Woodman, 2011b: 114). One explanation is that this is another contradiction within Beck's work, but it can also be understood within the individualisation framework as we have developed it in this book.

Seemingly validating Brannen and Nilsen's critique, both Beck-Gernsheim and Beck have separately proposed that there is increasing pressure to treat life as a planning project, a pressure that is 'forcing individuals into the future as they go about their daily lives' (Beck-Gernsheim, 2002: 45). Again, how-ever, there is strong evidence that the impact of individualisation on temporal orientation should be understood in more nuanced terms than that which has been attached to the choice biography:

> [T]hrough recurrent surges of individualization, a double effect occurs. On the one hand … the temporal horizons of perception narrow more and more, until finally in the limiting case *history* shrinks to *the (eternal) present* … On the other hand … the con-straints increase to shape one's own biography, and in precisely those areas where it is once again the product of new institutional conditions. (Beck, 1992: 135, emphasis in original)

As such, the individualisation thesis overlaps as much with theories that claim the possibility of long-term planning is being eroded (cf. Nowotny, 1994; Rosa, 2013) as it overlaps with Anthony Giddens's argument that people must now 'colonise the future for themselves as an intrinsic part of their life-planning' (1991: 125). In other words, planning appears both increasingly important due to the weakening of some taken-for-granted biographical pathways and increasingly difficult if not impossible because of institutional structures. This includes employment, which today gives few people the type of stability that makes planning and 'choice' making possible. We have tried to think about the dispositions that these conditions may invoke, drawing on parts of Bourdieu's writing that have focused on social change. In one of his later books, Bourdieu wrote about the rise of the type of 'non-standard' work patterns we have discussed in this chapter, highlighting 'that casualization is spreading across the work force, and can dismantle temporal horizons' (Bourdieu, 1998b: 82).

In the same 2008 interviews introduced earlier in this chapter we asked participants from the Life Patterns study about their hopes and plans for the future (Woodman, 2011b). Consistent with the type of generational habitus Bourdieu's writing about social change would lead us to expect among young people today, the participants had multiple, and often seemingly contradictory, ways of orienting towards the future. For example, a significant number said explicitly that they did not plan for the future because it was too uncertain, but nevertheless suggested that they were taking steps towards certain preferred futures. In contrast to the way that reflexivity is often conceptualised in youth studies, the most privileged were less likely to plan in detail for particular futures or to have strategies for managing uncertainty. This was because the types of uncertainties and contradictions at the core of individualisation have less impact on their lives. Upper middle-class participants in the Life Patterns study, defined by parents in professional work and with higher education, were concerned for their future but were less likely to say they explicitly planned. Instead they tended to take up possibilities when these were presented, opportunities that in many cases were facilitated by their social network, either family or friends (Woodman, 2011b: 119).

This finding from Life Patterns mirrors those of other studies that have shifted the focus of their analysis from individual temporal orientations to the way that school communities, families and local geographical communities collectively co-create a sense of future possibilities (Thomson and Taylor, 2005; McLeod and Yates, 2006; Wierenga, 2009). For example, Wierenga (2009) followed a small group of young people from one country town in Australia through secondary school in the late 1990s to investigate the ways that this group developed 'stories' about their personal futures. Wierenga's analysis shows that a personal narrative about the future is a co-creation with significant others built over time:

> Networks shape individuals' ideas about the world. Social interactions enrich the individual's stories with shared meanings and thicken stories with new ideas. Social relationships both supply ideas about goals, and supply ways of attaining them. (2009: 60)

In Wierenga's analysis trusted others are central to the ability to build a robust sense of preferred and possible futures. Our analysis in this chapter, supported by the Life Patterns research, reinforces and builds on this understanding of the role of significant others in two ways. First, narratives about the future and practices that enact futures can to some extent be the property of a network. These networks include, for example, parents, other kin or close friendship groups, people who can take on some of the responsibility for shaping the future in the context of uncertainty for young people (see for example Cuervo and Wyn, 2012). Second is the foundational role of shared time with significant others in this process, which draws on trust built up through practices that unfold over time. Developing with others a sense of the future, and building cultural (and subcultural) capital that can act as a resource in young people's lives, appear to be a process of embodied learning, and hence take time with others. This is one of the reasons why the temporal de-synchronisation we have described in this chapter matters for young lives.

Time has long been linked to inequality, including in the accumulation of cultural capital (Bourdieu, 1986), but the conditions facing young people today mean that this link has taken on new dimensions. Along these lines, Bourdieu calls the rise of insecure work 'a mode of domination of a new kind, based on the creation of a generalised and permanent state of insecurity' (1998b: 85). The increasing individualisation and changeability of work patterns in Australia is a primary element of the generational location of contemporary young people. One axis of inequality between young people can be conceptualised on the basis of the extent to which they can control or escape the types of work conditions that lead to this temporal individualisation. In this light, the existence of time-based inequality is not evidence against social change but is being reshaped through social change.

Conclusion

In this chapter we have explored biographical individualisation and its implications for young people's cultural practices by asking a question about time that has yet to be properly explored by youth researchers. This is the nature of the temporal structure of young people's everyday lives and the relationship of this structure to inequalities between young people. We have argued for attending to the implications of the temporal restructuring of everyday life as an example of how the dispositions towards the present and future that young people develop, as well as their cultural practices and the types of relationships they can form, are being reshaped for and by their generation.

Young people in contemporary Australia as well as many other parts of the world are likely to meet more people, and have more acquaintances and even 'friends', than at any previous point in history. Yet as the experiences of the participants discussed here show, it is regular and extended periods of shared time with close friends that many value and may matter most as a resource. Often combined with some form of post–school study, which has become a majority experience in Australia, an increasingly individualised work schedule is part of a new set of generational conditions shaping the lives of young people. The new temporal structures that are shaping this generation's lives are not primarily the result of greater freedom over their time but of a structured individualisation of time. This individualisation makes the scheduling of regular periods of time with a group of significant others difficult. Aligning the multiple, fragmented and varying timetables of each member's daily life is at times and for some almost impossible.

8

PLACE

The analysis of place provides a basis for understanding the complex ways in which change and continuity are experienced by individuals and communities. Our discussion of place deepens and extends our understanding of social generations through a consideration of the intersections of biography and history in specific locations. We argue that place, as a relational concept (that includes the flows of people, ideas and capital between different locations), is central to understanding how different groups of young people manage the fragmenting and individualising processes of late modernity in their social, economic and political contexts. In other words, analysis of place assists in the analysis of contemporary societies and how they are changing in significant ways.

It is timely for youth sociologists to give greater consideration to place. We are living in times that are frequently described by youth sociologists as involving mobilities of young people on an unprecedented scale, bringing into being new transnational aspirations, sensibilities and affiliations (Bauman, 1998; Ong, 1999; Rizvi, 2012) and involving changing landscapes of risk and opportunity (Evans and Helve, 2013). Increasingly, mobility is regarded as an intrinsic part of the transition to adulthood (Molgat, 2008). A sociological understanding of place and mobility (or a lack of mobility) enables us to understand more about the 'big issues' of social change and continuity. Patterns of mobility and migration operate through connections between *specific* places, and these mobilities have distinctive social and economic impacts on these places. In order to understand how individualisation processes create new ways of relating to institutions (for example labour markets and education, as well as family) and new ways of mobilising resources, we need to understand these processes in their local and global context. Rather than being freed from location and institutional constraints, analysing social change in local contexts helps us to see how the individualisation process brings new institutional constraints, creates new inequalities, and contributes to the making and remaking of place.

As we have argued in Chapter 4, the concept of social generation provides a conceptual device for understanding the intersections between biography and history. Although the idea of a social generation may imply a somewhat global notion, in reality social generations are forged through the interplay between people and their circumstances. For this reason, we need a well-theorised and explicit focus on place in order to understand the nature and meaning of social generations. As youth researchers have begun to analyse the relevance of place, it has become increasingly apparent that the meaning and value of mobility have been 'transformed' in the course of a generation (Devine et al., 2003). As Henderson and colleagues (2007) also note, research on intergenerational relationships within families shows that contemporary patterns of chain migration create complex relationships between generations, often involving ambivalence about social mobility.

We would argue that a deeper understanding of the significance of social generations can be accomplished by drawing on the already discussed concept of habitus as a tool for understanding how place is both constituted by and contributes to the emotions, attitudes and the embodied practices that form a generation. The value of considering habitus is that it enables us to grasp the way in which place is simultaneously material and subjective, in which the physical and semiotic domains are connected. In Chapter 2 we looked at changes in the experience of youth, tying these to our relational understanding of youth (Chapter 5). In this chapter we extend this approach through the use of a relational conceptualisation of place as a basis for understanding how generational effects are played out in different parts of the world, drawing among others on examples from communities in Romania, Nigeria and China.

In exploring these issues, we draw particularly on research that pertains to the complex interrelationships between what are loosely referred to as rural and urban places. Mobilities (national and transnational), one of the central features of youth in late modernity, are frequently associated with the unprecedented urbanisation of populations in many countries. Rural places (and urban places) are being transformed by changing global economic processes that are creating new urban areas and in some cases megacities. These changes are experienced locally in specific ways, even as they are part of and contribute to global economic, cultural and social processes. Young people are particularly implicated in these new mobilities, creating broad generational effects as they navigate new structures of opportunity and risk. This means that they are in the vanguard of creating new patterns of life, and in doing so they are forging distinctive ways of living that distinguish them from previous generations.

Yet place is surprisingly absent in contemporary sociological research. Reviewing the role of place in sociological literature, Gieryn (2000) concludes that sociologists have given the appearance of not being interested in place. Place, he argues, tends to be invisible in sociological literature, not because it is not present, but because it is seldom framed as 'place'. His review also highlights the tendency for sociologists to analyse urban sites, which, while identified in terms of their physical location, are seldom analysed from the point of view of what place means for understanding social life or for the development of theory. This is reflected in the paucity of rural sites in his comprehensive review of sociological studies of place. We would suggest that this oversight has contributed to the ubiquity of the urban in youth studies, and the failure to seek to understand the centrality of place in social relationships.

As Massey (1998) argues, place is not simply a backdrop to life – concurrently it constitutes and is constituted by relations. It is through engagement with others, and sometimes struggles, that spaces are turned into places that are unique and have significance for people. It is important to recognise the specific ways in which location (social, economic, historical), meaningfulness (culture and identity) and material form (buildings, parks, streets, mountains, rivers and trees) interrelate to create distinctive experiences. Place is much more than an assemblage of the 'natural' and material. Youth researchers along with others have explored the work that individuals and collectives do to create and maintain a sense of place, to build a territory of their own (Massey, 1998). This is part of the youth cultures tradition discussed in Chapter 6, and particularly in an environment that is changing rapidly, youth cultural forms can be understood as an attempt to recreate a sense of community and place (Cohen, 1972). Different struggles to define place and create a 'territory' can occur concurrently. Strategies that can be conceptualised as oppressive, creative or resistant can be potentially at play simultaneously in the one place (Massey, 1998; MacDonald et al., 2010: 4).

Against such a backdrop this chapter takes up emerging elements of the analysis of place for understanding young people's lives. The work of social geographers (for example, Massey, 1998; Skelton and Valentine, 1998; Hopkins and Pain, 2007; Hall et al., 2009) provides the basis of an understanding of the relational elements of place. Other insights about the significance of place have been developed through a focus on mobilities, adding to an understanding of the relational aspects of place. We also look to understandings of place developed through a critical analysis of the lives of young people in relation to rural locations. As such, this chapter draws on examples of research with young people in rural places, and examples from the Global South as well as from the North. We also look, if only briefly, at the relationship between indigenous young people and place in youth sociology.

The Invisibility of Place

A spatial, place-based focus in youth sociology that is critical of the way in which traditional sociological theory normalises 'northern' societies and social relations is gaining traction. For example, taking a different approach from that of Connell, Farrugia (2014) revisits sociological traditions to argue that the tendency to focus on globalised urban places as sites where exciting new developments in social relations and organisation can be investigated is based on a long tradition of seeing rural places as an undifferentiated 'other' and as representing the past. Reflecting the conceptual frameworks of the wider sociological milieu, much youth research has contributed to the assumption that urban and metropolitan spaces provide the setting for youth researchers to understand new trends, global processes, and the nature of new youth dispositions, cultures and patterns (Cuervo and Wyn, 2012).

The under-theorisation of place in youth research, and the marginalisation of experiences outside the metropole, are in part tied to the conceptual lenses that are used. Although youth researchers routinely acknowledge that youth is not a universal category, until recently there has been little consideration of geographic, historical and social location and when this has occurred it has been judged against the 'mainstream' urban experience. This is exacerbated by the fact that much of the theorising about social change has focused on 'new' youth through the wide range of studies of urban-based young people in the Global North. Urban youth tend to be seen as connected to global trends and flows in a way that their rural counterparts are not. This is often acknowledged, as Ball, Maguire and Macrae (2000) do in their study of youth transitions in the 'global city' of London in the 1990s, and as McLeod and Yates (2006) also acknowledge in their study of young Australians in metropolitan and regional areas of Australia in the 2000s. Leccardi and Ruspini's (2006) exploration of 'new youth' also focuses on young people in the urban areas across a range of western countries. This work can seem to suggest, if only implicitly, that identity is no longer based in locality (Farrugia, 2014), or if it is, it is only about disadvantage.

This trend is related to the divisions between mainstream and at-risk we discussed in Chapter 5. Policy-related research that draws on the idea of youth transitions has been especially influential in youth research and in institutionalising urban experience as the norm. It is not that transitions research has ignored young people outside of cities. However, the framework of transitions has in particular built an evidence base showing that, compared to patterns of transition through education and into employment for young people in metropolitan areas, young people in rural communities are disadvantaged, lacking the resources of educational and employment opportunities, health care, transport and the broad cultural engagement opportunities of metropolitan areas (Alston, 2005). The social and economic effects of the lack of these resources are often identified as a 'gap' between patterns of educational achievement and engagement and employment for rural young people and those of their urban counterparts, creating the foundation for policies that seek to align the patterns of the (rural) 'disadvantaged' with the (urban) mainstream. This gap is evident in distinctive patterns of transition involving lower rates of educational participation, higher proportions of young people with low socio-economic status (Lamb, 2011), and less stable employment (Alston and Kent, 2001) amongst young Australians who are living in rural areas, compared with their urban counterparts.

Highlighting these patterns is important. As we showed in Chapter 5, the lens of youth transitions has been especially influential in the creation of technologies of measurement for identifying standard and non-standard patterns of youth transition to adulthood. Yet, as we argue in this chapter, exploring the relevance of place in young people's lives brings a perspective that goes beyond the measuring of rural transitions against (normative) urban patterns. The transitions paradigm in interaction with the pervasive theme of 'new' youth in the global city has had the unintended effect of perpetuating a legacy of viewing rural areas as backward and as representing the past (Farrugia, 2014). Yet young people living in rural areas also need to have a sense of their connection to these global processes to build their lives (Cuervo and Wyn, 2012). Young people in rural communities are as much members of, and shapers of, their generation as their urban peers – and as we hope to highlight in this chapter are in many ways as much if not more affected by global economic and social processes.

Theorising Young People and Place

Youth researchers focusing on the ways in which young people engage with cultures and on the intersections of biographical and social-structural transformations have begun to bring place to the fore. Although this contribution is especially evident in the engagement by youth sociologists with young people's lives in rural places, it also has the potential to open up new understandings of place in urban and metropolitan settings. The focus on urban youth has a tendency towards assuming that urban settings and their global connections are undifferentiated, at the expense of understanding urban places as distinctive sites, despite (or perhaps because of) their particular location within global flows.

Gieryn argues that place matters for understanding almost every aspect of social life and historical change because it 'saturates social life' and all social phenomena are 'emplaced' (Gieryn, 2000: 467). Gieryn's suggestions for the framing of place, we would suggest, are useful for the sociology of youth. The three interrelated elements of location, material form and meaningfulness can be seen as the defining features of place. As Gieryn argues, '[p]lace has a plenitude, a completeness, such that the phenomenon is analytically and substantively destroyed if the three become unravelled, or one of them forgotten' (2000: 466). To put this another way, place is buildings, streets, trees and rivers at a particular geographic spot at a particular historical time, as well as their interpretations, representations and identifications by people (at a particular geographic spot at a particular historical time). Drawing on Bourdieu (1990), we would argue that acknowledging place means understanding the material and the interpretive elements of places as physical and semiotic domains that operate autonomously and yet are interdependent. These interrelated elements have been explored in a variety of ways. For example, 'place-based belongingness' refers to a feeling of being 'at home' (Antonsich, 2010), intersecting with the idea of 'home', which as Hage (1997) points out captures the temporal element of the idea of home as integral to hope for the future. In this sense 'home' is as much a symbolic space, a place of familiarity, belonging, attachment and security (Antonsich, 2010).

This means that place is not just a backdrop, it is also a force that has effects on social life – it mediates social life. As Gieryn explains, 'places are made through human practices and institutions, and they in turn help to make those practices and institutions' (2000: 467). One of the ways in which this works is that places give expression to social categories and practices, differences and hierarchies; they arrange patterns of face-to-face interaction and they embody and secure cultural norms and individual memories. In the following sections we draw on these conceptual foundations to provide a deeper analysis of how place matters to young people, and how it contributes to a more nuanced and effective conceptualisation of young people's lives.

Mobilities, Cultures and Place

Recently the concept of mobilities has been combined with reconceptu-alisations of home and belonging to explore the complex meaning of place in young people's lives in contemporary conditions. Rizvi (2012: 200), for example, argues that place is integrally related to global flows of ideas and cultural resources that create 'transnational' youth cultures and global mobili-ties so that young (cosmopolitan) people belong to several places at once, bringing the potential of new and flexible notions of citizenship. This theme is also taken up by Henderson and colleagues (2007). Using the biographi-cal approach we discussed in previous chapters, they analyse the transitions of young people in the UK to investigate how the idea of home plays a crucial role in providing them with a sense of personal security, arguing that the negotiation of home as a resource has become increasingly significant in the making of inequality, including the capacity for mobility. The security of 'home', as a symbolic and material place, is juxtaposed by the vulnerability of the street. For example, Pattman (2012) analyses how the stereotype of street children became a moral panic in the lead up to the 2010 football World Cup in South Africa, in which street children were viewed as a threat to the safety of international tourists as well as signifying Africa's failure to modernise.

For Henderson and her co-authors (2007; see also Thomson and Taylor, 2005), the suggestion of a binary between cosmopolitans and locals is too strong. Young people in many places are torn between different pressures and desires to stay and to move, and have multiple and sometimes contradictory identities available to them. They argue that 'urban and cosmopolitan identities are available to young people both within and outside cities and developed economies' (Henderson et al., 2007: 103). These writers instead use the concepts of localism and cosmopolitanism as interrelated elements of 'economies of mobility' (2007: 101), to understand the ways in which the meaning and value of mobility is being transformed by young people, contributing to new opportunities for some and new vulnerabilities for others, based on gender and class.

For example, Henderson and her colleagues (2007) show that while it was a common expectation amongst young people that they would move away from their local area, those whose families had previous experience of geographical mobility or who had the resources to support mobility were more likely to take up educational and employment opportunities outside their local area. They show how a traditional preference by young women for staying in close proximity to their mothers and a similar preference for 'localism' by young men from poorer families limited their educational and employment options, making them vulnerable to disadvantage.

Focusing on a Northern Irish city, these authors also show how generations of migration from particular localities mean that young people in particular areas have access to intergenerational knowledge of places other than their own home (Henderson, et al., 2007). For example, young Protestants in the Northern Irish city tended to know about Scotland and London, whereas Catholics in the city tended to have knowledge of the USA. As Salazar (2011) argues, people tend to travel to places they already 'know' (in other words, mobilities are highly specific and linked to the relationships that people have to place). For others local networks provide community and support but tie young people to particular identities in particular places that can be at odds with the demands of increasingly global transitions regimes that push them towards further education (Henderson et al., 2007: 106). A sense of home or belonging can hence for some young people be a resource that can provide the security that can seemingly paradoxically support mobility, but not for all (Wierenga, 2009).

In the face of these transition regimes, making one's way in life, for those in many localities including the outer suburbs of many cities, means leaving the locality where they currently live. This is a recurring theme in youth research, as we discuss below: moving away from one's place of origin has come to be seen as a necessary aspect of the making of adult lives. For example, Molgat's research on young people in the province of Quebec (Canada) analyses the institutionalisation of mobility associated with tertiary education. As in many countries there is a trend for young people to move to cities for secondary and tertiary studies, and this outward migration throws up concerns about creating a 'negative spiral effect on the viability of some regions and towns' (Molgat, 2008: 118).

The growing weight placed on extended education, combined with the changing youth labour market, can mean that young people in rural and regional areas face conflicting pressures. The important community goal of retaining their young people is often in tension with expectations, also shared by many within the community, that young people should and will need to pursue further education and credentialed and skilled employment (Gabriel, 2006: 36–7). City life can have certain attractions for young people due to the diversity of experience and relative anonymity possible, and parents and other significant others, well aware of the structural changes going on around them, will sometimes encourage them to leave. To understand these factors researchers utilised the concept of a 'culture of migration' to highlight that some young people live in a culture, either national or local, where migration is assumed or expected, particularly for the 'best and brightest' (Gabriel, 2002: 211). In this type of culture it is not leaving but staying that demands justification and not being mobile can mark young people out as educational failures (Looker and Naylor, 2009).

This association between mobility and success points to the way groups of young people who might be seen to be unaffected by the individualisation process are in fact among the most affected. Those who are negotiating the pressures to stay or to move must make decisions that metropolitan youth are not routinely required to do, because of their physical proximity to educational and employment opportunities. Metropolitan youth are not faced with the decisions about education that often bring a profound sense of anxiety for young people from rural areas (Geldens and Bourke, 2008: 288). Others have made similar points about the efforts young people make to belong in rural and regional areas in changing times (Kraack and Kenway, 2002; Nairn et al., 2003; Kenway et al., 2006; Hall et al., 2009). While researchers have often turned to metropolitan experience to explore the relationship between biography and change, 'new' youth is also found in non-urban areas (Cuervo and Wyn, 2012: 1).

Even the research we have discussed in this section, which attends to the nuances of place, can contribute to the perpetuation of stereotypes of a rural–urban divide. For example, the focus on rural youth can perpetuate the myth that place only matters to those living outside the city, in outer-metropolitan areas, in country towns and in isolated rural areas, and in particular that mobility from non-metropolitan areas is about 'leaving' (Hall et al., 2009; Cuervo and Wyn, 2012). Understandings of mobilities require a reflexive approach to the role that research plays in perpetuating stereotypes. Research on young people in different locations reveals that youth mobilities have very different meanings and outcomes, depending on the way in which mobility is connected to structures of inequality. For example, Molgat's (2008) exploration of mobilities of young people in the province of Quebec reveals that short-term migration from rural areas to gain educational qualifications can also be a strategy for building sustainable lives in rural areas. This same complexity is visible in the lives of Life Patterns participants from outside the metropolitan centres.

In 2012, Cuervo and Wyn reinterviewed a subset of 19 people from the first cohort of the Life Patterns research programme who had made their lives in rural areas, combining this with analysis of survey data and interview material collected through this cohort's 20s. The analysis reveals how the stereotype of rural disadvantage is simplistic. By investigating the participants' perspectives, decisions, attitudes and outcomes it was clear that they not only attached a sense of belonging to landscapes and locations, through an appreciation of a physical landscape, a way of life and strong intergenerational connections, but also that making a life in rural areas required a grasp of how global social and economic forces impacted on location (Cuervo and Wyn, 2012).

These young adults developed at least a practical sense that changes in rural Australia (for example the rise of new forms of agricultural production and integration of the rural economy into new markets) meant that the patterns followed by their parents were unlikely to provide a straightforward template for their own lives, even if they desired a similar lifestyle. Recognising shifts in the skill set and scale of farming today, there were examples of participants moving to metropolitan or regional centres to pursue degrees in agriculture or business and finance with the aim of acquiring credentials for employment with larger agricultural producers (Cuervo and Wyn, 2012: 163), or to pursue qualifications that would otherwise be useful in regional and rural areas, such as teaching (Cuervo and Wyn, 2012: 114). These educational decisions allowed the reproduction of some elements of their parents' lives (and their own childhood for their children) but in a new way for new times.

This goes some way to countering the idea that it is the 'best and brightest' who leave rural areas, contributing a more complex understanding of the pushes and pulls that shape the geographical movements of young people. Attending to the particularities of place, and the particularities of biography in this historical moment, is important for understanding the experiences of youth, whether in agriculture or elsewhere, as rural and regional experience does not look the same for this generation as it did for their parents.

Despite our efforts in Chapter 2 to acknowledge the importance of research and theorising from beyond the Global North, in this section, as in much of the book, we have drawn primarily on work from the Global North. In the coming sections of this chapter we return to scholarship with young people from the Global South. These empirical analyses of young people in different places contribute to an understanding of how social structures such as labour markets, citizenship, education and family are deeply implicated in what they consider possible, what they aim for, and for the strategies they use to make their lives. Through an examination of settings as diverse as Romania, China and Nigeria, we aim to gain an understanding of how new forces for mobility interface with and reconfigure older dynamics of inequality.

Work on mobility from scholars in the North tends to operate on the premise that those who are not mobile are hampered by a lack of cultural and material resources to engage in the individualised 'transition regimes' of contemporary education and work (Henderson et al., 2007: 111). Yet as the research by Horváth (2008) with young people in Romania, by Lou (2011) with young people in China, and by Hoechner (2013) with young people in Nigeria reveals, mobility can be a strategy for escaping poverty that nonetheless leaves young people relatively trapped in low-skill jobs and marginalised positions.

Making Place Visible

There is an emerging view that mobile youth represent a vanguard. For example, in his account of youth cultures and mobilities Rizvi argues that mobilities on a global scale are transforming youth cultures, and that young people's cultural practices 'are forged at the global intersection of these social, economic, political and cultural flows' (2012: 192). New times, Rizvi argues, mean that young people are forging identities 'that can no longer be interpreted through a pre-determined cultural script concerning relations of locality, traditions, family, class and community' (2012: 194). He also argues that even those who are not able to benefit from new, 'diverse mobilities' are implicated in the 'transnational spaces' that mobile youth create (2012: 202). While it is clear that young people in various parts of the world are contributing to new patterns of mobility, we would interpret this differently. Although processes of mobility are 'transnational' in the sense that they cross national boundaries and are also part of a wider global sensibility of mobility, the evidence suggests that more needs to be known about the different meanings and implications of different kinds of mobilities and their relationship to places, highlighting the contradictions that young people are navigating.

An example of this can be found in the way that young mobile lives reflect and contribute to the socio-historical-spatial relations of places. Horváth's study of the lives of young people in two groups of connected villages near industrial centres in Transylvania (in the western part of Romania) reveals the ways in which migration has, over the course of a generation, become normalised in young adulthood (Horváth, 2008). The analysis reveals the ways in which new habits, artefacts, perspectives and ideas that derive from connections with other places become integrated with the culture of a place, in turn reshaping the possibilities for subsequent generations. Horváth explores how the widescale trend of out-migration from Romania during recent decades has had very particular implications for young people in the clusters of villages known as Panit and Colonia where migration brings strong relational ties between specific places. These ties open up pathways for subsequent generations, and they also bring back a return – often financial, but also ways of thinking and being.

For young people in these village clusters, Horváth argues, migration has had the effect of normalising mobility as part of becoming an adult. The analysis of the fine-grain of these spatial relationships between people and place exposes the active role that young people play in interpreting and shaping these socio-spatial relationships. For example, in the early 1990s young people's migration was largely to Hungary, involving irregular and short episodes of labour migration. By the late 1990s, however, this had changed, with the length of the stay being extended and the inclusion of other destinations (Italy, Germany and Spain). To explain the significance of mobile labour in this region, Horváth states:

> In the two study areas, almost without exception, every extended family has at least one member definitively relocated abroad, and in both networks of villages we identified a sizeable group of persons (about 100–150 in each community) who spend a considerable time in a different country but do not relocate. (2008: 776)

For these young people migration is a familiar story, and drawing on the experiences of at least fifteen years of migration from their villages, they have extensive knowledge of their potential destinations. Although they are aware of the risks of exploitation in the destination countries, of the reality that they will work hard doing quite menial work and that there is often racism, migration offers an opportunity to benefit financially from the gap between the value of Romania currency and the currency of destination countries. Horváth found that young people in the villages had a nuanced understanding of the risks and benefits of migrating to different countries. Germany was generally regarded as the best option for migration because it offered the highest remuneration but was the most difficult to access. Spain on the other hand was the easiest to access but offered the lowest pay. He also found that young people were very sensitive to the meaning of work in relation to place. For example, as migrants they were prepared to work in menial and marginal low-skill jobs but they would not contemplate undertaking these kinds of jobs in their own country.

Labour migration to specific destinations by these Romanian young people is accepted as a way of generating resources for the families in their villages. Successive age cohorts of young people build on the knowledge of their older siblings and relations to make labour migration an accepted life-course experience for both young men and women. Migration after marriage is regarded less favourably, especially for women, and in these villages was the exception. The strategy of labour migration in these villages operates against a backdrop of increasing participation in university education amongst urban young people in Romania. Whereas only one in ten young Romanians attended tertiary education in the 1980s, by 2003 40 per cent were attending a tertiary institution (Horváth, 2008: 781). As Horváth alludes to, there is a sense in which the labour migration strategies that have served these villages over the last fifteen years are being overtaken by new dynamics involving a reinscribing of rural-urban inequalities through credentialism and access to tertiary education. Importantly, Horváth argues that the strategies used by the young people in these village clusters are a response to the reality that they have an increasingly marginalised labour market status in their own country.

His analysis of young people in rural Romania illustrates how mobility is a contradictory resource; it is a strategy for survival, but it can create the risk of ultimately being 'out of place'. This process is also analysed by Hoechner (2013) in her study of Qur'anic students in Nigeria. Yet again, this study analyses the strategies used by young people in rural areas that have gone into economic decline. Hoechner describes the social networks that link young men in particular villages with poor Qur'anic schools in Kano city in the Muslim north of Nigeria. Escaping the poverty of their rural homes, it is traditional for boys to be enrolled by their families in educational centres where they become *almajirai* (Qur'anic students). Hoechner's analysis shows how *almajirai* become implicated in complex navigations of belonging as they struggle to maintain a sense of dignity and (re)build their identities in a new place, one where by definition they lack a *gata* (a person who will stand up for them). As she explains, in a society in which individuals gain their social standing from the people they belong to (be it family members or patrons), being unable to display such belonging means they are vulnerable and defenceless (Hoechner, 2013: 9).

The implications of urbanisation and of the demise of traditional forms of rural economy are also playing out in China, with significant implications for young people. Lou (2011) fills a gap in studies of cultural formation amongst Chinese youth, arguing that youth culture in rural China can be character-ised as derivative of 'mainstream' urban youth cultures of materialism and individualistic values. This process, she argues, is facilitated by educational policies that locate middle schools in towns and cities (whereas elementary schools are located in villages). This means that rural students often have to board away from home in 'townships' that, as Lou explains, hover 'somewhere between the rural and the urban in both imagination and reality' (2011: 575). Townships are the product of rapid urbanisation and development processes and the depopulation of rural areas:

> A recent survey of 101 rural villages in five provinces reveals that 44% of them suffer environmental degradation due to rapid towni-zation … The rural population proportion has decreased to about 54% of the total Chinese population at the end of 2009, compared to 64% in 2000, 74% in 1990, and 81% in 1980. It is projected to be reduced to 35% by 2030. (Lou, 2011: 575)

In Longma, in the Hong County of Shaanxi in Northwest China where Lou's study was undertaken, *jiedau* (meaning roads and streets) have rapidly expanded to take over agricultural land. Lou states that these changes to the nature of rural places have had significant implications for young people – but that in turn young people are also having an impact on these locations. Her research with young people reveals their intense preoccupation with how places feel. They characterised the *jiedau* most consistently as chaotic and polluted, but also as noisy, crowded and dirty. At the same time though they appreciated the development of high-rise buildings, the many cars, the parks and the convenience of shopping (Lou, 2011: 576).

The curriculum of the middle schools, implemented in 2005, emphasises the cultivation of *suzhi*, or quality, in the rounded development of students. According to Lou (2011: 576), *suzhi* is associated with modernity and urbanity, formal education, cosmopolitanism, civility and discipline. Rural students are widely regarded as having low *suzhi* compared to their urban counterparts. This urban-centric curriculum, Lou argues, contributes to the displacing of rural students. They do not tend to perform well in a curriculum that is oriented towards the entrepreneurialism and innovation associated with urban subjectivities. Her research reveals the ways in which rural students attempt to develop a possible future for themselves through gaining educational credentials that will enable them to become professionals (lawyers, police) who can make a difference to the chaotic and polluting aspects of urban development. However, rural students are the most likely to fail school, increasing the proportion of students who become *erliuzi* or second-class citizens. These young people have no place to go: the farms their families occupied no longer exist and they are not qualified to work in the cities. In the following section we discuss how these studies expand our understanding of place and the wider social dynamics that are explored in this book.

Place and Global Generations

Taking a cautious approach to the idea of a global generation, we note that this idea is being explored (Edmunds and Turner, 2005; Beck and Beck-Gernsheim, 2009). For example, Beck and Beck-Gernsheim (2009) argue that if we are to take a global framework in discussing generations, this needs to be considered as an enforced 'cosmopolitanisation' rather than the universalisation of a value set. By cosmopolitanisation, Beck and Beck-Gernsheim mean that taken-for-granted ways of life come under challenge due to the impact of cultural flows across borders. This process can have positive outcomes, including for Beck and Beck-Gernsheim the promotion of more open flows of communication and the globalisation of understandings of rights discourses. They also point out that to the extent that 'transnational lifestyles' become evident, this can contribute to a de-legitimation of global inequality, or at least a need to explicitly defend the existence of inequality, because inequality is increasingly difficult to treat as fate (Beck and Beck-Gernsheim, 2009). However, cross-border flows also increase insecurity which cannot be understood as locally, nationally, or regionally bounded. As an example of this double-sided process, young people in Brazil increasingly cannot see why they are unable to live the lifestyles of young people in the USA or Australia while at the same time there is a 'Brazilianisation' of labour markets in the 'North' (Beck, 2000; Furlong and Kelly, 2005), as employment conditions such as temporary, uncontracted and otherwise insecure work once associated with the Global South, or the past of the North, spread through the economies of North America, Europe, New Zealand and Australia, particularly the youth labour market. More than global youth style cultures, it is 'insecurity that is turning into the key experience transcending borders' (Beck and Beck-Gernsheim, 2009: 33).

Beck and Beck-Gernsheim (2009: 33) suggest that contemporary young people live in a world of compulsory, potentially conflict-riven, interaction across borders, borders that are more difficult to maintain. On the one hand this allows new hybrid identities and nomadic youth movements across the globe (Nilan and Feixa, 2006), while on the other it creates new incentives to reestablish divisions; a defensiveness, as some try to hold on to previous affluence in the face of growing insecurity against others' aims to achieve the life they see portrayed in global media – an image that is at best a rapidly fading possibility for the majority even in the Global North (Beck and Beck-Gernsheim, 2009).

The workings of inequality in this context are potentially complex. As highlighted by Artini, Nilan and Threadgold (2011) in their study of young Balinese working in the cruise-ship industry, their research shows that young people who are not necessarily among the very elite, but possess relatively high levels of economic and cultural capital compared to many of their compatriots in their Balinese community, sometimes including having servants at home, are targeted by this industry to be service workers themselves because they have developed global and arguably 'western' dispositions.

The pay available from the multinational companies that staff these cruise ships seems high relative to local standards, and young Balinese can be encouraged by their family to take the opportunity to interact with westerners and for a small measure of upward mobility in terms of economic wealth, some of which may be returned to the family and community. However, wages quickly diminish with travel costs and recruitment agent fees and their time on the cruise-ships often interrupts an educational trajectory that may have included higher education and disrupts important social and cultural networks in their home communities (Artini et al., 2011: 5). Ironically, as international travel has become more affordable, this small and risky chance of economic mobility for middle-class young Balinese comes through serving customers who are often working-class people from the global North on holiday. These holiday-makers will return to increasingly insecure and arguably exploitative employment, particularly the younger workers, when their cruise is finished (Woodman and Threadgold, forthcoming).

Identifying both these young Balinese people and young working-class Australian holiday-makers as part of the same generation seems trivialising and perhaps suspect. Sometimes discussions of global inequality can make it seem like studying intra-national inequalities is illegitimate. However, understanding the creation of local, national and global inequality remains valuable (Roberts, 2010: 143; Threadgold, 2011). Drawing on a concept of social generation enables us to recognise cross-border interactions between young people in different parts of the world and cultural links across different parts of the world, as well as the extent to which both the young Balinese and young working-class Australians, despite the vast differences in their lives, are living in conditions shaped by new insecurities and global transition regimes. Across their diversity, these young lives in the vast majority of cases will be very different to those of their parents.

Young People Making a Place for Themselves

We would argue that the processes of individualisation are evident in each of the studies described above. In other words, the ways in which young people attempt to 'hold together' a biography vary in different places but a common thread can be seen in their strategies and imaginaries. Against a backdrop of the fragmentation of traditional institutions (for example rural labour markets in China and Romania, the Muslim religious institutions of Nigeria, and rural industry in Australia and Canada) young people forge strategies that enable them to have paid work and develop the kinds of dispositions and skills (through work and education) by which they can hope to gain a measure of social and economic security in changing times.

One way to interpret the empirical studies presented above is to use them to show how globalising processes are played out differently and with a range of consequences for young people. Yet this approach risks simply reducing place to a backdrop against which variations of significant processes occur;

a secondary consideration to placeless social forces. But as we explain at the outset of this chapter, when we analyse young people's experiences as they are embedded in place we gain a deeper understanding of the processes of social change and continuity, of individualisation, of regimes of transition and inequality, and of social generation. For example, Lou's (2011) study of young people in the rapidly urbanising areas of Northwestern China reveals how regimes of transition – institutionalised patterns of educational participation by young people – impact on the lives of young people and their community. In China, as in other countries like Australia and Canada, these institutionalised processes create patterns of migration and mobility that bring new opportunities to individuals and create new patterns of vulnerability (especially for the uneducated).

These institutionalised processes and the ways in which young people respond to them have generational effects. As we discussed in Chapter 3, social generations are forged via the operation of significant social processes that create distinctive new opportunities and risks compared with the previous generation. We can see from the examples of youth mobilities in Romania (Horváth, 2008) and rural Australia (Cuervo and Wyn, 2012), and urbanisation in Northwest China (Lou, 2011), the emergence of generational dispositions that mark out one generation from another. Lou's (2011) study shows the way in which regimes of transition that involve increasing levels of formal education for young rural Chinese encourage new dispositions involving *suzhi* (or cosmopolitanism). Lou's research also shows how some young people struggle to perform well in a curriculum that is designed to create more urban-centric, entrepreneurial subjects. Importantly, this struggle is emplaced – it is closely interrelated with the shift from rural places to urban ones, and also reflected in the students' tangible efforts to understand what (new) urban places mean for themselves and for rural places. Most of all, the students struggle to understand how they belong in the new physical places and social spaces that are being created. Whether they become integrated into the new ways or marginal to them, these young people are nonetheless part of a new social generation in China.

A social generation approach is also relevant to the study of mobility amongst Romanian young people in the rural villages in Transylvania. Horváth's (2008) study shows how new institutional constraints have marked the lives of a generation, and created new traditions that distinguish one social generation from another. The connections between the rural villages in Romania and labour markets in Germany, Spain, Hungary and Italy involve distinctive forms of belonging both in terms of (subjective) identification with landscapes and ways of living, and, institutionally, through the possibilities and limitations on citizenship.

Complex dynamics of continuity and change are implicated in each of these case studies. Through them we can see the ways in which new structural processes involving labour markets and educational participation create patterns of inequality. The *erliuzi* in Northwestern China are 'failures' – those who have not been able to manage to reinvent themselves as *suzhi*. In Romania, regimes of transition around international labour markets also mean that these mobile young people are likely to be excluded from gaining the educational qualifications they will need to gain secure employment in Romania's transforming economy. In Nigeria, Hoechner (2013) shows how the long-standing tradition for poor young men from rural areas to seek a livelihood in the traditional Muslim schools in urban areas by becoming *almajirai* has become a pathway to further alienation as these schools themselves become marginalised by new western systems of education. These examples provide a rich exploration of how new inequalities are created – layering onto and reconfiguring older structures of inequality based on religion, class, gender and race in new times.

A better theorisation of place calls for and supports a stronger theorisation of and engagement with time. In this book we have engaged with time and space in separate chapters yet the two are intertwined. We see both time and space relationally (Massey, 2005). Practices necessarily unfold over time in places, while creating particular senses of time and space. Even if some of these spaces for contemporary young people are 'cyber' this type of space is still created through social practices with particular temporalities. Massey denotes this intertwined constitution of place and time as the activity of 'spacialisation'. For Massey, rather than conceptualise 'space' as an a-priori dimension, space is the knitting together of multiple 'trajectories' or 'narratives' (Massey, 2005: 23–4).

Place is more than a setting within which new and old institutional processes and global forces are played out over time. In the end the challenge of place and temporality in youth studies is not just about looking to 'different' places or 'different' times, but equally about what an engagement with space and time can bring to our understanding of young lives. In the context of our focus in this chapter, we believe youth studies will benefit from a stronger theorisation and deeper analysis of place and its significance in the lives of young people. One group of young people has long been identified as connected to place, and this research can inform future efforts to better understand place in young lives. Connection to land is central to all indigenous cultures, although the complex ways in which this connection is forged are far from fully understood. A recent study of young indigenous Australians by Biddle and Swee (2012) found that those who were connected to their homelands and were able to participate regularly in hunting or fishing and in land sustainability practices tended to have higher levels of (western) educational qualifications and to be more healthy than their counterparts.

To properly understand the significance of place to indigenous young people may require going beyond empirical research. We hope to have shown that it is possible to do much through reworking the existing 'Northern' conceptual apparatus, and that this can provide a basis for rethinking contemporary youth studies. It may be, however, that into the future we will need to turn to concepts from the Global South; it may be here that youth research finds a guide to a better understanding of the temporal-spatial dimensions of life. For example, although Maori concepts cannot be translated easily into western words, it is instructive to explore the inter-relatedness of Maori identity with place and in time. For example, the term *whakapapa*, often used as a genealogical device, is a cultural discourse that enables people to establish the relationships between individuals, *whanau* (families), *hapu* (local tribes) and *iwi* (regional tribal bodies). Individuals and groups gain their respect and authority (*manu*) through an ongoing relationship with the land. *Tangata whenua* is the concept used to express this relationship with the land. It is often translated as 'people of the land' and refers to the specific place that Maori have a relationship with through their tribal ancestry, and through which they gain the confidence and authority to relate to the world. The current generation of indigenous young people are both drawing on and working to maintain this relationship to place, in the face of social change that brings new challenges (and potentially new possibilities) for doing so.

Conclusion

Place is not just a backdrop for more important considerations, or the container in which activities take place, it is also a force that mediates social life. Yet traditionally place has been attributed little explicit significance in sociological research. This chapter addresses the traditional invisibility of place through a focus on the lives of young people in rural areas and a considera-tion of the idea of mobilities, and we have argued that it is timely for youth sociologists to focus on place.

The focus on young people in rural areas highlights the urban-centric nature of much youth sociology – both in terms of the focus of research and theorising, and the location of those who do the theorising. Despite the tradition of the invisibility of place, a focus on place is increasingly evident in youth sociology. This is in part forged through a critique of the urban-centric traditions of youth studies, recognising the tendency for sociologists to understand 'new' youth in terms of the global city, perpetuating the idea that rural areas are mere backwaters with little relevance for the present. But more importantly, an increasing volume of research on young people in the Global South or majority world and on young people from non-metropol-itan areas in the South as well as the North reveals that their lives and the quality of their communities are significantly impacted by global economic and social processes. This research reveals that young people in rural com-munities are as much members of, and shapers of, their generation as their urban peers – and are in many ways as much if not more affected by global economic and social processes.

Research on mobilities of youth is also an increasingly significant focus in youth studies. The idea of mobilities refers to the movement of young people on an unprecedented scale, bringing into being new transnational sensibili-ties and affiliations in changing landscapes of risk and opportunity, in which mobility itself is becoming an intrinsic part of transition regimes. However, we would caution against jumping to the conclusion that mobile youth rep-resent a vanguard. It is important to consider the ways in which the position of young people at the global intersection of social, political and cultural 'flows' transform youth cultures, but these processes do not mean that loca-tion and institutional connection are no longer relevant.

Indeed, the research on young people's relationships to place across a wide range of countries reveals the central, if changing, significance of location to their lives. Various forms of youthful mobility are driven by transition regimes (of education and labour markets) that link young people to increasingly complex institutional processes. Young people's mobilities are often associ-ated with established social, cultural and economic links between places. They are often based on strong relational ties between specific places, which cre-ate ongoing connections and involve the exchange of ways of thinking and being. Thus, although processes of mobility are 'transnational', more needs to be known about the different meanings and implications of different kinds of mobilities and their relationship to places, and how new forces for mobility are implicated in new expressions of inequality. Analysing young people's experiences in place contributes to a deeper understanding of the processes of individualisation, inequality, and of generation.

9

CONCLUSION

This book aims to contribute to the sociological project of understanding young people's lives in contemporary conditions. In writing it we have engaged in depth with a central concern within contemporary youth studies: the complex relationship between change and continuity. This is reflected in a range of ways in the book's focus on the impact of new (global) education and labour-market transition regimes, new economic forms and global connections, and the proliferation of (fragmenting) institutional processes that we characterise as individualisation. It is also reflected in our methodology, including the range of empirical studies of young people's lives that we draw on, and our analysis of the legacies of youth sociology to build a forward-looking and robust youth studies.

While forward-looking, this book has provided the scope to return in some depth to the legacy of the work of Bourdieu, Mannheim and the individualisation theorists (particularly Beck and Beck-Gernshiem) to cast new light on the value of the concepts of social generation, individualisation and habitus. These concepts offer a rich framework by which to understand young people's experiences, because it is crucial to ask, as Richard Sennett (2006: 3) asks, what values and attitudes can hold people together as the institutions in which they live fragment? As youth researchers have so often highlighted, young people tend to be in the vanguard of the cultural and subjective expressions of new economic and political developments. To recognise this is not to deny that inequality exists, or that youth is a significant social status, it is to attempt to understand what inequality and youth look like now. Hence the leitmotifs of our analysis are the recognition of social change and the recognition of age as a social relation. However, like Sennett (2006), we would say that experience matters, and that a sociology of youth that does not take young people's own understandings of their situation seriously risks imposing the 'violence' of theory without the reflexivity of good social science practice (Ball, 2006). Through young people's attitudes, behaviours and cultural expressions we may see the ways in which new forms of institutional practice, global changes in labour markets and the redistribution of economic wealth 'mark' their lives, revealing opportunities as well as the hidden injuries that young people bear (Sennett and Cobb, 1972).

Within the field of youth studies, a significant body of research now exists to document how economic and cultural globalisation are reshaping young people's lives in both the Global South and North. Globalisation is creating new forms of connection that transcend the traditional cultural divisions of North/South/East/West, and yet at the same time are reinscribing local cultures, affiliations and divisions. These relationships are supported by the digital revolution, enabling young people to have a new awareness about how others are living and to create new imaginaries. Local, and increasingly global, transition regimes, based on institutionally sanctioned trajectories through education into labour markets, create normative youth transitions, yet the neoliberal promise of the benefits of global economic development has emerged for a minority only, creating new forms of inequality in and across national boundaries. As we discussed in Chapter 2, these inequalities impact directly and disastrously on young people. While there is little disagreement about such developments, there is intense debate about how to interpret their impact on the nature and meaning of youth. In drawing on existing theories we confront central disputes within the field.

In recognition of the enormity, but also the necessity, of the task of understanding young people's lives against a backdrop of these transformative dynamics, we note that the discipline of sociology has tended to gain its impetus from social change. The task of understanding social change and identifying the perils of social division along class, cultural, religious and gender lines inspired Marx, Durkheim, Weber and many first wave feminists (including Virginia Woolf, Mary Wollstonecraft and Marie Stopes) and second wave feminists (for example, Simone de Beauvoir, Betty Friedan, Juliet Mitchell, Luce Irigaray, Nancy Chodorow). Patterns of social life, especially those that reflect and contribute to inequality, can endure in various forms while their meaning and the processes that create these patterns change. This is true in relation to race, gender, class or geographical location, as well as other social divisions that have not been our focus in this book. This creates a challenge for sociologists of youth to recognise changing (or actively reproduced) patterns and also understand the dynamics that create these patterns and what they mean for young people.

Take for example the success that young women have enjoyed within new transition regimes of post-secondary education, in many western countries achieving higher participation rates than their male peers. This change in gender relations needs to be understood in relation to the processes that manage to maintain significant forms of gender inequality in employment alongside and despite young women's growing credentials, especially in some countries such as Australia (Andres and Wyn, 2010; Cuervo et al., 2012) and the USA (Gerson, 2010). Despite these complexities, the public intellectuals of the New Right, shock jocks, and many economists and policy makers in the neoliberal tradition emphasise the 'choices' that young women are now free to take, and proclaim that the dynamics of gender, as well as class and race, are becoming less significant. In the wider public discourse the ideology of choice remains strong. Against this backdrop the sociology of youth has an important role in speaking back to these disempowering discourses, yet all too often the critique has been aimed inward as claims for social change by some are interpreted by others as implying the end of social divisions. Hence we would take issue with the too simple caricaturing of the concept of individualisation (as indicating the end of social division) and with simplistic understandings of the concept of social generations (as a denial of intra-generational social division) that have characterised debates about change and continuity in youth sociology.

Our analysis suggests that the individualisation thesis has a significant overlap with many other recent theoretical innovations, including some unexpected resonances with postcolonial theory, with post-structuralist theories of identity, and even with some aspects of Bourdieu's thinking about action and the habitus in times of social change. We would suggest that as a result the individualisation thesis is not only less innovative than many critics of this concept assume, but that it also provides an underutilised tool for understanding how contemporary life is riddled with inequalities that are classed, gendered and raced; inequalities that are produced in new ways. The individualisation thesis issues a challenge to youth studies, and to sociology, broadly, to understand how people must now actively shape their biographies in response to the broad-scale processes that have created new conditions of life in recent decades.

While largely avoiding debates about whether the world, or parts of it, is in the midst of a shift from one form of modernity to another, we have argued that the conditions of life have changed in significant ways for young people around the world, thereby creating the conditions for a new generation. While the lives of young people across different places and social positions remain very different from each other, what they share is that their lives will, for most, look very different from those of their parents. Our specific goal has been to move beyond the theoretical impasse that has built up around the conflation of inequality with continuity (of social 'structures' and processes) as well as the conflation of 'freedom', 'choice' and 'equality' with social change. To do so we have developed the concept of social generation as proposed by Mannheim for contemporary challenges, using it to rethink debates about youth transitions, cultures, and time and place in young lives.

Generations, Transitions, Cultures

Over the last quarter of a century or more, youth sociologists have been drawn to the concept of youth transitions to analyse and describe the (changing) patterns of participation in education and employment in response to new transition regimes. In response to criticism, researchers using this framework have in recent times focused on other aspects of life, such as wellbeing and housing transitions. Nonetheless, the transitions metaphor makes it difficult to avoid reifying adulthood as a transition destination, and we would argue that the concept of transitions is a limited tool for understanding the changing meaning and experience of youth. This is because while a transitions framework enables the measurement of young people's trajectories against normative (institutional) markers, such as various stages of educational achievement and engagement with the labour market, it provides little grasp of the interrelationship between biography and history.

To put this another way, a transitions approach, while noting that the 'standard' transition from education to full-time engagement in the labour market has been a more extended process for young people today than it was for the generation born in the late 1940s and 1950s (called the Baby Boomers), nonetheless assumes that 'youth' is a universal category and stage of life that precedes a 'standard', if also classed, gendered and raced, adulthood. Research working with the transitions metaphor too easily treats youth as a category rather than a relationship.

Our theme of understanding youth in the context of change and continuity has also been central to debates in youth cultural studies. Resonating with contemporary disputes about individualisation, which have taken place particularly within youth transitions studies, debates over the past two decades about the relative merits of a subcultural or post-subcultural understanding of young people's cultural practices have coalesced around the relationship between social change, social structure and identity. By the early 1990s it was clear that the traditional class basis for youth subcultures had become far more complex and this was a foundation for post-subcultural conceptualisations of neo-tribes and scenes. Yet a nuanced analysis of this complexity and its relationship to inequality has been in large part neglected as the literature on youth cultures became a site for a debate about the extent to which changing cultural forms and the disappearance of 'traditional' class-based affiliations meant that young people were now 'freer' and class was less 'relevant'.

In both cultures and transitions research a particular way of thinking about the relationship between continuity and change has become common, making the nuanced relationship between youth transitions, cultural forms and social position more difficult to see. As an alternative, we have suggested thinking about transitions and cultures through the lens of generation and biography. The concept of social generation has assisted us to trace the way the possibilities available to young people in general are remade over time, and with their responses to these possibilities, create and recreate patterns of inequality. Old divisions have to be actively reinforced, or even made anew. Importantly, social generations are not simply 'age groupings' and they are not homogeneous. Investigating the challenges faced, the resources available to, and the dispositions developed by, different young people within a generation can provide a basis for researching how people actively negotiate, in everyday life, inconsistent and changeable rules and guidelines across various biographical spheres and how processes of inequality, including class, gender and race, emerge through this.

In this advocacy for the value of a sociology of generations, we are of course not asking researchers to abandon these other highly productive research traditions. Indeed, research approaches that explore 'transitions' and 'cultures' and particularly their intersection are valuable tools for deepening our understanding of social generations. The methods and research questions of the Life Patterns study, for example, from which we have drawn throughout this book to develop our sociology of generations, were designed to track the transitions of Australian youth. This shares with other studies in both the transitions and cultures tradition the goal of tracking young people through social institutions, including but not limited to school and work. As with much recent 'cultural' research, this study uses qualitative methods to research participants' understanding of their lives. This can provide a picture of which young people are most advantaged and what it means today to be excluded from the possibilities available to other members of this generation.

Time, Place and the Future

We have expanded on the concept of social generation through an exploration of time and place. By focusing on temporal dynamics, we have explored the nature of the biographical individualisation facing the contemporary generation of young people in Australia, highlighting its implications for young people's cultural practices and how it is implicated in inequalities between young people. Young people in contemporary Australia, and in many other parts of the world, have an unprecedented capacity to connect with others. Despite this the types of sociality that may be most important to quality of life and that many people (both young and old) appear to value most highly, extended and frequent periods of shared time with close friends, are not so easy to arrange. The increasingly individualised schedules of work and study that are part of the generational conditions shaping the lives of young people make creating and maintaining this type of quality relationship with others newly challenging. We have used the experiences of participants in the Life Patterns research programme to argue that this temporal individualisation leads to fragmented and varying timetables of everyday life for many young people, which for those without the resources to counter this individualisation can diminish their social networks and ability to engage in cultural practices.

Similarly, place should not be understood as the background to more important considerations, it mediates social life in consequential ways and is centrally implicated in the nature of social generations and inequalities. Our focus on young people in rural areas aimed to counter the urban-centric focus of research and theorising in youth studies and to highlight where most of those who do this theorising are based. The research continuing to emerge on the lives of young people in the majority world, outside the North and its metropolitan centres, as well as research with rural and regional young people in the North, shows that they are far from left out of the global processes that we argue are creating new generational conditions. In fact within these groups are likely to be found the young people most impacted by new institutional (global) transitions regimes and labour markets. They are just as much a part of the forging of a new generation.

In drawing this book to a conclusion, we are aware that in attempting to meet the challenge of understanding young people's lives without slipping into simplistic understandings or convenient shortcuts we may raise more questions than we can answer, including what the 'Asian Century' might mean for youth studies and its 'Northern theories'. The challenge for us has been to recognise that as the world changes the processes that produce inequalities also change. In documenting these changes we can see that gender, race, class and geographic location, to name just the most obvious examples, and the divisions we have focused on in this book, as well as others that we have not been able to properly attend to such as disability and sexuality, continue to provide a basis for stark and consequential inequalities. Yet it is also crucial to understand that the dynamics that produce these inequalities, and the ways that they are experienced, are not consonant across time (or place). To understand how social generations are produced, and experienced, both now and in the future, is therefore an important task for youth sociologists. Our hope is that this book not only contributes to the ongoing debates about youth, change and inequality but also makes the task of understanding these dynamics easier.

REFERENCES

Abbott, A. (2001) *Chaos of Disciplines*. Chicago: University of Chicago Press.

Abbott, D. (2007) 'Poverty and pro-poor policies in Pacific Island countries', *Asia-Pacific Population Journal*, 22(3): 59–74.

ABS – see Australian Bureau of Statistics.

Adam, B. (2009) 'Cultural future matters: an exploration in the spirit of Max Weber's methodological writings', *Time and Society*, 18(1): 7–25.

Adkins, L. (2004) 'Reflexivity: freedom or habit of gender?', in L. Adkins and B. Skeggs (eds), *Feminism after Bourdieu*. Oxford: Blackwell. pp. 191–210.

Allan, G. (2008) 'Flexibility, friendship and family', *Personal Relationships*, 15(1): 1–16.

Allen, S. (1968) 'Some theoretical problems in the study of youth', *The Sociological Review*, 16(3): 319–31.

Alston, M. (2005) 'Social exclusion in rural Australia', in C. Cocklin and J. Dibden (eds), *Sustainability and Change in Rural Australia*. Sydney: UNSW Press. pp. 157–70.

Alston, M. and Kent, J. (2001) *Generation X-pendable: Young, Rural and Looking for Work: An Examination of Young People's Perceptions of Employment Opportunities in Rural Areas*. Wagga Wagga: Centre for Rural Social Research, Charles Sturt University.

Althusser, L. (1971) *Lenin and Philosophy and Other Essays*. London: New Left Books.

Anderson, M., Bechhofer, F., McCrone, D., Jamieson, L., Li, Y. and Stewart, R. (2005) 'Timespans and plans among young adults', *Sociology*, 39(1): 139–55.

Andres, L. and Wyn, J. (2010) *The Making of a Generation: The Children of the 1970s in Adulthood*. Toronto: University of Toronto Press.

Andres, L., Anisef, P., Krahn, H., Looker, D. and Thiessen, V. (1999) 'The persistence of social structure: cohort, class and gender effects on the occupational aspirations and expectations of Canadian youth', *Journal of Youth Studies*, 2(3): 261–82.

Antonsich, M. (2010) 'Searching for belonging – an analytical framework', *Geography Compass*, 4(6): 644–59.

Archer, L. (2003) 'The "value" of higher education', in L. Archer, M. Hutchings and A. Ross (eds), *Higher Education and Social Class: Issues of Exclusion and Inclusion*. London: RoutledgeFalmer. pp. 119–36.

Archer, M. (2012) *The Reflexive Imperative in Late Modernity*. Cambridge: Cambridge University Press.

Arnett, J. (2004) *Emerging Adulthood: The Winding Road from the Late Teens through the Twenties*. New York: Oxford University Press.

Artini L.P., Nilan, P. and Threadgold, S. (2011) 'Young Indonesian cruise workers, symbolic violence and international class relations', *Asian Social Science*, 7(6): 3–14.

Ashton, D. and Field, D. (1976) *Young Workers*. London: Hutchinson.

Atkinson, W. (2007) 'Beck, individualization and the death of class: a critique', *British Journal of Sociology*, 58(3): 349–65.

Australian Bureau of Statistics (2013) 4102.0 – *Australian Social Trends: Young Adults Then and Now*. Canberra: Australian Bureau of Statistics.

Australian Bureau of Statistics (2012a) 6227.0 – *Education and Work, Australia*. Canberra: Australian Bureau of Statistics.

Australian Bureau of Statistics (2012b) 4704.0 – *The Health and Welfare of Australia's Aboriginal and Torres Strait Islander Peoples*, online resource last updated Dec 2012 – viewed 13 September 2013. www.abs.gov.au/AUSSTATS/abs@.nsf/Latestproducts/ 4704.0Main%20Features1Oct%202010?opendocument&tabname=Summary&pro dno=4704.0&issue=Oct%202010&num=&view=

Australian Bureau of Statistics (2012c) 4102.0 – *Australian Social Trends: Education Differences between Men and Women*, Sept 2012. Canberra: Australian Bureau of Statistics.

Australian Bureau of Statistics (2010) 4102.0 – *Are Young People Earning or Learning, Social Trends*, March 2010. Canberra: Australian Bureau of Statistics.

Australian Bureau of Statistics (2009a) 4102.0 – '*Patterns in Work*', in *Australian Social Trends*, December 2009. Canberra: Australian Bureau of Statistics.

Australian Bureau of Statistics (2009b) 4250.0.55.001 – *Perspectives on Education and Training: Social Inclusion, 2009*. Canberra: Australian Bureau of Statistics.

Australian Bureau of Statistics (2008) 4326.0 – *National Survey of Mental Health and Wellbeing: Summary of Results, 2007*. Canberra: Australian Bureau of Statistics.

Australian Bureau of Statistics (2006) 4153.0 – *How Australians Use Their Time, 2006*. Canberra: Australian Bureau of Statistics.

Australian Bureau of Statistics (2005) 4102.0 – *Australian Social Trends 2005*. Canberra: Australian Bureau of Statistics.

Australian Institute of Health and Welfare (2011) *Young Australians: Their Health and Wellbeing 2011*. Canberra: Australian Institute of Health and Welfare.

Ball, S. (2006) 'The necessity and violence of theory', *Discourse: Studies in the Cultural Politics of Education*, 27(1): 3–10.

Ball, S., Maguire, M. and Macrae, M. (2000) *Choice, Pathways, Transitions: New Youth, New Economies in the Global City*. London: RoutledgeFalmer.

Barry, M. (2006) *Youth Offending in Transition: The Search for Social Recognition*. Oxon: Routledge.

Baudrillard, J. (2002) *The Spirit of Terrorism and Other Essays* (trans. C. Turner). London: Verso.

Baudrillard, J (1983) *Simulations*. New York: Semiotext(e).

Bauman, Z. (2007a) *Liquid Times*. Cambridge: Polity.

Bauman, Z. (2007b) *Consuming Life*. Cambridge: Polity.

Bauman, Z. (2001) *The Individualized Society*. Cambridge: Polity.

Bauman, Z. (2000) *Liquid Modernity*. Cambridge: Polity.

Bauman, Z. (1998) *Globalization: The Human Consequences*. Cambridge: Polity.

Beck, U (2009) *World at Risk*. Cambridge: Polity.

Beck, U. (2007) 'Beyond class and nation: reframing social inequalities in a globalizing world', *The British Journal of Sociology*, 58(4): 679–705.

Beck, U. (2006) *Cosmopolitan Vision*. Cambridge: Polity.

Beck, U. (2002) 'The cosmopolitan society and its enemies', *Theory, Culture & Society*, 19(1–2): 17–44.

Beck, U. (2000) *The Brave New World of Work*. Cambridge: Polity.

Beck, U. (1992) *Risk Society: Towards a New Modernity*. London: Sage.

Beck, U. and Beck-Gernsheim, E. (2009) 'Global generations and the trap of methodological nationalism for a cosmopolitan turn in the sociology of youth and generation', *European Sociological Review*, 25(1): 25–36.

Beck, U. and Beck-Gernsheim, E. (2002) *Individualization: Institutionalized Individualism and its Social and Political Consequences*. London: Sage.

Beck, U. and Beck-Gernsheim, E. (1996) 'Individualization and "precarious freedoms": perspectives and controversies of a subject-oriented sociology', in P. Heelas, S. Lash and P. Morris (eds), *Detraditionalization: Critical Reflections on Authority and Identity*. Oxford, Blackwell. pp. 23–48.

Beck, U. and Lau, C. (2005) 'Second modernity as a research agenda: theoretical and empirical explorations in the meta-change of modern society', *The British Journal of Sociology*, 56(4): 525–57.

Beck-Gernsheim, E. (2002) *Reinventing the Family: In Search of New Lifestyles*. Cambridge: Polity.

Bennett, A. (2012) 'Dance parties, lifestyle and strategies for ageing', in A. Bennett and P. Hodkinson (eds), *Ageing and Youth Cultures: Music, Style and Identity*. London/New York: Berg. pp. 95–104.

Bennett, A. (2011) 'The post-subcultural turn: some reflections 10 years on', *Journal of Youth Studies*, 14(5): 493–506.

Bennett, A. (2006) 'Punk's not dead: the continuing significance of punk rock for an older generation of fans', *Sociology*, 40(2): 219–35.

Bennett, A. (2005) 'In defence of neo-tribes: a response to Blackman and Hesmondhalgh', *Journal of Youth Studies*, 8(2): 255–9.

Bennett, A. (2000) *Popular Music and Youth Culture: Music, Identity and Place*. London: Macmillan.

Bennett, A. (1999) 'Subcultures or neo-tribes? Rethinking the relationship between youth, style and musical taste?', *Sociology*, 33(3): 599–617.

Bennett, A. and Hodkinson, P. (eds) (2012) *Ageing and Youth Cultures: Music, Style and Identity*. London/New York: Berg.

Bennett, T. (2007) 'Habitus clivé: aesthetics and politics in the work of Pierre Bourdieu', *New Literary History*, 38(1): 201–28.

Bergmann, W. (1992) 'The problem of time in sociology: an overview of the literature on the state of theory and research on the "sociology of time", 1900–82', *Time and Society*, 1(1): 81–134.

Berlant, L. (2011) *Cruel Optimism*. Durham: Duke University Press.

Bessant, J. (2008) 'Hard wired for risk: neurological science, "the adolescent brain" and developmental theory', *Journal of Youth Studies*, 11(3): 347–60.

Bhabha, H. (1994) *The Location of Culture*. New York: Routledge.

Biddle, N. and Swee, H. (2012) 'The relationship between wellbeing and indigenous land, language and culture', *Australia, Australian Geographer*, 43(3): 215–32.

Biggart, A. and Walther, A. (2006) 'Coping with yo-yo transitions: young adults' struggle for support – between family and state in comparative perspective', in C. Leccardi and E. Ruspini (eds), *A New Youth? Young People, Generations and Family Life*. Aldershot: Ashgate. pp. 41–62.

Bittman, M. (2005) 'Sunday working and family time', *Labour and Industry*, 16(1): 59–81.

Blackman, S. (2005) 'Youth subcultural theory: a critical engagement with the concept, its origins and politics, from the Chicago School to postmodernism', *Journal of Youth Studies*, 3(1): 1–20.

Blatterer, H. (2007) *Coming of Age in Times of Uncertainty*. New York: Berghahn.

Boden, D. and Molotch, H. (1994) 'The compulsion to proximity', in R. Friedland and D. Boden (eds), *Nowhere: Space, Time and Modernity*. Berkeley: University of California Press. pp. 257–86.

Bourdieu, P. (2008) *Sketch for a Self-Analysis*. Chicago: University of Chicago Press.

Bourdieu, P. (2000a) *Pascalian Meditations*. Cambridge: Polity.

Bourdieu, P. (2000b) 'Making the economic habitus: Algerian workers revisited', *Ethnography*, 1(1): 17–41.

Bourdieu, P. et al. (1999) *The Weight of the World: Social Suffering in Contemporary Society*. Cambridge: Polity.

Bourdieu, P. (1998a) *Practical Reason: On the Theory of Action*. Cambridge: Polity.

Bourdieu, P. (1998b) *Acts of Resistance*. Cambridge: Polity.

Bourdieu, P. (1993) *Sociology in Question*. London: Sage.

Bourdieu, P. (1990) *The Logic of Practice*. Stanford: Stanford University Press.

Bourdieu, P. (1986) 'The forms of capital', in J. Richardson (ed.), *Handbook of Theory and Research for the Sociology of Education*. New York: Greenwood. pp. 241–58.

Bourdieu, P. (1984) *Distinction: A Social Critique of the Judgement of Taste*. London: Routledge & Kegan Paul.

Bourdieu, P. (1979 [1963]) *Algeria 1960*. Cambridge: Cambridge University Press.

Bourdieu, P. (1977) *Outline of a Theory of Practice*. Cambridge: Cambridge University Press.

Bourdieu, P. (1962) *The Algerians*. Boston, MA: Beacon.

Bourdieu, P. and Passeron, J.C. (1979 [1964]) *Reproduction in Education, Society and Culture*. London: Sage.

Bourdieu, P. and Sayad, A. (2004) 'Colonial rule and cultural sabir', *Ethnography*, 5(4): 445–86.

Boyd, D.M. and Ellison, N.B. (2008) 'Social network sites: definition, history, and scholarship', *Journal of Computer-Mediated Communication*, 13(1): 210–30.

Brannen, J. and Nilsen, A. (2007) 'Young people, time horizons and planning: a response to Anderson et al.', *Sociology*, 41(1): 153–60.

Brannen, J. and Nilsen, A. (2005) 'Individualisation, choice and structure: a discussion of current trends in sociological analysis', *The Sociological Review*, 53(3): 412–28.

Brannen, J. and Nilsen, A. (2002) 'Young people's time perspectives: from youth to adulthood', *Sociology*, 36(3): 513–37.

Brooks, R. and Everett, G. (2008) 'The prevalence of "life planning": evidence from UK graduates', *British Journal of Sociology of Education*, 29(3): 325–37.

Brown, P., Lauder, H. and Ashton, D. (2011) *The Global Auction: The Broken Promises of Education, Jobs and Incomes*. New York: Oxford University Press.

Buchler, S., Baxter, J., Haynes, M. and Western, M. (2009) 'The social and demographic characteristics of cohabiters in Australia', *Family Matters*, 82: 22–9.

Buchmann, M. (1989) *The Script of Life in Modern Society: Entry into Adulthood in a Changing World*. Chicago: University of Chicago Press.

Buckingham, D. (2006) 'Is there a digital generation?', in D. Buckingham and R. Willett (eds), *Digital Generations: Children, Young People and New Media*. Mahwah, NJ: Erlbaum.

Burnett, M.J. (2010) *Generations: The Time Machine in Theory and Practice*. Farnham: Ashgate.

Butler, J. (1990) *Gender Trouble and the Subversion of Identity*. New York and London: Routledge.

Bynner, J. (2005) 'Rethinking the youth phase in the life-course: the case for emerging adulthood?', *Journal of Youth Studies*, 8(4): 367–84.

Campbell, I. (2004) 'Casual work and casualisation: how does Australia compare?', *Labour and Industry*, 15(2): 85–111.

Canclini, N.G. (1995) *Hybrid Cultures: Strategies for Entering and Leaving Modernity*. Minneapolis: University of Minnesota Press.

Castells, M. (2012) *Networks of Outrage and Hope: Social Movements in the Internet Age*. Cambridge: Polity.

Castells, M. (2000) *The Rise of the Network Society: The Information Age: Economy, Society and Culture Vol. I* (2nd edition). Cambridge, MA/Oxford, UK: Blackwell.

Chauvel, L. (2010) 'The long-term destabilization of youth, scarring effects, and the future of the welfare regime in post-*trente glorieuses* France', *French Politics, Culture & Society*, 28(3): 74–96.

Chauvel, L. (2006) 'Social generations, life chances and welfare regime sustainability', in P.D. Culpepper et al. (eds), *Changing France: The Politics that Markets Make*. Basingstoke: Palgrave Macmillan. pp. 150–75.

Christensen, P. and James, A. (2001) 'What are schools for? The temporal experience of children's learning in Northern England', in A. Alanen and B. Mayall (eds), *Conceptualising Adult-Child Relations*. London: Routledge Falmer. pp. 70–85.

Cieslik, M. and Pollock, G. (2002) 'Introduction', in M. Cieslik and G. Pollock (eds), *Young People in Risk Society*. Aldershot: Ashgate. pp. 1–21.

Clarke, G. (1990) 'Defending ski jumpers: a critique of theories of youth subculture', in S. Frith and A. Goodwin (eds), *On Record: Roc, Pop and the Written Word*. London: Routledge, pp. 81–96.

Clarke, J., Hall, S., Jefferson, T. and Roberts, B. (2006 [1976]) 'Subcultures, cultures and class: a theoretical overview', in S. Hall and T. Jefferson (eds), *Resistance Through Rituals* (2nd edition). London: Hutchinson.

Coffey, J. (2013) '"Body pressure": negotiating gender through body work practices', *Youth Studies Australia*, 32(2): 39–48.

Coffey, J. and Farrugia, D. (2014) 'Unpacking the black box: the problem of agency in the sociology of youth', *Journal of Youth Studies*, 17(4): 461–74.

Cohen, A.K. (1956) *Delinquent Boys: The Culture of the Gang*. London: Routledge & Kegan Paul.

Cohen, P. (2003) 'Mods and shockers: youth cultural studies in Britain', in A. Bennett, M. Cieslik and S. Miles (eds), *Researching Youth*. Basingstoke: Palgrave Macmillan. pp. 29–51.

Cohen, P. (1999) *Rethinking the Youth Question: Education, Labour and Cultural Studies*. Basingstoke: Macmillan.

Cohen, P. and Ainley, P. (2000) 'In the country of the blind? Youth studies and cultural studies in Britain', *Journal of Youth Studies*, 3(1): 79–95.

Cohen, S. (1972) *Folk Devils and Moral Panics: The Creation of Mods and Rockers*. London: MacGibbon & Kee.

Coleman, J. (1990) *Foundations of Social Theory*. Cambridge: Harvard University Press.

Coleman, J. (1961) *The Adolescent Society: The Social Life of the Teenager and its Impact on Education*. New York: Free Press of Glencoe.

Coles, B. (1986) 'Gonna tear your playhouse down: towards reconstructing a sociology of youth', *Social Science Teacher*, 15(3): 78–80.

Collins, W.A. and van Dulmen, M. (2006) 'Friendships and romance in emerging adulthood: assessing distinctiveness in close relationships', in J.J. Arnett and J.L. Tanner (eds), *Emerging Adults in America: Coming of Age in the 21st Century*. Washington, DC: American Psychological Association Books. pp. 219–34.

Connell, W.F., Francis, E.P. and Skilbeck, E.E. (1957) *Growing Up in an Australian City: A Study of Adolescents in Sydney*. Melbourne: Australian Council for Educational Research.

Connell, R. (2013) 'The neoliberal cascade and education: an essay on the market agenda and its consequences', *Critical Studies in Education*, 54(2): 99–112.

Connell, R. (2007) *Southern Theory: The Global Dynamics of Knowledge in Social Science*. Cambridge: Polity.

Corsten, M. (1999) 'The time of generations', *Time & Society*, 8(2–3): 249–72.

Côté, J. (2000) *Arrested Adulthood: The Changing Nature of Maturity and Identity*. New York: New York University Press.

Côté, J. and Allahar, A. (1996) *Generation on Hold: Coming of Age in the Late Twentieth Century*. New York: New York University Press.

Côté, J. and Levine, C. (2005) *Identity, Formation, Agency, and Culture: A Social Psychological Synthesis*. Mahwah, NJ: Erlbaum.

Cruces, G., Ham, A. and Viollaz, M. (2012) *Scarring Effects of Youth Unemployment and Informality: Evidence from Argentina and Brazil*. Working Paper Centre for Distributive, Labour and Social Studies (CEDLAS), Buenos Aires, Argentina: Universidad Nacional de La Plata.

Cuervo, H., Crofts, J. and Wyn, J. (2013) *Generational Insights into New Labour Market Landscapes for Youth* (Research Report 42). Melbourne: Youth Research Centre, University of Melbourne.

Cuervo, H. and Wyn, J. (2012) *Young People Making it Work: Continuity and Change in Rural Places*. Melbourne: Melbourne University Publishing.

Cuervo, H. and Wyn, J. (2014) 'Reflections on the use of spatial and relational metaphors in youth studies', *Journal of Youth Studies*, 17(7): 901–915.

Cuervo, H., Wyn, J. and Crofts, J. (2012) *Gen X Women and the Gender Revolution: Pioneers or Traditionalists?* (Research Report 36). Melbourne: Youth Research Centre, University of Melbourne.

Cummings, J. (2006) 'It's more than a t-shirt: neo-tribal sociality and linking images at Australian indie music festivals', *Perfect Beat*, 8(1): 65–84.

Davis, M. (1999) *Gangland: Cultural Elites and the New Generationalism* (2nd edition). Sydney: Allen and Unwin.

de Certeau, M. (1984) *The Practices of Everyday Life*. Berkeley: University of California Press.

Department of Education, Employment and Workplace Relations (2009) *The Higher Education Report 2008*. Canberra: Department of Education, Employment and Workplace Relations.

Devadason, R. (2008) 'To plan or not to plan? Young adult future orientations in two European cities', *Sociology*, 42(6): 1127–45.

Devine, F. (2004) *Class Practices: How Parents Help Their Children Get Good Jobs*. Cambridge: Cambridge University Press.

Devine, F., Britton, N., Halfpenny, P. and Mellor, R. (2003) 'Family and community ties in space and time', in G. Allan and G. Jones (eds), *Social Relations and the Lifecourse*. Basingstoke: Palgrave. pp. 172–86.

Devlin, M., James, R. and Grigg, G. (2008) 'Studying and working: a national study of student finances and student engagement', *Tertiary Education and Management*, 14(2): 111–22.

Dixon, J., Woodman, D., Strazdins, L., Banwell, C., Broom, D. and Burgess, J. (2013) 'Flexible employment, flexible eating and health risks', *Critical Public Health*: DOI: 10.1080/09581596.2013.852162.

Driver, C. (2011) 'Embodying hardcore: rethinking "subcultural" authenticities', *Journal of Youth Studies*, 14(8): 975–90.

Du Bois, W.E.B. (1994 [1903]) *The Souls of Black Folk*. New York: Dover.

du Bois-Reymond, M. (1998) '"I don't want to commit myself yet": young people's life concepts', *Journal of Youth Studies*, 1(1): 63–79.

du Bois-Reymond, M. (1995) 'Future orientations of Dutch youth: the emergence of a choice biography', in A. Cavalli and O. Galland (eds), *Youth in Europe*. London: Pinter. pp. 201–22.

du Bois-Reymond, M. and Stauber, B. (2005) 'Biographical turning points in young people's transitions to work across Europe', in H. Helve and G. Holm (eds), *Contemporary Youth Research: Local Expressions and Global Connections*. Aldershot: Ashgate. pp. 63–75.

du Bois Reymond, M. and te Poel, Y. (2006) 'Work and care in the life-course of young adults in the Netherlands', in C. Leccardi and E. Ruspini (eds), *A New Youth? Young People, Generations and Family Life*. Aldershot: Ashgate. pp. 164–86.

Dunham, C. (1998) 'Generation units and the life course: a sociological perspective on youth and the anti-war movement', *Journal of Political and Military Sociology*, 26(2): 137–55.

Dwyer, P. and Wyn, J. (2001) *Youth, Education and Risk: Facing the Future*. London/ New York: RoutledgeFalmer.

Eckersley, R. (2011) 'A new narrative of young people's health and wellbeing', *Journal of Youth Studies*, 14(5): 627–38.

Edmunds, J. and Turner, B. (2005) 'Global generations: social change in the twentieth century', *The British Journal of Sociology*, 56(4): 559–77.

Edmunds, J. and Turner, B. (eds) (2002) *Generations, Culture and Society*. Buckingham: Open University Press.

Ehn, B. and Löfgren, O. (2009) 'Routines – made and unmade', in E. Shove, F. Trentman and R. Wilk (eds), *Time, Consumption and Everyday Life*. Oxford: Berg. pp. 99–114.

Elder, G.H. and Pellerin, L.A. (1998) 'Linking history and human lives', in J.Z. Giele and G.H. Elder (eds), *Methods of Life Course Research: Qualitative and Quantitative Approaches*. London: Sage. pp. 264–94.

Elias, N. (2000) *The Civilizing Process* (revised edition). Oxford: Blackwell.

Elias, N. (1992) *Time: An Essay*. Oxford: Blackwell.

Engels, F. (1993, German original 1845) *The Condition of the Working Class in England*. Oxford: Oxford University Press.

Erikson, E.H. (1968) *Identity, Youth and Crisis*. New York: Norton.

Erikson, E.H. (1965) *Childhood and Society*. Harmondsworth: Penguin.

Esping-Andesen, G. (2009) *The Incomplete Revolution: Adapting Welfare States to Women's New Roles*. Cambridge: Polity.

Evans, K. (2007) 'Concepts of bounded agency in education, work, and the personal lives of young adults', *International Journal of Psychology*, 42(2): 85–93.

Evans, K. (2002) 'Taking control of their lives: agency in young adult transitions in England and the new Germany', *Journal of Youth Studies*, 5(3): 245–69.

Evans, K. and Furlong, A. (1997) 'Metaphors of youth transitions: niches, pathways, trajectories or navigations', in J. Bynner, L. Chisholm and A. Furlong (eds), *Youth, Citizenship and Social Change in a European Context*. Aldershot: Ashgate. pp. 17–41.

Evans, K. and Helve, H. (2013) 'Youth and work transitions in changing social landscapes', in H. Helve and K. Evans (eds), *Youth and Work Transitions in Changing Social Landscapes*. London: Tufnell.

Everatt, D. (2013) '"Ring of fire or a puff of (commentators') smoke"? Youth unemployment and transitions in Guateng, South Africa', in H. Helve and K. Evans (eds), *Youth and Work Transitions in Changing Social Landscapes*. London: Tufnell.

Eyerman, R. and Turner, B.S. (1998) 'Outline of a theory of generations', *European Journal of Social Theory*, 1(1): 91–106.

Farrugia, D. (2014) 'Towards a spatialised youth sociology: the rural and the urban in times of change', *Journal of Youth Studies*, 17(3): 293–307.

Farrugia, D. (2011) 'Youth homelessness and individualised subjectivity', *Journal of Youth Studies*, 14(7): 761–75.

Farrugia, D. and Watson, J. (2011) '"If anyone helps you then you're a failure": youth homelessness, identity, and relationships in late modernity', in S. Beadle, R. Holdsworth and J. Wyn (eds), *For We Are Young and…? Young People in a Time of Uncertainty*. Melbourne: Melbourne University Press, pp 142–57.

Feixa, C. and Cangas, Y.G. (2005) 'The socio-cultural construction of youth in Latin America: achievements and failures', in H. Helve and G. Holm (eds), *Contemporary Youth Research: Local Expressions and Global Connections*. Aldershot: Ashgate. pp. 39–48.

Feuer, L.S. (1969) *The Conflict of Generations*. New York: Basic Books.

Foucault, M. (1982) 'The subject and power', *Critical Inquiry*, 8(4): 777–95.

Foundation for Young Australians (FYA) (2013) *How Young Australians are Faring 2013*. Melbourne: Foundation for Young Australians.

France, A. (2007) *Understanding Youth in Late Modernity*. Maidenhead: Open University Press.

Fraser, N. (2005) 'Mapping the feminist imagination: from redistribution to recognition to representation', *Constellations*, 12(3): 295–307.

Furlong, A. (2009) 'Revisiting transitional metaphors: reproducing social inequalities under the conditions of late modernity', *Journal of Education and Work*, 22(5): 343–53.

Furlong, A. (2013) *Youth Studies: An Introduction*. New York: Routledge.

Furlong, A. and Cartmel, F. (2007 [1997]) *Young People and Social Change: New Perspectives* (2nd edition). Maidenhead: Open University Press.

Furlong, A. and Cartmel, F. (1997) *Young People and Social Change: Individualization and Risk in Late Modernity*. Buckingham: Open University Press.

Furlong, A. and Kelly, P. (2005) 'The Brazilianisation of youth transitions in Australia and the UK?', *Australian Journal of Social Issues*, 40(2): 207–25.

Furlong, A., Woodman, D. and Wyn, J. (2011) 'Changing times, changing perspectives: reconciling "transition" and "cultural" perspectives on youth and young adulthood', *Journal of Sociology*, 47(4): 355–70.

Gabriel, M. (2006) 'Youth migration and social advancement: how young people manage emerging differences between themselves and their hometown', *Journal of Youth Studies*, 9(1): 33–46.

Gabriel, M. (2002) 'Australia's regional youth exodus', *Journal of Rural Studies*, 18(2): 209–212.

Geldens, P. and Bourke, L. (2008) 'Identity, uncertainty and responsibility: privileging place in a risk society', *Children's Geographies*, 6(3): 281–94.

Geldens, P., Lincoln, S. and Hodkinson, P. (2011) 'Youth: identities, transitions, cultures', *Journal of Sociology*, 47(4): 347–53.

Gerson, K. (2010) *The Unfinished Revolution: How a New Generation is Reshaping Family, Work, and Gender in America*. New York: Oxford University Press.

Giddens, A. (1991) *Modernity and Self-identity: Self and Society in the Late Modern Age*. Stanford: Stanford University Press.

Giddens, A. (1990) *The Consequences of Modernity*. Stanford: Stanford University Press.

Giddens, A. (1984) *The Constitution of Society: Outline of the Theory of Structuration*. Cambridge: Polity.

Giddens, A. (1971) *Capitalism and Modern Social Theory: An Analysis of the Writings of Marx, Durkheim and Max Weber*. Cambridge: Cambridge University Press.

Gieryn, T. (2000) 'A space for place in sociology', *Annual Review of Sociology*, 26: 463–96.

Go, J. (2013) 'Decolonizing Bourdieu: theory in Pierre Bourdieu's early work', *Sociological Theory*, 31(1): 49–74.

Goodwin, J. and O'Connor, H. (2009) 'Youth and generation: "in the midst of an adult world"', in A. Furlong (ed.), *Handbook of Youth and Young Adulthood: New Perspectives and Agendas*. London: Routledge. pp. 22–30.

Goodwin, J. and O'Connor, H. (2005) 'Exploring complex transitions: looking back at the "golden age" of youth transitions', *Sociology*, 39(2): 201–20.

Gramsci, A. (1971) *Selections from the Prison Notebooks*. London: Lawrence and Wishart.

Gregg, M. (2011) *Work's Intimacy*. Cambridge: Polity.

Gregory, J. (2012) 'Ageing rave women's post-scene narratives', in A. Bennett and P. Hodkinson (eds), *Ageing and Youth Cultures.* Oxford: Berg. pp. 37–49.

Gregory, K. and Clarke, M. (2003) 'High-stakes assessment in England and Singapore', *Theory into Practice*, 42(1): 66–74.

Griffin, C. (2011) 'The trouble with class: researching youth, class and culture beyond the "Birmingham School"', *Journal of Youth Studies*, 14(3): 245–59.

Griffin, C. (1993) *Representations of Youth*. Cambridge: Polity.

Griffin, C. (1985) *Typical Girls? Young Women from School to the Job Market*. London: Routledge and Kegan Paul.

Haenfler, R. (2012) '"More than the X's on my hands" – older straight edgers and the meaning of style', in A. Bennett and P. Hodkinson (eds), *Ageing and Youth Cultures: Music, Style and Identity*. Oxford: Berg. pp. 9–23.

Haenfler, R. (2010) *Goths, Gamers, and Grrrls: Deviance and Youth Subcultures*. Oxford: Oxford University Press.

Hage, G. (1997) 'At home in the entrails of the West', in H. Grace, G. Hage, L. Johnson, J. Langsworth and M. Symonds (eds), *Home/World: Space, Community and Marginality in Sydney's West*. Annandale, NSW: Pluto. pp. 99–153.

Hall, G. Stanley (1904) *Adolescence*. New York: Appleton.

Hall, S. and Jefferson, T. (2006) 'Once more around *Resistance through Rituals*', in S. Hall and T. Jefferson (eds) *Resistance through Rituals: Youth Subcultures in Post-war Britain* (2nd Edition). London: Routledge.

Hall, T., Coffey, A. and Lashua, B. (2009) 'Steps and stages: rethinking transitions in youth and place', *Journal of Youth Studies*, 12(5): 547–61.

Harvey, D. (1989) *The Condition of Postmodernity: An Enquiry into the Origins of Cultural Change*. Cambridge, MA: Blackwell.

Hassan, R. and Purser, R.E. (2007) 'Introduction', in R. Hassan and R.E. Purser (eds), *24/7: Time and Temporality in the Network Society*. Stanford: Stanford University Press. pp. 1–24.

Hayes, D. (2012) 'Re-engaging marginalised young people in learning: the contribution of informal learning and community-based collaborations', *Journal of Education Policy*, 27(5): 641–53.

Hayward, K. (2013) '"Life stage dissolution" in Anglo-American advertising and popular culture: Kidults, Lil' Britneys and Middle Youths', *The Sociological Review*, 61(5): 525–48.

Hayward, K. (2012) 'Pantomime justice: a cultural criminological analysis of "life stage dissolution"', *Crime, Media, Culture*, 8(2): 213–29.

Heath, S. (2009) 'Young, free and single?', in A. Furlong (ed.), *Handbook of Youth and Young Adulthood: New Perspectives and Agendas*. Oxfordshire: Routledge. pp. 211–16.

Hebdige, D. (1979) *Subculture: The Meaning of Style*. London: Methuen.

Heinz, W.R. (1992) 'Introduction: institutional gatekeeping and biographical agency', in W.R. Heinz (ed.), *Institutions and Gatekeeping in the Life Course*. Weinheim: Deutscher Studien Verlag.

Heinz, W.R. (ed.) (1991) *Theoretical Advances in Life Course Research*. Weinheim: Deutscher Studien Verlag.

Henderson, S., Holland, J., McGrellis, S., Sharpe, S., Thomson, R. with Grigoriou, T. (2007) *Inventing Adulthoods: A Biographical Approach to Youth Transitions*. London: Sage.

Herrera, L. (2012) 'Youth and citizenship in the digital age: a view from Egypt', *Harvard Educational Review*, 82(3): 333–52.

Hesmondhalgh, D. (2005) 'Subcultures, scenes or tribes? None of the above', *Journal of Youth Studies*, 8(1): 21–40.

Hinrichs, K., Roche W. and Sirianni C. (1991) 'From standardization to flexibility: changes in the political economy of working time', in K. Hinrichs, W. Roche and C. Sirianni (eds), *Working Time In Transition: The Political Economy of Working Hours in Industrial Nations.* Philadelphia: Temple University Press. pp. 3–25.

Hochschild, A.R. (1997) *The Time Bind: When Work Becomes Home and Home Becomes Work*. New York: Metropolitan Books.

Hodkinson, P. (2012) 'Beyond spectacular specifics in the study of youth (sub) cultures', *Journal of Youth Studies*, 15(5): 557–72.

Hodkinson, P. (2011) 'Ageing in a spectacular "youth culture": continuity, change and community amongst older goths', *The British Journal of Sociology*, 62(2): 262–82.

Hodkinson, P. (2003) '"Net.Goth": online communication and (sub)cultural boundaries', in D. Muggleton and R. Weinzeirl (eds), *The Post-Subcultures Reader*. Oxford: Berg. pp. 285–97.

Hodkinson, P. (2002) *Goth: Identity, Style and Subculture*. Oxford: Berg.

Hodkinson, P. and Lincoln, S. (2008) 'Online journals as virtual bedrooms? Young people, identity and personal space', *Young*, 16(1): 27–46.

Hoechner, H. (2013) 'Mobility as a contradictory resource: peripatetic Qur'anic students in Kano, Nigeria', *Children's Geographies*, online before print DOI:10.1 080/14733285.2013.827876

Holland, S. (2012) 'Alternative women adjusting to ageing, or how to stay freaky at 50', in A. Bennett and P. Hodkinson (eds), *Ageing and Youth Cultures: Music, Style and Identity*. Oxford: Berg. pp. 119–32.

Hollands, R. (2002) 'Division in the dark: youth cultures, transitions and segmented consumption spaces in the night-time economy', *Journal of Youth Studies*, 5(2): 153–73.

Hopkins, P. (2010) *Young People, Place and Identity*. London: Routledge.

Hopkins, P. and Pain, R. (2007) 'Geographies of age: thinking relationally', *Area*, 39(3): 287–94.

Horváth, I. (2008) 'The culture of migration of rural Romanian youth', *Journal of Ethnic and Migration Studies*, 34(5): 771–86.

Howe, N. and Strauss, W. (1997) *The Fourth Turning: An American Prophecy*. Portland: Broadway Books.

Huq, R. (2006) *Beyond Subculture: Pop, Youth and Identity in a Postcolonial World*. London: Routledge.

International Labour Organisation (ILO) (2013) *Global Employment Trends for Youth 2013: A Generation At Risk*. Geneva: International Labour Office.

International Labour Organisation (ILO) (2010) *Global Employment Trends for Youth: Special Issue on the Impacts of the Global Economic Crisis on Youth*. Geneva: International Labour Organisation.

International Labour Organisation (ILO) (2008) *World of Work Report 2008: Income Inequalities in the Age of Financial Globalization*. Geneva: International Institute for Labour Studies.

International Labour Organisation (ILO) (2004) *A Fair Globalization: Creating Opportunities for All*. Report of the World Commission on the Social Consequences of Globalization. Geneva: International Labour Organisation.

International Monetary Fund (IMF) (2007) *World Economic Outlook: Globalization and Inequality*. Washington, DC: International Monetary Fund.

Ito, M. and Okabe, D. (2006) 'Intimate connections: contextualising Japanese youth and mobile messaging', in R. Kraut, M. Brynin and S. Kiesler (eds), *Computers, Phones and the Internet: Domesticating Information Technology*. Oxford: Oxford University Press. pp. 235–50.

James, R. (2001) 'Participation disadvantage in Australian higher education: an analysis of some effects of geographical location and socioeconomic status', *Higher Education*, 42: 455–72.

James, R., Baldwin, G., Coates, H., Krause, K-L. and McInnis, C. (2004) *An Analysis of Equity Groups in Higher Education 1991–2002*. Canberra: Department of Education, Science and Training, Commonwealth of Australia.

Jameson, F. (1991) *Postmodernism: The Cultural Logic of Late Capitalism*. Durham, NC: Duke University Press.

Jenkins, R. (1992) *Pierre Bourdieu*. London: Routledge.

Jenkins, R. (1983) *Lads, Citizens and Ordinary Kids: Working-class Youth Lifestyles in Belfast*. London: Routledge and Kegan Paul.

Jones, G. (2009) *Youth*. Cambridge: Polity.

Jones, G. (1995) *Leaving Home*. Buckingham: Open University Press.

Jones, G. and Wallace, C. (1992) *Youth, Family and Citizenship*. Buckingham: Open University Press.

Kahn-Harris, K. (2007) *Extreme Metal: Music and Culture on the Edge*. London: Berg.

Kelly, P. (2006) 'The entrepreneurial self and "youth at-risk": exploring the horizons of identity in the twenty-first century', *Journal of Youth Studies*, 9(1): 17–32.

Kelly, P. (2001) 'Youth at risk: processes of individualisation and responsibilisation in the risk society', *Discourse*, 22(1): 23–33.

Kenway, J., Kraack, A. and Hickey-Moody, A. (2006) *Masculinity Beyond the Metropolis*. London: Palgrave Macmillan.

Kenyon, S., Lyons, G. and Rafferty, J. (2002) 'Transport and social exclusion: investigating the possibility of promoting inclusion through virtual mobility', *Journal of Transport Geography*, 10(3): 207–19.

Khalaf, S. and Khalaf, R.S. (2011) *Arab Youth: Social Mobilisation in Times of Risk*. Lebanon: Saqi.

Klatch, R.E. (1999) *A Generation Divided: The New Left, The New Right, and the 1960s*. Berkeley: University of California Press.

Kraack, A. and Kenway, J. (2002) 'Place, time and stigmatised youthful identities: bad boys in paradise', *Journal of Rural Studies*, 18: 145–55.

Kraas, F. (2007) 'Megacities and global change: key priorities', *The Geographical Journal*, 173(1): 79–82.

Lahire, B. (2011) *The Plural Actor*. Cambridge: Polity.

Lahire, B. (2003) 'From the habitus to an individual heritage of dispositions: towards a sociology at the level of the individual', *Poetics*, 31(5–6): 329–55.

Laidi, Z. (2001) 'Urgency: the sacred present', *Queen's Quarterly*, 108(4): 531–7.

Lamb, S. (2011) 'School dropout and completion in Australia', in S. Lamb, E. Markussen, R. Teese, N. Sandberg and J. Polesel (eds), *School Dropout and Completion: International Comparative Studies in Theory and Policy*. Springer: Dordrecht. pp. 1–20.

Lasén, A. (2006) 'How to be in two places at the same time: mobile phone uses in public places', in J. Höflich and M. Hartman (eds), *Mobile Communication in Everyday Life: Ethnographic Views, Observations and Reflections*. Berlin: Frank & Timme. pp. 227–52.

Leccardi, C. (2012) 'Young people's representations of the future and the acceleration of time: a generational approach', *Diskurs Kindheits-und Jungenforschung Heft*, 1: 59–73.

Leccardi, C. (2007) 'New temporal perspectives in the "high-speed society"', in R. Hassan and R.E. Purser (eds), *24/7: Time and Temporality in the Network Society*. Stanford: Stanford Business Books. pp. 25–36.

Leccardi, C. (2006) 'Facing uncertainty: temporality and biographies in the new century', in E. Ruspini and C. Leccardi (eds), *A New Youth? Young People, Generations and Family Life*. Aldershot: Ashgate. pp. 15–40.

Leccardi, C. and Ruspini, E. (eds) (2006) *A New Youth? Young People, Generations and Family Life*. Aldershot: Ashgate.

Lefebvre, H. (2004) *Rhythmanalysis: Space, Time and Everyday Life*. London: Continuum.

Lehmann, W. (2004) '"For some reason, I get a little scared": structure, agency, and risk in school – work transitions', *Journal of Youth Studies*, 7(4): 379–96.

Lesko, N. (1996) 'Denaturalizing adolescence: the politics of contemporary representations', *Youth & Society*, 28(2): 139–61.

Levin, J. (2013) *Blurring the Boundaries: The Declining Significance of Age*. New York and London: Routledge.

Ley, K. (1984) 'Von der Normal – zur Wahlbiographie', in M. Kohili and G. Roberts (eds), *Biographie und Soziale Wirklichkeit*. Stuttgart: Metzler.

Lingard, B. (2011) 'Policy as numbers: accounting for educational research', *Australian Educational Researcher*, 38: 355–82.

Looker, E.D. and Naylor, T.D. (2009) '"At risk" of being rural? The experience of rural youth in a risk society', *Journal of Rural and Community Development*, 4(2): 39–64.

Lou, J. (2011) 'Transcending an urban–rural divide: rural youth's resistance to townization and schooling, a case study of a middle school in Northwest China', *International Journal of Qualitative Studies in Education*, 24(5): 573–80.

Luckman, S. (2003) 'Going bush and finding one's "tribe": raving, doof and the Australian landscape', *Continuum: A Journal of Media and Cultural Studies,* 17(3): 318–32.

Lyotard, J.F. (1984). *The Postmodern Condition: A Report on Knowledge*. Minneapolis: University of Minnesota Press.

MacDonald, R. (2011) 'Youth transitions, unemployment and underemployment: plus ça change, plus c'est la même chose?', *Journal of Sociology*, 47(4): 427–44.

MacDonald, R. and Marsh, J. (2005) *Disconnected Youth? Growing up in Britain's Poor Neighbourhoods*. Basingstoke: Palgrave.

MacDonald, R., Mason, P., Shildrick, T., Webster, C., Johnston, L. and Ridley, L. (2001) 'Snakes & ladders: in defence of studies of youth transition', *Sociological Research Online*, 5(4), available at www.socresonline.org.uk/5/4/macdonald.html

MacDonald, R., Shildrick, T. and Blackman, S. (eds) (2010) *Young People, Class and Place*. London: Routledge.

MacLean, S. (2011) 'Managing risk and marginality', in S. Beadle, R. Holdsworth and J. Wyn (eds), *For We Are Young and…? Young People in a Time of Uncertainty*. Melbourne: Melbourne University Press, pp. 158–73.

Maffesoli, M. (1996) *The Time of the Tribes: The Decline of Individualism in Mass Society*. London: Sage.

Malbon, B. (1999) *Clubbing: Dancing, Ecstasy and Vitality*. London: Routledge.

Males, M. (2009) 'Does the adolescent brain make risk taking inevitable? A skeptical appraisal', *Journal of Adolescent Research*, 24(1): 3–20.

Mannheim, K. (1952 [1923]) 'The problem of generations', in *Essays on the Sociology of Knowledge*. London: Routledge. pp. 276–322.

Marquardt, R. (1996) *Youth and Work in Troubled Times: A Report on Canada in the 1990s*. Ottawa: Canada Policy Research Networks.

Mason, A. and Lee, S. (2012) 'Youth and their changing economic roles in Asia', *Asia Pacific Population Journal*, 21(1): 61–81.

Massey, D. (2005) *For Space*. London: Sage.

Massey, D. (1998) 'The spatial construction of youth cultures', in T. Skelton and G. Valentine (eds), *Cool Places: Geographies of Youth Cultures*. London and New York: Routledge. pp. 122–30.

McDonald, K. (1999) *Struggles for Subjectivity*. London: Cambridge.

McLeod, J. and Yates, L. (2006) *Making Modern Lives: Subjectivity, Schooling, and Social Change*. Albany: State University of New York Press.

McNay, L. (1999) 'Gender, habitus and the field: Pierre Bourdieu and the limits of reflexivity', *Theory Culture & Society*, 16(1): 95–117.

McRobbie, A. (1991) *Feminism and Youth Culture: From Jackie to Just Seventeen*. Macmillan: London.

McRobbie, A. (1978) *Jackie: An Ideology of Adolescent Femininity*. Discussion Paper. Birmingham: University of Birmingham.

McRobbie, A. and Garber, J. (1976) 'Girls and subcultures', in T. Jefferson and S. Hall (eds), *Resistance Through Rituals: Youth Subcultures in Post-war Britain*. London: Huchinson. pp. 209–22.

Mentré, F. (1920) *Les generations sociales*. Paris: Bossard.

Merton, R.K. (1938) 'Social structure and anomie', *American Sociological Review*, 3(5): 672–82.

Miles, S. (2000) *Youth Lifestyles in a Changing World*. Buckingham: Open University Press.

Mills, C.W. (1959) *The Sociological Imagination*. New York: Oxford University Press.

Mizen, P. (2004) *The Changing State of Youth*. New York: Palgrave.

Mizen, P. (2002) 'Putting the politics back into youth studies: Keynesianism, monetarism and the changing state', *Journal of Youth Studies*, 5(1): 5–20.

Molgat, M. (2008) 'Youth, mobility and work in Canada: internal migration, immigration and public policy implications', in R. Bendit and M. Hahn-Bleibtreu (eds), *Youth Transitions: Processes of Social Inclusion and Patterns of Vulnerability in a Globalised World*. Opladen and Farmington Hills: Barbara Budrich. pp. 115–31.

Muggleton, D. (2000) *Inside Subculture: The Postmodern Meaning of Style*. Oxford: Berg.

Muggleton, D. (1997) 'The post-subculturalist', in S. Readhead, D. Wynne and J. O'Connor (eds), *The Clubcultures Reader: Readings in Popular Cultural Studies*. Oxford: Blackwell, pp. 185–203.

Murdock, G. and McCron, R. (2006) 'Consciousness of class and consciousness of generation', in S. Hall and T. Jefferson (eds), *Resistance Through Rituals* (2nd edition). London and New York: Routledge. pp. 162–76.

Musgrove, F. (1969) 'The problems of youth and the social structure', *Youth and Society*, 11: 35–58.

Musgrove, F. (1964) *Youth and the Social Order*. London: Routledge and Kegan Paul.

Nairn, K., Higgins, J. and Sligo, J. (2012) *Children of Rogernomics: A Neoliberal Generation Leaves School*. Dunedin: Otago University Press.

Nairn, K., Panelli, R. and McCormack, J. (2003) 'Destabilizing dualisms: young people's experiences of rural and urban environments', *Childhood*, 10(1): 9–42.

Nayak, A. (2003) *Race, Place and Globalization: Youth Cultures in a Changing World*. Oxford: Berg.

Nayak, A. and Kehily, M.J. (2008) *Gender, Youth and Culture: Young Masculinities and Femininities*. Basingstoke: Palgrave Macmillan.

Nilan, P. (2012) 'Hybridity', in N. Lesko and S. Talburt (eds), *Youth Studies: Keywords and Movements*. New York: Routledge. pp. 252–6.

Nilan, P. and Feixa, C. (eds) (2006) *Global Youth? Hybrid Identities, Plural Worlds*. London: Routledge.

Nisbet, R.A. (1962) 'Sociology as an art form', *Pacific Sociological Review*, 5(2): 67–74.

Nowotny, H. (1994) *Time: The Modern and Postmodern Experience*. Cambridge: Polity.

Oinonen, E. (2003) 'Extended present, faltering future: family formation in the process of attaining adult status in Finland and Spain', *Young*, 11(2): 121–40.

Omerbasic, G. (2012) *Being Young and Precarious in Denmark*. Copenhagen: Solidar.

Ong, A. (1999) *Flexible Citizenship: The Cultural Logics of Transnationality*. Durham: Duke University Press.

Organisation for Economic Co-operation and Development (OECD) (2011) *Education at a Glance 2011: OECD Indicators*. Paris: OECD.

Organisation for Economic Co-operation and Development (OECD) (2010) *Education at a Glance 2010: OECD Indicators*. Paris: OECD.

Organisation for Economic Cooperation and Development (OECD) (2008) *Growing Unequal? Income Distribution and Poverty in OECD Countries*. Paris: OECD.

Organisation for Economic Cooperation and Development (OECD) (1996) *Lifelong Learning for All*. Paris: OECD.

Ortega y Gasset, J. (1961 [1923]) *The Modern Theme*. New York: Harper.

Pais, J.M. (2003) 'The multiple faces of the future in the labyrinth of life', *Journal of Youth Studies*, 6(2): 115–26.

Pattman, R. (2012) 'Street children', in N. Lesko and S. Talbut (eds), *Keywords in Youth Studies*. New York: Routledge. pp. 262–7.

Perrone, E. (1991) 'On standardised testing', *Childhood Education*, 67: 132–42.

Piaget, J. (1954) *The Construction of Reality in the Child*. New York: Basic Books.

Pilcher, J. (1994) 'Mannheim's sociology of generations: an undervalued legacy', *British Journal of Sociology*, 45(3): 481–95.

Pocock, B. (2003) *The Work/Life Collision: What Work is Doing to Australians and What to Do about It*. Sydney: Federation Press.

Pocock, B., Buchanan, J. and Campbell, I. (2004) 'Meeting the challenge of casual work in Australia: evidence, past treatment and future policy', *Australian Bulletin of Labour*, 30(1): 16–32.

Pocock, B., Skinner, N. and Williams, P. (2012) *Time Bomb: Work, Rest and Play in Australia Today*. Sydney: NewSouth.

Polesel, J., Dulfer, N. and Turnbull, M. (2012) *The Experience of Education: The Impact of High Stakes Testing on School Students and their Families*. Sydney: Whitlam Institute.

Polhemus, T. (1997) 'In the supermarket of style', in S. Redhead, D. Wynne and J. O'Connor (eds), *The Clubcultures Reader: Readings in Popular Cultural Studies*. Oxford: Blackwell, pp. 148–51.

Pollock, G. (2008) 'Youth transitions: debates over the social context of becoming an adult', *Sociology Compass*, 2(2): 467–84.

Powell, R. and Clarke, J. (1976) 'A note on marginality', in T. Jefferson and S. Hall (eds), *Resistance Through Rituals: Youth Subcultures in Post-war Britain*. London: Huchinson. pp. 223–9.

Presser, H.B. (2004) *Working in a 24/7 Economy: Challenges for American Families*. New York: Russell Sage Foundation.

Price, R., McDonald, P., Bailey, J. et al. (2011) 'A majority experience: young people's encounters with the labour market', in R. Price, P. McDonald and J. Bailey et al. (eds), *Young People and Work*. Aldershot: Ashgate. pp. 1–17.

Pusey, M. (2007) 'The changing relationship between the generations ... It could even be good news?', *Youth Studies Australia*, 26(1): 9–16.

Quinlan, M. (2012) 'The "pre-invention" of precarious employment: the changing world of work in context', *The Economic and Labour Relations Review*, 23(4): 3–24.

Rattansi, A. and Phoenix, A. (2005) 'Rethinking youth identities: modernist and postmodernist frameworks', *Identity*, 5(2): 97–123.

Ravallion, M. (2008) *Bailing out the World's Poorest*. Policy Research Working Paper 4763. Washington, DC: World Bank.

Redhead, S. (1990) *The End-of-the-Century Party*. Manchester: Manchester University Press.

Reich, W. (1972) *The Greening of America*. Harmondsworth: Penguin.

Rizvi, F. (2012) 'Mobilities and the transnationalization of youth cultures', in N. Lesko and S. Talbut (eds), *Keywords in Youth Studies*. New York: Routledge. pp. 191–202.

Robards, B. and Bennett, A. (2011) 'MyTribe: post-subcultural manifestations of belonging on social network sites', *Sociology*, 45(2): 303–17.

Roberts, B. (2006 [1975]) 'Naturalistic research into subcultures and deviance', in S. Hall and T. Jefferson (eds), *Resistance Through Rituals* (2nd edition). London and New York: Routledge. pp. 207–15.

Roberts, B. (2002) *Biographical Research*. Buckingham: OUP.

Roberts, K. (2007) 'Youth transitions and generations: a response to Wyn and Woodman', *Journal of Youth Studies*, 10(2): 263–9.

Roberts, K. (2003) 'Problems and priorities for the sociology of youth', in A. Bennett, M. Cieslik and S. Miles (eds), *Researching Youth*. Basingstoke: Palgrave Macmillan. pp. 131–28.

Roberts, K. (1997) 'Structure and agency: the new youth research agenda', in J. Bynner, L. Chisholm and A. Furlong (eds), *Youth, Citizenship and Social Change in a European Context*. Aldershot: Ashgate. pp. 56–65.

Roberts, K. (1995) *Youth and Employment in Modern Britain*. Oxford: Oxford University Press.

Roberts, K. (1968) 'The entry into employment: an approach towards a general theory', *Sociological Review*, 16(2): 165–84.

Roberts, K. and Pollock, G. (2009) 'New class divisions in the new market economies: evidence from the careers of young adults in post-Soviet Armenia, Azerbaijan and Georgia', *Journal of Youth Studies*, 12(5): 579–96.

Roberts, S. (2013) 'Boys will be boys… won't they? Change and continuities in contemporary young working-class masculinities', *Sociology*, 47(4): 671–86.

Roberts, S. (2012) 'One step forward, one step Beck: a contribution to the ongoing conceptual debate in youth studies', *Journal of Youth Studies*, 15(3): 389–401.

Roberts, S. (2011) 'Beyond "NEET" and "tidy" pathways: considering the "missing middle" of youth transition studies', *Journal of Youth Studies*, 14(1): 21–39.

Roberts, S. (2010) 'Misrepresenting "choice biographies"? A reply to Woodman', *Journal of Youth Studies*, 13(1): 137–49.

Rogers, G. and Rogers, J. (eds) (1989) *Precarious Jobs in Labour Market Regulation: The Growth of Atypical Employment in Western Europe*. Belgium: International Institute for Labour Studies.

Rosa, H. (2013) *Social Acceleration: A New Theory of Modernity*. New York: Columbia University Press.

Ryder, N.B. (1965) 'The cohort as a concept in the study of social change', *American Sociological Review*, 30(6): 843–61.

Said, E. (1989) 'Representing the colonized: anthropology's interlocutors', *Critical Inquiry*, 15(2): 205–225.

Salazar, N.B. (2011) 'The power of imagination in transnational mobilities, identities', *Global Studies in Culture and Power*, 18(6): 576–98.

Sassen, S. (2008) *Territory, Authority, Rights: From Medieval to Global Assemblages* (updated edition). Princeton: Princeton University Press.

Sassen, S. (2002) 'Women's burden: counter-geographies of globalization and the feminization of survival', *Nordic Journal of International Law*, 71(2): 255–74.

Scarpetta, S. and Sonnett, A. (2012) 'Challenges facing European labour markets: is a skill upgrade the appropriate instrument?', *Intereconomics*, 47(1): 4–30.

Schneider, J. (2000) 'The increasing financial dependency of young people on their parents', *Journal of Youth Studies*, 3(1): 5–20.

Schroeder, L. (2006) *What High-Stakes Testing Means for the Emotional Wellbeing of Students and Teachers*. Unpublished PhD thesis, Claremont Graduate University.

Seaton, E. (2012) 'Biology/nature', in N. Lesko and S. Talburt (eds), *Keywords in Youth Studies*. New York: Routledge. pp. 24–8.

Sennett, R. (2006) *The Culture of the New Capitalism*. New Haven: Yale University Press.

Sennett, R. and Cobb, J. (1972) *The Hidden Injuries of Class*. New York: Knopf.

Sharpe, S. (1976) *Just Like a Girl: How Girls Learn to be Women*. Harmondsworth: Penguin Books.

Shildrick, T. and MacDonald, R. (2006) 'In defence of subculture: young people, leisure and social divisions', *Journal of Youth Studies*, 9(2): 125–40.

Shilling, C. and Mellor, P.A. (2007) 'Cultures of embodied experience: technology, religion and body pedagogics', *The Sociological Review*, 55(3): 531–49.

Shomos, A., Turner, E. and Will, L. (2013) *Forms of Work in Australia*, Productivity Commission Staff Working Paper. Canberra: Productivity Commission.

Shove, E. (2009) 'Everyday practice and the production and consumption of time', in E. Shove, F. Trentman and R. Wilk (eds), *Time, Consumption and Everyday Life*. Oxford: Berg. pp. 17–33.

Silva, J.M. (2012) 'Constructing adulthood in an age of uncertainty', *American Sociological Review*, 77(4): 505–22.

Skelton, T. and Valentine, G. (eds) (1998) *Cool Places: Geographies of Youth Cultures*. London: Routledge.

Skrbis, Z. et al. (2011) 'Expecting the unexpected: young people's expectations about marriage and family', *Journal of Sociology*, 47(2): 1–21.

Slade, T., Johnston, A., Oakley Browne, M., Andrews, G. and Whiteford, H. (2009) '2007 National Survey of Mental Health and Wellbeing: methods and key findings', *Australian and New Zealand Journal of Psychiatry*, (43): 594–605.

Sørensen, M.P. and Christiansen, A. (2013) *Ulrich Beck: An Introduction to the Theory of Second Modernity and the Risk Society*. London: Routledge.

Southerton, D. (2009) 'Re-ordering temporal rhythms: coordinating daily practices in the UK in 1937 and 2000', in E. Shove, F. Trentman and R. Wilk (eds), *Time, Consumption and Everyday Life*. Oxford: Berg. pp. 49–64.

Southerton, D. (2006) 'Analysing the temporal organization of daily life: social constraints, practices and their allocation', *Sociology*, 40(3): 435–54.

Spencer, L. and Pahl, R. (2006) *Rethinking Friendship: Hidden Solidarities Today*. Princeton: Princeton University Press.

Standing, G. (2011) *The Precariat: The New Dangerous Class*. London: Bloomsbury Academic.

Stiggins, R. (1999) 'Assessment, student confidence and school success', *Phi Delta Kappan*, 81(3): 191–8.

Stokes, H. (2012) *Imagining Futures: Identity Narratives and the Role of Part Time Work, Family and Community*. Melbourne: Melbourne University Press.

Stokes, H. and Wyn, J. (2007) 'Constructing identities and making careers: young people's perspectives on work and learning', *International Journal of Lifelong Education*, 26(5): 495–511.

Sutcliffe, B. (2004) 'World inequality and globalization', *Oxford Review of Economic Policy*, 20(1): 15–37.

Symes, C. (1999) 'Chronicles of labour: a discourse analysis of time diaries', *Time and Society*, 8(2): 357–80.

Talburt, S. and Lesko, N. (2012) 'An introduction to seven technologies of youth studies', in N. Lesko and S. Talburt (eds), *Youth Studies: Keywords and Movements*. New York: Routledge, pp. 1–10.

Tapscott, D. (1998) *Growing up Digital: The Rise of the Net Generation*. New York: McGraw-Hill.

te Riele, K. (2004) 'Youth transition in Australia: challenging assumptions of linearity and choice', *Journal of Youth Studies*, 7(3): 243–57.

Thomson, R. and Taylor, R. (2005) 'Between cosmopolitanism and the locals: mobility as a resource in the transition to adulthood', *Young*, 13(4): 327–42.

Thomson, R., Kehily, M., Hadfield, L. and Sharpe, S. (2009) 'The making of modern motherhoods: storying an emergent identity', in M. Wetherell (ed.), *Identity in the 21st Century: New Trends in Changing Times*. Basingstoke: Palgrave Macmillan. pp. 197–212.

Thomson, R., Holland, J., McGrellis, S., Bell, R., Helderson, S. and Sharpe, S. (2004) 'Inventing adulthoods: a biographical approach to understanding youth citizenship', *The Sociological Review*, 52(2): 218–39.

Thornton, S. (1996) *Club Cultures: Music, Media and Subcultural Capital*. Hanover: Wesleyan University Press.

Thrasher, F.M. (1927) *The Gang: A Study of 1,313 Gangs in Chicago*. Chicago: University of Chicago Press.

Threadgold, S. (2011) '"Should I pitch my tent in the middle ground?" On "middling tendency", Beck and inequality in youth sociology', *Journal of Youth Studies*, 14(4): 381–93.

Threadgold S. and Nilan, P. (2009) 'Reflexivity of contemporary youth, risk and cultural capital', *Current Sociology*, 57(1): 47–68.

Thrift, N. and May, J. (eds) (2001) *Timespace: Geographies of Temporality*. London: Routledge.

Thrupp, M. (2001) 'School-level education policy under New Labour and New Zealand Labour: a comparative update', *British Journal of Educational Studies*, 49(2): 187–212.

Tilleczek, K. (2010) *Approaching Youth Studies: Being, Becoming and Belonging*. Toronto: Oxford University Press.

Tranberg-Hansen, K., Dalsgaard, A.L., Gough, K., Madsen, U.A., Valentin, K. and Wildermuth, N. (eds) (2008) *Youth and the City in the Global South*. Bloomington: Indiana University Press.

UNESCO Institute for Statistics (UIS) (2009) *Global Education Digest 2009: Comparing Education Statistics Across the World*. Montreal: UNESCO.

UNICEF (2011) *Global Inequality: Beyond the Bottom Billion – A Rapid Review of Income Distribution in 141 Countries.* New York: UNICEF.

United Nations (2005) *The Inequality Predicament: Report on the World Social Situation 2005.* New York: United Nations Department of Economic and Social Affairs.

United Nations Economic and Social Commission for Asia and the Pacific (UNESCAP) (2013a) *Population Trends in Asia and the Pacific.* New York: United Nations.

United Nations Economic and Social Commission for Asia and the Pacific (UNESCAP) (2013b) *Urbanisation Trends in Asia and the Pacific.* New York: United Nations.

Urry, J. (2002) 'Mobility and proximity', *Sociology*, 36(2): 255–74.

Valentine, G. and Skelton, T. (2007) 'Re-defining "norms": D/deaf young people's transitions to independence', *The Sociological Review*, 55(1): 104–23.

Vincent, J.A. (2005) 'Understanding generations: political economy and culture in an ageing society', *British Journal of Sociology*, 56(4): 579–99.

Vosko, L.F. (2003) 'Precarious employment in Canada: taking stock, taking action', *Just Labour*, 3(Fall): 1–5.

Wacquant, L. (2014) 'Homines in extremis: what fighting scholars teach us about habitus', *Body & Society*, 20(2): 3–17

Wagner, P. (2001) *A History and Theory of the Social Sciences: Not All that is Solid Melts into Air.* London: Sage.

Walkerdine, V. and Jiménez, L. (2012) *Gender, Work and Community after De-Industrialisation: A Psychosocial Approach to Affect.* Basingstoke: Palgrave Macmillan.

Wang, H., Kong, M., Shan. W. and Vong, S.K. (2010) 'The effects of doing part time jobs on college student academic performance and social life in a Chinese society', *Journal of Education and Work*, 23(1): 79–94.

Watson, I., Buchanan, J., Campbell, I. and Briggs, C. (2003) *Fragmented Futures: New Challenges in Working Life.* Sydney: The Federation Press.

Watson, J. (2011) 'Understanding survival sex: young women, homelessness and intimate relationships', *Journal of Youth Studies*, 14(6): 639–55.

Webster, C., MacDonald, R. and Simpson, M. (2006) 'Predicting criminality? Risk factors, neighbourhood influence and desistance', *Youth Justice*, 6(1): 7–22.

White, R. and Wyn, J. (2013) *Youth and Society* (3rd edition). Melbourne: Oxford University Press.

Whyte, W.F. (1943) *Street Corner Society: The Social Structure of an Italian Slum.* Chicago: University of Chicago Press.

Wierenga, A., Landstedt, E. and Wyn, J. (2013) *Revisiting Disadvantage in Higher Education.* Melbourne: Youth Research Centre.

Wierenga, A. (2009) *Young People: Making a Life.* Basingstoke: Palgrave Macmillan.

Willis, P. (1978) *Profane Culture.* London: Routledge & Kegan Paul.

Willis, P. (1977) *Learning to Labour: How Working Class Kids Get Working Class Jobs*. Farnbrough: Saxon House.

Woodman, D. (2013) 'Young people's friendships in the context of non-standard work patterns', *The Economic and Labour Relations Review*, 24(3): 416–32.

Woodman, D. (2012) 'Life out of synch: how new patterns of further education and the rise of precarious employment are reshaping young people's relationships', *Sociology*, 46(6): 1074–90.

Woodman, D. (2011a) 'A generations approach to youth research', in S. Beadle, R. Holdsworth and J. Wyn (eds), *For We Are Young and…? Young People in a Time of Uncertainty*. Melbourne: Melbourne University Press. pp. 29–48.

Woodman, D. (2011b) 'Young people and the future: multiple temporal orientations shaped in interaction with significant others', *Young*, 19(2): 11–128.

Woodman, D. (2010) 'Class, individualisation and tracing processes of inequality in a changing world: a reply to Steven Roberts', *Journal of Youth Studies*, 13(6): 737–46.

Woodman, D. (2009) 'The mysterious case of the pervasive choice biography: Ulrich Beck, structure/agency, and the middling state of theory in the sociology of youth', *Journal of Youth Studies*, 12(3): 243–56.

Woodman, D. (2004) 'Responsibility and time for escape: the meaning of wellbeing to young Australians', *Melbourne Journal of Politics*, 29(1): 82–95.

Woodman, D. and Threadgold, S. (forthcoming) 'Critical youth studies in an individualised and globalised world: making the most of Bourdieu and Beck', in P. Kelly and A. Kamp (eds), *A Critical Youth Studies for the 21st Century*. Leiden: Brill.

Woodman, D. and Threadgold, S. (2011) 'The future of the sociology of youth: Institutional, theoretical and methodological challenges', *Youth Studies Australia*, 30(3): 8–12.

Woodman, D. and Wyn, J. (2013) 'Youth policy and generations: why youth policy needs to "rethink youth"', *Social Policy and Society*, 12(2): 265–75.

Worth, N. (2009) 'Understanding youth transition as "becoming": identity, time and futurity', *Geoforum*, 40(6): 1050–60.

Wyn, J. and Andres, L. (2011) 'Navigating complex lives: a longitudinal, comparative perspective on young people's trajectories', *Early Intervention in Psychiatry*, 33 (Supplement 1): pp. 1–5.

Wyn, J. and Cuervo, H. (forthcoming) 'Reflections on the use of spatial and relational metaphors in youth studies', *Journal of Youth Studies*.

Wyn, J., Cuervo, H. and Landstedt, E. (2014) 'The limits of wellbeing', in K. Wright and J. McLeod (eds), *Re-thinking Youth Wellbeing: Critical Perspectives*. Singapore: Springer.

Wyn, J., Lantz, S. and Harris, A. (2012) 'Beyond the "transitions" metaphor: family relations and young people in late modernity', *Journal of Sociology*, 48(1): 1–20.

Wyn, J., Smith, G., Stokes, H., Tyler, D. and Woodman, D. (2008) *Generations and Social Change: Negotiating Adulthood in the 21st Century: Report on the Life-Patterns*

Research Program: 2005–2007 (Research Report 29). Melbourne: Youth Research Centre, University of Melbourne.

Wyn, J. and Woodman, D. (2007) 'Researching youth in a context of social change: a reply to Roberts', *Journal of Youth Studies*, 10(3): 373–81.

Wyn, J. and Woodman, D. (2006) 'Generation, youth and social change in Australia', *Journal of Youth Studies*, 9(5): 495–514.

INDEX